Discourse and Literature:
The Interplay of Form and Mind

Guy Cook

Oxford University Press 1994

Oxford University Press
Walton Street, Oxford OX2 6DP

Oxford New York Toronto Madrid
Delhi Bombay Calcutta Madras Karachi
Kuala Lumpur Singapore Hong Kong Tokyo
Nairobi Dar es Salaam Cape Town
Melbourne Auckland

and associated companies in
Berlin Ibadan

Oxford and Oxford English are trade marks of
Oxford University Press

ISBN 0 19 437185 9

Set by Wyvern Typesetting Ltd, Bristol
Printed in Hong Kong

To Elena

Contents

Acknowledgements

There are a number of people to whom this book owes a great deal.

Tony Cowie supervised the thesis from which this book derives, and gave me, while I was writing, constant help, detailed advice, and the benefit of his wide knowledge and understanding of language and literature. At the same time, as a colleague, he was always ready to give me his warm-hearted encouragement, friendship, and support.

Henry Widdowson has, in many discussions over many years, made a deep impression on my ideas about literature, and I hope this is reflected here. Tony Smith has always been willing, at all hours, to sort out problems generated by this book, ranging from the most philosophical, to the most frustrating misbehaviour of computers.

Lastly, although it is a cliché of an academic preface to say that views expressed by my students have influenced my writing, in this case it is true: most true, I hope, of those opponents of the academic formalization of literary experience with whom I seemed to disagree most fiercely.

The author and publisher are grateful to the following for permission to reproduce extracts and figures from copyright material

Addison-Wesley Publishing Company Inc. for figure from *The Handbook of Artificial Intelligence Volume 1* (p. 302) by Avron Barr and Edward A. Feigenbaum, © 1981 by William Kaufman, Inc.

Daniel G. Bobrow for extract from 'Notes on a schema for stories' by D. E. Rumelhart in *Representation and Understanding* by D. G. Bobrow and A. M. Collins (Academic Press 1975).

The Bodleian Library, University of Oxford, for extract from *Songs of Experience* by William Blake (17078.d391).

Curtis Brown Group Ltd and Phoebe Larmore Literary Agency for poem 'You fit into me' by Margaret Atwood from *Power Politics*, © 1971 Margaret Atwood, © Margaret Atwood 1990, Oxford University Press, Canada, and © 1976 Margaret Atwood, Simon & Schuster Inc., United States. Reprinted with permission of the poet.

Lawrence Erlbaum Associates, Inc. and the authors for figure from *Scripts, Plans, Goals, and Understanding* by R. C. Schank and R. Abelson (1977).

W. L. Gore & Associates (UK) Limited for advertisement for Gore-Tex fabrics.

Hamish Hamilton Ltd and Random House Inc. for extract from *The Long Goodbye* by Raymond Chandler (Hamish Hamilton/Alfred Knopf 1953) copyright © Raymond Chandler 1953.

Methuen, London for poem 'First World War Poets' by Edward Bond from *Theatre Poems and Songs* (1978).

Oxford University Press and the author for extract from poem 'The behaviour of dogs' by Craig Raine from *The Onion, Memory* (OUP 1978), © Craig Raine 1978.

Parfums International for advertisement for 'Passion'.

Writers' House Inc. on behalf of the author for extract from *A Brief History of Time* by Stephen Hawking (Bantam Press 1988).

Introduction

The last two decades in applied linguistics have seen a very considerable growth of interest in discourse analysis—the study of how stretches of language take on meaning, purpose, and unity for their users. A substantial proportion of this interest has focused upon the discourse of literature. This is appropriately so, for discourse analysis must be able to account for *all* types of discourse, and, among discourse types, literature is widely if not universally considered to be one of the most important and the most powerful.

The discourse analyst's interest in literature is motivated not only by its potential to augment our understanding of discourse in general, but also by its relevance to pedagogy. The study of literary discourse forms a substantial part of the curriculum in both first and second language education. Our conceptions of literature are bound to influence the way in which we teach it. Continuing exploration of the nature of literature is thus crucial in the applied as well as the theoretical sphere.

Discourse analysis has focused very much upon the social nature of communication, stressing contextual aspects of meaning which are interactive and negotiated, determined by the social relations and identities of the participants in communication. Under the influence of this approach, something of a consensus has emerged in recent years, that literature is just one more genre among equals, functioning in much the same way as others. Particularly influential in the formation of this view has been the Hallidayan conception of language as a social semiotic, and the belief that the function of all discourse is a blend of the interpersonal and ideational. This consensus considers that literature too is primarily a mode of social interaction, reflecting and creating its own institutions and power relations. In this view there is nothing distinctive about either the language of literary discourse or its representations of the world; it is rather that some texts become literary when presented as such by institutions or when read in certain ways by readers,[1] and that is all. Which texts these are will thus always be relative to a specific social milieu.

This view (let us call it for ease of reference the 'social approach') has developed in understandable reaction against other views of literature, each of which has emphasized some element of the literary experience at the expense of others, or taken an element which is present (perhaps only incidentally) in some literary works, and elevated it into a defining characteristic of all literature, often with particularly damaging effects in the classroom.

Firstly, the social approach has rejected the idea that through literature a particularly perceptive or accurate view of the world is somehow transmitted to the reader with an overall improving effect, either moral or intellectual. This view, in addition to its rather unpleasant reduction of literature to the role of moral tutor or vicarious experience, has a number of weaknesses, which can be revealed by both theory and direct experience. On the theoretical side, it subscribes to a very simple transmission view of communication, and ignores the problem of how superior perception or judgement, if authors do possess these qualities, are conveyed through language. In addition, experience tells us that there are many literary works which seem to be neither moral nor informative, and whose authors were anything but exemplary individuals. In pedagogy, this approach can lead to a rather patronizing morality, a hero-worshipping of authors, and a lack of emphasis on the pleasures (as opposed to the improving effect) of literature.

Secondly, the social approach has rejected the idea that literariness resides in a particular use of language, that it is—in other words—a feature of text rather than discourse. This view is hardly tenable, for a number of reasons which have often been pointed out. Taking a canon of literary works as a whole, one would be hard-pressed to pinpoint any particular uses of language which are common to all of them. Many literary works, on the contrary, seem pointedly to borrow the language of non-literary discourses. Even in the case of the short lyric poem, which is often used to exemplify this view, the linguistic features which may seem distinctive (such as parallelism and creative deviation) are too readily found in supposedly non-literary discourses such as advertisements, journalism, songs, nursery rhymes, political speeches, prayers, chants, and graffiti to make it convincing. In pedagogy a purely linguistic approach can lead to a mechanistic and soulless description of literary texts which leaves the individual reader, and the relevance of literature to his or her world, completely out of account.

Thirdly, the social approach has rejected the idea of literature as a canon of texts interpreted in ways which clearly reflect the values and the identity of a particular nation or social class.[2] This view reduces what could be an instrument of understanding and tolerance between peoples to one which reinforces prejudice. Its pedagogical effects are harmful: when a canon interpreted in this way is imposed upon outsiders it can deny them access to their own cultural heritage, while to insiders, by presenting only texts interpreted in ways which reflect their own values, it denies the ability of literature to allow us access to ways of seeing which are not our own.

The rejection of these views, each regarding literature as discourse with its own distinctive features, has been strengthened by growing doubts about the validity of a literary canon: a body of texts, clearly circumscribed and separable from others, which are generally agreed to constitute 'Literature' (with a capital 'L')! The first source of doubt has been the growing realization that 'Literature', as conceived in contemporary Western society, is a fairly modern invention (Williams 1983: 183; Foucault [1969] 1979); the second is that the contents of the canon — exactly which texts are deemed to be literature — will vary from age to age and place to place. As the notion of a fixed and unproblematic canon is so central to the literature curriculum, these doubts have either been vituperatively rejected by literature teachers and course designers, or — where they have been taken on board — they have caused a crisis of confidence. The borders between literature and non-literature have become vague and confused, and there seems little left to distinguish the study of literature from the study of language and communication in general.

The force of these arguments against the notion of literature as a fixed or easily identifiable body of texts cannot be denied, and it would be foolish not to take them into account. Clearly any literary canon is relative to a particular time and place, and a particular, socially defined, group of readers. Yet despite the coldly convincing rigour of the social approach and the validity of the points which it raises, there are elements which it leaves out of account. It is not that the social approach, with its emphasis on the relativity of literary judgements, is wrong, but rather that it is incomplete. In addition, like the reigning literary ideologies which it overturned in its day, it too is now in danger of becoming stifling and dogmatic (as perhaps all theories must become in time). Too much emphasis on the social relativity of literature may distract us from the heartening fact that people often *do* seem to find something accessible, beautiful, understandable, enjoyable, and uplifting when they reach out to the literary traditions of societies and social groups which are not their own, and that they can (albeit in the light of background information) recognize in those traditions a common experience which cuts across the boundaries of nation, culture, and history. The social approach, by stressing divisions between people, often seems to deny this.

An aspect of literature which the social approach finds hard to explain is the paradox presented, in widely differing social contexts, by the contradiction between the apparent uselessness of literary works and the high value placed upon them. Though they may incidentally offer us information, or create social relations and institutions, this does not seem to be the primary motivation for either the writing or the reading of literature. On the contrary, literary texts, in all kinds of societies, often tell us at great length of worlds and people who do not exist, of emotions and experiences which do not affect us. They dwell at length on banal facts which we know already (death is sad, nature is beautiful, love is joyful, etc.), or they create patterns and play with expectations for no apparent reason at all. A theory is needed to explain the extraordinary value and pleasure accorded to such features by very different readers.

What I want to suggest in this book is that there is a type of discourse which has a particular effect on the mind, refreshing and changing our mental representations of the world. While the texts which perform this function will be different for particular individuals or social groups, the effect itself may be universal and answer a universal need. It derives, I believe, from an interaction of textual form with a reader's pre-existing mental representations. It is not, therefore, to be found in a description of either literary form or the reader in isolation, but only in a description of the two together. The value of this effect explains the value attached to the discourses which cause it—hence the high value placed upon some apparently useless discourses. I believe that discourse conventionally classified as literary often fulfils this function, and for this reason the texts I have used to exemplify this effect are from what is generally accepted as the literary canon. But this does not preclude the possibility that works outside the conventional canon may also achieve this effect (though in my view, to avoid the argument becoming circular, this would in fact make them literary).

My argument demands descriptions both of literary forms and of readers' minds, so it will range across a number of theories of literature, psychology, and discourse from different periods of the twentieth century, seeking insights which will provide components of the theory I wish to develop. As these areas are so diverse, it may be helpful to give an outline of the structure of the book and the focus of each chapter in advance.

Part One considers a number of approaches both to discourse in general and to literature in particular, assessing both their strengths and weaknesses in the description of literary effect. Chapter 1, which provides a basis for a description of mental representations and the effect of literature upon them, considers schema theory, which has its origins in the Gestalt psychology of the 1920s, and has since become firmly established in applied linguistics and discourse analysis. Chapter 2 considers contemporary approaches to discourse analysis, highlighting not only the contribution they may make to a description of literature, but also their incapacity to account for many of its features. Chapter 3 returns in more detail to the issue of how representations of the world are derived from, and brought to bear upon, the interpretation of texts. It explores in detail some of ideas from Artificial Intelligence (AI) and discusses both how they may contribute to a description of literary discourse, and also some of their incapacity to do so. In Chapter 4, these modes of analysis are brought to bear upon two problematic texts: a translation, whose literariness seems to survive the complete change of form implicit in translation from one language to another, and an advertisement which, while it makes use of literary techniques, is unlikely to be considered by most readers literary. Chapter 5 surveys and assesses some twentieth-century literary theories which claim to provide both a description of literary language and form, and of their effect on the reader. It traces a tradition from Russian formalism, through structuralism and stylistics, to reader response and reception theory. Chapter 6 continues the history begun in Chapter 5. In an analysis of two problematic texts, a synthesis is attempted between an analysis of form and of the mental representations of a reader, attempting to show how literary effect cannot be confined to one or the other, but demands a description of both.

Part Two brings together ideas and techniques of analysis from all the approaches discussed in Part One. Chapter 7 examines some psychological theories of a dynamic interaction between experience and mental representation, and proposes a theory of how mental representations interact with, and are altered by, literary discourse. Chapter 8 demonstrates this theory in the detailed analysis of three literary texts (William Blake's 'The Tyger', Henry James' *The Turn of the Screw* and Gerard Manley Hopkins' 'The Windhover') all of which are both favourites in literary pedagogy and have attracted considerable scholarly analysis and disagreement.

The implications of this approach for pedagogy, which have been put to one side during the development of the argument, are considered again in Chapter 9.

Notes

1 My use of the term 'reader' rather than 'audience' is deliberate. I deal throughout with the experience of literature as one of reading, and my theory does not necessarily extend to non-literate societies. In literate societies, though poems and plays—and even novels—may be performed, they are also read.

2 Carey (1992), in a survey of late nineteenth- and early twentieth-century literary reputations, provides a convincing and extremely well-documented account of how the British literary educational establishment has excluded works of high quality written by or for the newly literate middle classes.

PART ONE

1 A basis for analysis: schema theory, its general principles, history, and terminology

Introduction

This book considers the relationship between literary language and our mental representations of the world. Its starting point is schema theory, a body of ideas which has passed from psychology, through Artificial Intelligence (AI), and into discourse analysis. It is appropriate to give a general description of the origins and main ideas of the theory in this opening chapter. The many problems of the theory, and in particular its failure to say anything very precise about the relation between schemata and specific linguistic choices (which are so important in literature) will not be dwelt on here, but will be returned to in later chapters.

Schema theory has its origins in the Gestalt psychology of the 1920s and 1930s. Its basic claim is that a new experience is understood by comparison with a stereotypical version of a similar experience held in memory. The new experience is then processed in terms of its deviation from the stereotypical version, or conformity to it. The theory applies both to the processing of sensory data and to the processing of language. After a long eclipse, schema theory received an enormous amount of attention in the AI work of the 1970s and 1980s, where it was developed for the help which it provides in the two crucial AI problems of visual recognition and the understanding of texts. It is only the latter of these two problems which concerns us here.

AI work on text understanding, inspired by schema theory, was in turn seized upon by discourse analysis and reading theory, and it has continued to exert a strong influence in both these areas ever since (see for example Carrell and Eisterhold 1983; Carrell 1988; Widdowson 1983, 1984:95–137; McCarthy 1991:68–71; Wallace 1992:33–8; Hatch 1992:85–120). This enthusiasm arises largely from the powerful insight which schema theory provides into the problem of 'coherence'; in other words, how texts take on unity and meaning for their receivers. In discourse analysis the theory has been joined with existing approaches to coherence, such as the study of cohesion, text structure, and pragmatics (areas which have in turn attracted the reciprocal interest of AI). As such, schema theory forms an indispensable part of an emerging overall theory of discourse.

Such a theory of discourse must inevitably include an approach to that group of texts which are categorized as 'literary' (though which texts are included within that category will vary among individuals and social groups). It must also address the difficult problem of what it is which leads individuals and social groups to classify certain texts in this way. There is thus a considerable overlap between discourse analysis and literary theory, particularly those literary theories which, like discourse analysis, have taken their inspiration from linguistics. And just as discourse analysis has benefited from the insights of schema theory, so theories of literature may do the same. But the influence and benefit of an interaction of schema theory and literary analysis is by no means one-way. There are many insights stemming from approaches to literature which can contribute to AI. There are also many interactions between linguistic form and schematic representation which AI theory overlooks. It is the nature of these interactions which is the focus of attention here.

The argument in this book is that literary texts are not merely a category which needs to be included in an overall theory for the sake of completeness. It is rather that they are different in kind, representative of a type of text which may perform the important function[1] of breaking down existing schemata, reorganizing them, and building new ones.

AI has demonstrated how schemata are essential to text processing, and this idea has been accepted in discourse analysis as a partial explanation of coherence. Schemata are also, however, at times a potential barrier to understanding. The mind must build new schemata and adjust existing ones if it is to adapt to new experience—a point much emphasized in recent work on the relationship between neurology and mental categorization (Edelman 1992). It is often assumed that the main functions of human language are to manipulate the environment and to create and maintain social relationships. The argument here is that a further function of language is to build new schemata and 'play with' existing ones. The best time to do this is clearly not at moments of practical urgency or social delicacy, hence the need to withdraw from practical and social pressures for this purpose, and the existence of a type of discourse whose function is to promote this change. Schemata play a well-documented role in processing text, but certain texts may also play a role in building and adjusting schemata. Clearly, the two are complementary and, for an intelligent organism, equally important. In my development of these ideas I shall suggest that discourse may be divided into three major types: 'schema reinforcing', 'schema preserving', and 'schema refreshing'. Discourse of the last type will deviate from schematic expectations. Linguistic deviation and structural deviation may be side-effects or causes of schematic deviation, but are not enough to disrupt schemata on their own. Discourse which is acclaimed as 'literary' is often of this 'schema refreshing' type, and it is this that accounts for the high value placed upon it.

Schema theory: general principles

Pragmatic analysis of discourse assumes both shared knowledge and processing rules. Both are assumed in speech-act theory and discourse analysis based upon it, though there is considerable difference in emphasis among analysts. There are in effect two schools of (not incompatible) thought, the one stressing inferencing procedures, the other shared knowledge of the world. Major works on pragmatics, such as Levinson (1983), and Leech (1983), or on relevance theory, such as Sperber and Wilson (1986), deal at length with inferencing, but less fully with shared knowledge of the world. Yet though there may be different emphases, it is widely agreed that *both* shared knowledge of the world and shared inferencing procedures must apply if participants are to reach similar pragmatic interpretations of discourse. The approach in this book dwells more upon the nature of shared knowledge of the world than upon inferencing procedures, which, for the sake of argument, I shall treat as constant and universal, though without implying that they are either.

A theory of knowledge in interaction with text is provided by the notion of 'schemata'. These are mental representations of typical instances, and the suggestion is that they are used in discourse processing to predict and make sense of the particular instance which the discourse describes. The idea is that the mind, stimulated either by key linguistic items in the text (often referred to as 'triggers' (see Pitrat [1985] 1988)), or by the context, activates a schema, and uses it to make sense of the discourse.[2] In this sense schemata are 'norms' and individual facts are 'deviations'. This psychological view of 'norm' and 'deviation' will be of use to us later when we discuss the use of these terms in the analysis of literary discourse.

Examples demonstrating schemata in discourse processing

How schemata operate in discourse is best illustrated by an example. In Cook (1989), a book which contains a simplified introduction to schema theory, I gave the following. Imagine a witness in a trial, who is asked to tell the court about his movements during the morning. In accordance with legal custom, he is asked to tell the court everything—'the whole truth'. He begins as follows:

> I woke up at seven forty. I made some toast and a cup of tea. I listened to the news. And I left for work at about eight thirty.

Such a description might well be enough to satisfy the court. But suppose the witness had said:

> I woke up at seven forty. I was in bed. I was wearing pyjamas. After lying still for a few minutes, I threw back the duvet, got out of bed, walked to the door of the bedroom, opened the door, switched on the landing light, walked across the landing, opened the bathroom door, went into the bathroom, put the basin plug into the plughole, turned on the hot tap, ran some hot water into the washbasin, looked in the mirror . . .

Although this is also true, it is clearly, even facetiously, 'too much'. But how does the witness assess the amount of detail required? And if the court want to know 'the whole truth', why are they prepared to allow some details to be omitted? There is an infinity of extra detail that could be added, even to the second version. The witness did not mention every time he blinked, for example, or the fact that he was breathing— and even these actions can be broken down into constituent muscular movements which can themselves be reduced to chemical changes.

Schema theory can explain omission by postulating that the 'default elements' of the schema activated can be taken as known. Thus it is not that the superfluous information in the second version of our example is not true, but rather that it is assumed—and that the witness can, and should, assume it is assumed. (Here I, the writer, am assuming, quite reasonably, that you, the reader, and the court and the witness I have invented, all have a similar schema to my own.) When the sender of a message judges an interlocutor's schema to correspond to a significant degree with his or her own, then it is only necessary to mention specific features which are not contained in it (the time of getting up and the contents of the breakfast for example); other features (like getting out of bed and getting dressed) will be assumed to be present by default, unless otherwise stated. (That is why it seems more reasonable to say 'I went to work in my pyjamas' than 'I went to work in my clothes'.) In this light, the impossible judicial demand for 'the whole truth' should not be taken too literally.

Evidence for schemata

There are a number of pieces of evidence that the mind does employ schemata in the interpretation of discourse. One is the fact that people questioned about a text or asked to recall it frequently fill in details not contained in the text but drawn from their relevant schema (Bartlett

1932:47–95; Bower, Black, and Turner 1979; Miller and Kintsch 1980). If we were shown the first version of the testimony, and asked what the witness ate for breakfast, we would be likely to reply that he ate toast, although this is not stated. (He said only that he made some toast, but not that he ate it.) Readers tend to assume that if someone makes breakfast, it is eaten, and, if nobody else is mentioned, that the speaker ate the breakfast himself. It is important to note that this conclusion cannot be reached by any logical inferencing rules operating on text without reference to specific knowledge. This mental ability to 'read in' details is particularly relevant to literary narrative, in which readers are given points of reference and left to fill in the gaps 'from imagination'.[3]

A second piece of evidence for schemata is provided by certain uses of the definite article with nouns which have neither a unique referent, nor are determined by previous mention.

Flight 715 has been unable to take off. The pilot has been taken ill.

Here the use of the definite article with 'pilot' seems quite appropriate (in a way which, say, 'farmer' would not) even though this pilot is mentioned for the first time.[4] If a pilot is part of our schematic knowledge of aircraft, he or she can be treated as given.

Many literary narratives, especially in their opening sentences, do however use the definite article as determiner in noun phrases which neither refer to earlier indefinite noun phrases, nor are default elements of schemata. François Mauriac's novel *Thérèse Desqueyroux*, for example, like many others, has a definite article for its very first word:

L'avocat ouvrit une porte.
(The lawyer opened a door.)

One effect of this is to make the reader process the discourse as though the relevant schema were shared with the narrator or characters when in fact it is unknown. This achieves both a degree of involvement, by assuming a kind of unwarranted intimacy, and also drives the reader forward to construct the necessary schema as quickly as possible. In addition it produces the sensation of entering into a mental world other than one's own, in which the reader is simultaneously an outsider and intimately involved.

Further evidence for schemata is provided by interpretation of homonymy and polysemy in discourse. Lehnert (1979:80) gives as an example, among others, the interpretation of the word 'seal' in the sentence

The royal proclamation was finished. The king sent for his seal.

Here, readers interpret the word 'seal' as 'a device which produces an official stamp of some sort' rather than as an animal (although the king could well have had a pet seal, and no logical inferencing rule will conclude that he did not), presumably because the former meaning belongs to a schema containing kings and proclamations. Constant exposure to actual or described situations in which kings had pet seals would lead to a different interpretation. The schema activated by the opening leads to one interpretation of 'seal'—a phenomenon referred to as 'expectation-driven understanding'—and is upset by an unexpected continuation, causing processing delays (Sanford and Garrod 1981:114–15; Haberlandt and Bingham 1982).

Literary texts sometimes exploit the expectation-driven understanding of homonyms and polysemes to create surprise and 'jolt' the reader into re-processing, as in this short poem by Margaret Atwood:

You fit into me

You fit into me
Like a hook in an eye—
A fish hook
An open eye

Indeed, such processing delay is a feature sometimes considered characteristic of literature, and was described by the Russian formalist Victor Shklovsky, as the 'device of impeded form'' (Shklovsky [1917] 1965: 13). It is also, however, a common feature of other discourse types such as advertisements (Cook 1992), graffiti (Blume 1985), and jokes (Chiaro 1992), as in the following children's joke:

Q: Why are people never hungry in the desert?
A: Because of all the sand which is there.

This phenomenon of expectation-driven understanding applies to all linguistic levels and ranks. Unexpected phonetic sounds are heard as the expected phoneme (Slobin 1979:37), while at the grammatical level, the formally ambiguous phrases, clauses, and sentences of the kind much discussed by linguists who eschew context are unlikely to cause the activation of rival interpretations in context (Cruse 1986:101). Again this is not always true of all discourse types, including many literary ones, where ambiguity may remain through the absence of sufficient disambiguating co-text or context.

World schemata and text schemata

Further evidence for schemata, and indeed for shared schemata, though of a different kind from those above, seems to be provided by instances in which speakers or writers follow the same ordering of information. This may be specific to a particular text type or discourse function. In a series of experiments, Linde and Labov (1975) showed how almost all subjects who were asked to describe the house or flat where they lived followed the order of describing the entrance, and then rooms branching off the entrance, returning to the hallway when they came to a dead end. Only after describing all the rooms would they then proceed to detail their contents. Their descriptions, in other words, seemed to follow a set pattern, which we would describe as a 'schema for describing one's home'.[6]

Such recurring orderings, however, raise a number of complex and largely unresolvable issues concerning the nature of the schema in operation. Do such patterns reflect schematic organization of knowledge of the world, or of certain text types—in this case description? I shall call these 'world schemata' and 'text schemata' respectively. By 'text schema' here I mean a typical ordering of facts in a real or fictional world. This neglected level of schematic knowledge is not the same as a typical ordering of functional units, which, in my terminology is better described as a 'discourse schema' (and corresponds to the 'rhetorical schemata' described by Carrell (1988) or the 'formal schemata' described by Carrell and Eisterhold (1983), or the notion of genre as developed in Swales 1990).

Though it might seem reasonable to suggest that world schemata and text schemata interact, and that, for example, descriptions of residences follow the order they do because that is how they are perceived and/or remembered, or because the speaker imagines conducting a visitor around his or her home, there is also the strong possibility that certain text types may impose their own organization upon information, and that this organization may be at odds with its storage prior to verbalization. Such a dichotomy is clear if one imagines narrating the events of a murder as evidence to the police or as a mystery story. In the latter case, the chronology of events would be disrupted by the demands of the text schema, and the initial event, which in a chronological narrative would come first, would be displaced to the end (Todorov [1966] 1988: 157–66). In such instances, different text schemata seem to be imposed upon a single world schema.

The origins of schema theory

The origin of schema theory in the current sense is most frequently attributed to the British psychologist Frederick Bartlett,[7] although Bartlett (1932: 199–201) himself gives credit for the idea to an earlier researcher, Henry Head, referring to the notion as one which had, even in the 1920s, been current for some time. In fact it seems unlikely that the notion of schemata could be said to have a definite point of origin or to be the invention of any one individual. In philosophy, the use of the word 'schema' goes back to Kant (the German word is also '*Schema*').

As such it is closely related to 'scheme' in the sense of 'a plan or map' and the two terms are often used interchangeably. Thus one problem with tracing the history of the term is separating its rigorous philosophical or psychological uses from casual ones as a high-flown synonym of 'scheme'.

Bartlett was a psychologist working within the Gestalt tradition, and his theories of memory, like Head's, must be seen against that background. As such, he shared the existing Gestalt emphasis on a 'top down' approach to understanding, and belief that perception creates a whole from otherwise disparate parts. Like other psychologists with a Gestalt approach to memory, he was concerned to demonstrate the inadequacies of theories of episodic memory relying on 'traces' of unique experiences (1932:204–5), and to stress the need for a theory of semantic memory instead.[8] Gestalt work in this vein owes much to the phenomenological approach in philosophy and psychology. The idea of schemata, and in particular the idea that discourse picks out new elements while leaving default ones to be filled in, may owe something to Husserl's theory of the 'manifold' ('the sum of the particulars furnished by sense before they have been unified by understanding' (Holub 1984:39)).[9]

A further reason for difficulty in fixing a point of origin for schema theory is that the notion that we interpret present experience in the light of organized past experience is both intuitively true—and a truism. As Bartlett himself observes:

> All people who have at any time been concerned with the nature and validity of everyday observation must have noticed that a good deal of what goes under the name of perception is, in the wide sense of the term, recall [. . .] the observer [. . .] fills up the gaps of his perception by the aid of what he has experienced before in similar situations, or [. . .] by describing what he takes to be 'fit' or suitable for such a situation.
> (Bartlett 1932:14)

So it is difficult to be precise about the dividing line between this commonplace observation and its innovative scientific development. It is not the idea of schematic memory which is radical, but its detailed explication.

Bartlett's *Remembering*

Bartlett worked upon perception in general, but it is only his work on the perception of text which concerns us here. In *Remembering* (1932: 63–95), he describes a series of experiments in which subjects were asked to recall material, either visual or textual, after ever longer and longer periods. In another series of experiments, referred to as 'serial reproduction' (op.cit.: 118–86), a subject was asked to reproduce an original, and that reproduction handed on to another subject to read and then later recall, and so on, in a process similar to the game of 'Chinese whispers'. Bartlett's aim was to study the changes which occurred in recall. He makes no particular distinction between textual and visual material, beyond noting the influence of certain narrative expectations on recall, such as the need for the weather to be 'sympathetic' to the plot in accordance with the so-called 'pathetic fallacy', i.e. 'the attribution by writers of human emotions [. . .] to inanimate objects or nature' (Wales 1989: 342).

The text Bartlett used was a translation of a native North American folk tale of a type which poses several comprehension problems for Europeans (the subjects were British). Bartlett noted the tendency of subjects to omit or rationalize details which they cannot tailor to their own expectations (such as supernatural events), to infer connections which are not stated, and to add detail which accords with stories they are familiar with (the time of death changes from sunrise to sunset for example, and the setting of a frightening story becomes a 'deep, dark forest'). He also noted how they remembered details most relevant to their own experience: his subjects, who had all lived through the First World War, while forgetting many other details, all remembered that one of the characters in the tale is distressed to leave his relatives for battle. From this series of experiments, Bartlett proceeded to his 'Theory of Remembering' (Chapter 10: 197–215) in which he propounds the basic principle of schema theory applied to language comprehension: that text is interpreted with the help of a knowledge structure activated from memory, capable of filling in details which are not explicitly stated.

However, at this point we should note some differences between Bartlett's schema theory and later versions. Firstly, there is no distinction made between the remembering of text and the remembering of sensory or kinesic data. Though texts were used in the experiments, language is treated as a transparent medium; in other words, no distinction is drawn between remembering the supposed facts of the story and a verbal representation of those facts. Secondly, schemata are treated as serial: representations of data whose elements are in (chronological) order, and there is no proposed hierarchical structure of different types of schemata which would enable movement from one element to another without following through the original order. There is thus no theoretical basis for explaining why certain details are omitted and others retained, either through failed recall or when deliberately summarizing, though both of these tendencies are noticed. Thirdly, prophetically, Bartlett several times (op.cit.: 202–12) expresses concern that the theory can in no way explain how the mind creates, destroys, and reorganizes schemata, though he does reiterate the need for the theory to explain this. Exactly such a concern with how the mind adapts its representations to new experience has become a focus of recent neurological theory (Edelman 1989, 1992). The central hypothesis of this book, proposed in detail in Chapters 8 and 9, is that a major function of certain discourses, notably literary discourses, may be to effect exactly such changes.

The eclipse of schema theory

As a psychologist of the Gestalt tradition, Bartlett relied heavily upon introspection concerning mental processes. Such an approach was soon to be eclipsed in psychology during the later 1930s, 40s and 50s by behaviourism, and more generally in the sciences by positivism, both of which forbade any appeal to the phenomenology of mental life. The linguistics of this period was keen to claim scientific status as defined by the academic norms of its time, and also adopted the behaviourist approach (Bloomfield [1933] 1935:21–41), limiting itself moreover to the analysis of sentences (Lyons 1968:172). Work on discourse was rarely undertaken in this mould of linguistics.[10]

The revival of schema theory

However, the 1970s witnessed an explosion of revived interest. Attempts to produce computer models of human text processing led to the realization that this involves not only knowledge of language, but also organized knowledge of the world (see for example Charniak (1975), Minsky (1975), Rumelhart (1975, 1977), Petofi (1976), Winograd (1977), Rumelhart and Ortony (1977), Schank and Abelson (1977)). Schema theory, as originated by Bartlett, was seized upon as an idea which might provide some insight into how this is done. Quite how knowledge is represented in schemata, whether in natural language or some other form of representation, need not concern us for the moment, though it is the assumption of AI that the latter possibility is the true one, and that some means of translation backwards and forwards between natural language and a conceptual representation is needed in both artificial and human intelligence (see Chapter 3). This assumption was based upon the fact that the most successful attempts to model human-like intelligence on computer made use of some form of conceptual representation (for a survey, see McTear 1987:15–39). The suggestion was that humans process discourse in a similar way to computers—although the complexity of the interaction of human language competence and knowledge is far greater than that of any computer programme.

AI work in this tradition was thus of two kinds: speculation on the nature of human intelligence and experimentation on the modelling of that intelligence in computers, conducted in the belief that each illuminates the other. If this hypothesis is true—that these pursuits are of the same object—then the old debate between behaviourist and cognitive psychology is to some degree bypassed. A behaviourist approach to psychology must limit itself to behaviour (the external manifestations of intelligence) only when it asserts, as it did in the 1940s and 50s, that the internal workings of an intelligence are impenetrable. In fact, this definition of behaviour rests upon the assumption that the mental processes behind behaviour are beyond analysis. One of the hopes of the strong AI approach to psychology is to render that distinction unnecessary by building intelligences whose mental processes are known and accessible, if only because they have been constructed by the analyst. (The leap from artificial to human intelligence still depends upon acceptance of an analogy between the two.) It is not that AI rejected the behaviourist approach to intelligence, but rather that it claimed to extend its frontiers. It is thus able to rehabilitate the ideas of Bartlett, while seeming in many ways akin to the more materialist views of his usurpers, sharing for example the essentially behaviourist view that similar behaviour indicates similar intelligence. The strong version of the AI thesis of course depends entirely upon the truth of the initial assumption of analogy, of which there are many opponents, notably the philosophers John Searle (Searle [1980] 1987) and Hilary Putnam (1988), the physicist Roger Penrose (1989), and the neurologist Gerald Edelman (1992). And the debate, though stimulated by the emotive issue of AI, is essentially an old one, well-established in philosophy, leading back to the rival claims and methods of rationalism and empiricism.

My own intention is to avoid this dispute by treating AI versions of schema theory as speculation about human intelligence, having the same status as any other theory of cognitive psychology, whether or not they are also reproducible in whole or part by computer. Indeed recent years have seen some fading of the initial hopes for AI and a diminution in the scope of its ambition to replicate human intelligence. Techniques of representation have also changed and the workings of the brain are no longer so widely regarded as analogous to those of a computer.[11] This, however, is not of concern here. The schema theory of AI has become firmly established as a contributory element in discourse analysis, a discipline which studies how people achieve meaning through texts, and it is with the interaction of text and human schematic representations of the world that this book is concerned.

The terminology of schema theory

Before we proceed, it may be wise to say a word about terminology. Ironically, in this area, the academic study of language often creates unnecessary confusion. This is endemic in linguistics, where theorists seem wilfully impervious to the fact that other people's definitions will persist alongside and in spite of their own. The simple solution would be always to employ a new term for a new concept rather than one which is already in use—but such an elementary insight into language seems beyond many who seek to explain its obscurer reaches!

Schema theory suffers from the same vice, and abounds in new usages of established terms, new terminologies which repeat old ideas, and redefinitions of terms by those who coined them.[12] Among those commonly used are 'frame', which dates back to Marvin Minsky's (1975) work on visual perception, 'global concepts',[13] 'scenarios',[14] and 'encyclopaedic entries'.[15] These are all general terms, roughly synonymous to 'schemata' as I have been using it above. This creates one kind of terminological problem. A different kind of problem arises when the term 'schema' is used in a narrower way than I am using it here. Thus one may find the term 'schema' used in text-generation theory to mean only 'rhetorical techniques' (McKeown 1985:10; Mann 1984; 1987), and in cognitive linguistics the term is sometimes used in the description of the rules of syntax as 'sentence schemata' (Winograd 1983:57–9, 347).

What is needed, in all this confusion, is firstly a general term, capable of referring to all types of postulated knowledge structures, and then a number of terms for sub-classes. The most favoured general term which has emerged over the years, especially in discourse analysis and applied linguistics,[16] seems now to be 'schema' (plural 'schemata') and that is why I have adopted it here. Later, I shall also distinguish three main types of schema: 'world schema', 'text schema', and 'language schema'. The large issue of the difference and interrelation between these three will, I hope, become clearer and more important as the argument develops.

Notes

1 'Function' here is used to mean 'function for the receiver' rather than 'function for the sender'. The comments here thus refer more to the effect of a discourse—what it does—rather than the intention behind it—what its sender wants it to do.

2 It may be that the mind also has representations of individual facts, perhaps stored along with the relevant typical instances which they most closely resemble (Schank 1982a:37–47).

3 This idea forms the basis of the 'reception theory' of literature (developed by Wolfgang Iser and others) which, significantly, has its roots in the same phenomenological approach to psychology as the Gestalt work on perception which is the origin of schema theory (Holub 1984).

4 Large-scale scholarly grammars have for a long time both recognized and attempted to tackle this question (Kruisinga 1932:242; Jespersen 1949:479–80), making some reference to the idea of shared knowledge in explanation, as do more recent grammars based on linguistics (Quirk et al. 1972:154–5; 1985:266–9). The usage can be accounted for by schema theory with particular elegance, however, simply by saying that our 'aeroplane schema' contains a 'pilot', and we assume that he or she has to be there for the plane to take off. It is as though he or she has already been mentioned.

5 An idea closely related to the formalist notion of 'defamiliarization' which I shall discuss in more detail in Chapter 5.

6 Van Dijk (1977:80) suggests a number of other general orders for description: that we tend, for example, to move from the general to the particular; the whole to the part; the including to the included; the large to the small; the outside to the inside. The degree to which such shared schemata may be universal or culture-specific is a question for continuing investigation and debate.

7 For example by de Beaugrande and Dressler 1981:90; van Dijk and Kintsch 1983:3; Widdowson 1984:124; Atkinson, Atkinson, Smith, and Hilgard 1987:275; Greene 1987:41; Garnham 1988:45.

8 For a summary of the rival theories of episodic and semantic memory, see Loftus and Loftus 1976.

9 An idea which itself derives from Kant, and, through a different line of descent, gave rise to Roman Ingarden's phenomenological theory of literature (Ingarden [1931] 1973:12), which has in turn profoundly influenced the 'reception theory' of the Geneva School of literary theory led by Wolfgang Iser (1974; 1978). The definition of the term 'manifold' here is from the *Shorter Oxford English Dictionary* (3rd edn.).

10 Bartlett's work, as van Dijk and Kintsch point out, 'only occasionally inspired psychologists during the [next] forty years' (1983:3). In effect, there is a lacuna in the development of the theory between Bartlett and the revival of the 1970s. Various attempts to trace the survival of Bartlett's idea through the literature of the intervening decades only emphasizes its absence. Van Dijk and Kintsch (1983: 3), and Schank and Abelson (1977:10), for example, both give their own histories by listing a series of papers, but curiously, their lists have no single author in common, suggesting that the theory was indeed 'on ice'. Schachtel (1949), in a study of Freud and Proust, used the term 'schemata' to describe adult categorization of memories which block the intensity of childhood experience from recall. Gibson (1950) drew a distinction between 'schematic perception' and 'literal perception', describing the former as casual and inattentive, and the latter as more detailed and precise (see Miller 1966:120). These uses,

however, are rather different from that described above. Nor is this diversity of attribution a feature of these two sources alone. Slobin (1979:155), for example, in describing Bartlett's work, links it only with a work on the psychology of rumour (Allport and Postman: 1947), as do Edwards and Middleton (1987).

11 Much AI work on schemata predates connectionist theories of 'Parallel Distributed Processing' which have gained wide currency in Cognitive Science (Rumelhart and McLelland 1986a and b; Johnson-Laird 1988:174–94). In this connectionist view of knowledge there are no separate 'stores' of rules or 'facts'. The knowledge and the rules are 'in' the connections of a neural network, and knowledge is thus distributed rather than localized. The strengths (or 'weightings') of connections are increased by exposure to data which activate them. The network thus acts 'as though it knows the rules' (Rumelhart and McLelland 1986:32) though those rules exist only as an abstraction by an outside analyst. Schema theory is in general quite compatible with this view of cognitive processing, although there is debate about the degree to which language knowledge may be stored in this way (Lachter and Bever 1988; Pinker and Prince 1988).

12 Though Bartlett may be credited with introducing the term in its current sense, he also rejected it as one 'I strongly dislike ... at once too definite and too sketchy' (1932:200–1)!

13 De Beaugrande and Dressler 1981:90.

14 First used by Sanford and Garrod 1981.

15 Sperber and Wilson (1986:138). Although Sperber and Wilson are slightly cursory in their summary of schema theory (op.cit.:138), taking 'context' to be 'the set of assumptions used in interpreting an utterance' (op.cit.:15), they define relevance (op.cit.:147) as 'that which has the greatest contextual effects and requires the smallest processing effort'. This view is not, however, incompatible with schema theory as described here. Schema theory could define 'relevance' as that which is not predicted by the schema, but will change it ('has the greatest contextual effects'); on the other hand, the existence of a schema which can accommodate new information makes processing easier ('requires the smallest processing effort'). Sperber and Wilson's lists of 'assumptions' brought to bear on a situation (for example op.cit.:142), are, therefore, rather like schemata.

16 Following Widdowson 1983.

2 A first bearing: discourse analysis and its limitations

Introduction

As outlined in the last chapter, schema theory originated in the Gestalt psychology of the 1920s and was later revived in the Artificial Intelligence work of the 1970s and 1980s. It has since become firmly established and further developed in applied linguistics, where schematic knowledge is seen as a crucial component of a language user's competence (Widdowson 1983) and therefore also of central importance in language acquisition (Skehan 1989:46). It is also an accepted component of discourse analysis—the study of what it is that makes texts meaningful and coherent for their users. Here again an emphasis on schematic knowledge is seen as an essential element in the development of discourse skills by the language learner (Widdowson 1983; Cook 1989; McCarthy 1991; Hatch 1992; Wallace 1992).

The aim of this book is to suggest and demonstrate that in certain discourse, of which literature is the prime example, the relation between schema and language is of a particular—and particularly important— kind. The argument is, put succinctly, that certain uses of language can change our representations of the world; that certain texts, in other words, can alter our schemata. As a background to this argument, this chapter discusses some of the main approaches to discourse. Its purpose is to examine, critically, some of the main tenets of discourse analysis, and to assess their potential role in the analysis of literature. Initially, the kind of discourse analysis examined is that which derives from and shares some of the 'scientific' premises of linguistics; and I am primarily concerned (as throughout this book) with written text experienced through reading. I hope to show how these approaches cannot always cope with literary discourse, and must lead to a search for some different relation between text and knowledge from that which is currently accepted.

'Text', 'context', and 'discourse'

Discourse analysis concerns the interaction of texts with knowledge of context to create discourse. As these terms 'text', 'context', and 'discourse' are used so variously and even interchangeably elsewhere,[1] it seems sensible to state clearly, at the outset, how they are used in this book.

By 'a text', I mean the linguistic forms in a stretch of language, and those interpretations of them which do not vary with context. I use the general term 'text' to mean language regarded in this way. In linguistics, texts have often been discussed as though their meanings were constant for all users. As has often been observed, valid objections may be raised to this notion of text as fixed. Firstly, it may be generalizing to the point of distortion to talk of different speakers' language competence as homogeneous. (Do a James Joyce and a six-year-old child really have so much in common?) Secondly, as many literary theorists have observed, it may be misleading to separate receiver and text in any way, since each comes into being through the other (Bakhtin[2] [1929] 1973:103; Barthes [1970] 1974). Text is dependent on its receiver, and therefore variable. Nevertheless, I believe the term is sufficiently constant to be used in the sense defined above.

Text interacts with 'context', which in my definition is a form of knowledge of the world. The ability to use a given language is a form of (tacit) knowledge too, yet there is an important distinction to be made between knowledge of the language and other knowledge. When I later emphasize the importance of describing the knowledge of a receiver as well as the text, I am not referring to linguistic knowledge.

The term 'context' can be used in both a broad and a narrow sense. In the narrow sense it refers to (knowledge of) factors outside the text under consideration. In the broad sense it refers to (knowledge of) these factors and to (knowledge of) other parts of the text under consideration, sometimes referred to as 'co-text'.[3]

'Context', in the broad sense, may be considered to be either external to language users, composed of elements existing independently of them, or internal, composed of their knowledge of them (Dascal 1981; Cook 1990a; Duranti and Goodwin 1992).[4] In practice, the two will usually be the same, and the distinction may be felt to be pedantic. Yet there are times when the distinction is important—when interactants distort, ignore, or fail to perceive elements of the context (as it is judged to exist by the analyst). I shall favour the second interpretation of context and define it as knowledge of relevant features of the world and co-text, rather than the world and co-text themselves. As such, context in the broad sense consists of knowledge of:

1 co-text
2 paralinguistic features
3 other texts (i.e. 'intertext')
4 the physical situation
5 the social and cultural situation

6 interlocutors and their schemata (knowledge about other people's knowledge)

'Discourse', as opposed to text, is a stretch of language in use, taking on meaning in context for its users, and perceived by them as purposeful, meaningful, and connected. This quality of perceived purpose, meaning, and connection is known as 'coherence'. 'Discourse analysis' is the study and the explanation of this quality of coherence. A discourse *is* a coherent stretch of language.

Defined in this way as a 'perceived' quality, the coherence of a given stretch of language will vary both with its perceiver and with its context. Discourse analysis must therefore be both a study of the formal linguistic qualities of stretches of language (texts), and a study of the variable perception of these stretches of language by individuals and groups.

Acceptability above the sentence

One starting point for 'scientific' analysis of written discourse is to consider the possibility that there are in texts rules and constraints on the selection and ordering of elements above the sentence—in other words, to consider whether grammar can be extended upwards. This was frequently a major concern of early attempts at discourse analysis (Harris 1952) and of 'text linguistics'. It will be useful to the argument here to look at some of the shortcomings of this approach.

It is not difficult to think up a string of sentences which seem odd to competent speakers of the language. Writing of narrative, Rumelhart put the standard case succinctly, as follows:

> Just as simple sentences can be said to have an internal structure, so too can stories be said to have an internal structure. This is so in spite of the fact that no one has ever been able to specify a general structure that will distinguish the strings of sentences which form stories from the strings which do not. Nevertheless, the notion of 'well-formedness' is nearly as reasonable for stories as it is for sentences. Consider the following examples:
>
> (1) Margie was holding tightly to the string of her new balloon. Suddenly, a gust of wind caught it. The wind carried it into a tree. The balloon hit a branch and burst. Margie cried and cried.
> (2) Margie cried and cried. The balloon hit a branch and burst. The wind carried it into a tree. Suddenly a gust of wind caught it. Margie was holding tightly to the string of her beautiful new balloon.
>
> Here I find two strings of sentences. One, however, also seems to form a sensible whole, whereas the other seems to be analysable into little more than a string of sentences. These examples should make

clear that some higher level of organization takes place in stories that does not take place in strings of sentences.
(Rumelhart 1975:211–12)

A number of points can be raised in objection, or at least in qualification, of Rumelhart's reasoning. Firstly, what is said here applies to narrative, and perhaps to narrative only. Indeed, an excessive concentration on narrative, to the exclusion of other discourse types, is a limitation of much textual analysis. It might be that ordering rules for sentences *can* be formulated for narratives, but that this formulation can not be generalized to other discourse types. This particular narrative, moreover, is one which follows a strict chronological sequence: the order of events in the world, and the order of events in the text are the same. But there are many other principles governing the ordering of events, especially in literature (as we shall see in Chapter 5), and indeed, as Fleischman (1990:132) observes, the frequent assumption in linguistics that a chronological sequencing of events in narrative is the usual or expected order may well be wrong.

Secondly, it might be argued that the rules governing the ordering of sentences in Rumelhart's example are dependent on knowledge of the world rather than any kind of 'text grammar'. One has to consider whether the oddity of the second version is really of the same kind as a departure from sentence grammar, such as:

*Carrot in gone my under does whose the ran.

One of the major factors in the coherence of Rumelhart's story derives not from formal co-occurrence restrictions, but from belief about the nature of time and continuity, and reversible as opposed to irreversible change. The balloon, competent speakers believe, cannot both 'have burst' and 'be carried by the wind'. Another source of coherence in this passage is our knowledge of children: they like balloons and are upset when they burst. (Rumelhart makes similar points himself.) Though these facts may always hold in our present experience however, one can imagine worlds, especially literary worlds, in which they would not. Science fiction, by definition, describes worlds about which our beliefs are significantly different, necessitating both an increase in the amount of explicit reference to background knowledge needed for interpretation, and the creation of coherence in texts which, interpreted through knowledge of the real world, would appear incoherent (Pitrat [1985] 1988:8). The same is true to some extent of any fictional world. Schematic expectation can be broken in fiction without destroying coherence. Rumelhart's second story might well be coherent in a number of fantastic fictional worlds. In Chapter 2 of Lewis Carroll's *Through the Looking Glass*, for example, time runs backwards, and expected sequences of events happen in reverse order. Another example is a *Superman* story in which the villain wins decisively, but is then defeated when Superman causes a period of time to be rerun. (Superman does this by flying up into Space and then orbiting so fast around the earth that he creates a gravitational pull strong enough to stop the Earth's rotation and make it spin in the opposite direction. Time returns to an earlier point in the story and the denouement is repeated, this time with a victory for Superman.) The oddity of Rumelhart's second sequence is thus relative to a given context, i.e. discoursal. A string of sentences which may initially appear unacceptable can be made to appear 'well-formed' by a change of context, including that of being presented as 'fantastic'.[5] Discourse analysis, in other words, demands a description of the knowledge of a specific receiver, of the kind which can be provided by schema theory.

One amusing example of coherence being established between sentences through knowledge of context is widely believed to occur in *Finnegans Wake,* in which the word '*entrez*' is supposed to have been mistakenly included by Joyce's amanuensis (Samuel Beckett) when somebody knocked at the door during dictation (Ellman [1959] 1982:649; Kennedy 1971: 207). Knowledge of this anecdote—whether true or not—would be one way of making this sentence coherent with its co-text when encountered.[6] Again, a literary example defies the general rule.

The situation is further complicated by the fact that discourse does not have to consist of strings of sentences, and that therefore a statement of combination rules for such sentences would not be enough, even if it were possible. Take, for example, the following:

> Mario Vargas Llosa. *Aunt Julia and the Scriptwriter.* Translated by Helen Lane. Picador. Published by Pan Books. To Julia Urquidi Illanes, to whom this novel and I owe so much. One. In those long ago days, I was very young and lived with my grandparents in a villa with white walls in the Calle Ocharan, in Miraflores.

Here, an application of knowledge about the layout and conventions of novels will make this a coherent discourse (just as knowledge about balloons, wind, and children makes Rumelhart's example coherent) despite the fact that of the eight units marked orthographically as sentences, only one conforms to the rules of sentence grammars. In this example it is true that I have run together a number of quite separate functional parts of the same discourse (distinguished by textual features such as typography, page position, and the spaces between them) but we do not have to cut across discourse parts (title page, dedication, etc.) so radically to find texts which are not composed of sentences. Many literary texts, including narrative, contain sequences which do not conform to the usual rules of sentence grammars. The orthographic sentences of the opening of Charles Dickens' novel *Bleak House*, for example, are without main verbs (Leech and Short 1981:138), as is this entire poem by Robert Browning:

Meeting at Night

The gray sea and the long black land;
And the yellow half-moon large and low;
And the startled little waves that leap
In fiery ringlets from their sleep,
As I gain the cove with pushing prow,   5
And quench its speed i' the slushy sand.

Then a mile of warm sea-scented beach;
Three fields to cross till a farm appears;
A tap at the pane, the quick sharp scratch
And blue spurt of a lighted match,   10
And a voice less loud, thro' its joys and fears,
Than the two hearts beating each to each!

Here, the two orthographic sentences, despite their departure from the 'normal' grammar of written English, are clearly connected as the two stages of the lover's journey, on sea and then on land, while their verblessness, perhaps, lends to the scene a static quality as the perspective gradually focuses from the panoramic to close-up, and the sense appealed to changes from sight to touch.

Whatever rules there may be for well-formed sequences, then, they cannot only be regarded as rules for the combination of sentences. Rumelhart's approach, in the extract quoted above, makes the rather naïve assumption that they can.[7]

This is not to say, however, that the rules of sentence grammars are of no relevance to discourse analysis, but only that whatever units exist above the sentence are different in kind. Nor is it to say that sentence grammar and context do not affect each other. Syntactic ordering to obtain focus on particular pieces of information, for example, is affected by a sender's knowledge of the knowledge of an interlocutor. When we come to examine the relationship between 'deviant' linguistic choices in literature of the kind emphasized by Jakobsonian stylistics, and 'deviant' conceptual representations in terms of the schemata of a given reader, one of the main points of the argument will be the futility of examining either in isolation. Description of linguistic choices at the level of grammar is undoubtedly important, but is significant only when related to a description of the receiver.

Cohesion

Cohesion may be defined as the formal linguistic realization of semantic and pragmatic relations between clauses and sentences in a text (Quirk, Greenbaum, Leech, and Svartvik 1985:1423). Catalogues of cohesive links are well known (Halliday and Hasan 1976; Halliday 1985) and summarized in many places; it is not my intention to rehearse them again here. It is, however, relevant to examine firstly the degree to which particular uses of cohesion may be typical of literary texts, and thus distinguish them as a text type, and secondly the degree to which a description of cohesion may contribute to the fundamental issue of discourse analysis: the explanation of coherence and the relationship between language and knowledge.

Aspects of literary cohesion: parallelism

Despite definitions of cohesion as the realization of semantic and pragmatic links (Quirk et al. 1985:1423), we may—if we define a cohesive device as a formal feature capable of creating a connection between sentences—validly include under the heading of cohesion a device which is often purely formal, and which is not included in these definitions. This is 'parallelism', a device frequently used in literary and related discourses, in which the repetition of form suggests a connection to the reader, through isomorphism (the principle whereby similarity of form suggests or reflects similarity of meaning). Syntactic parallelism occurs when the form of one sentence, clause, or phrase repeats the form of another;[8] morphological parallelism is when morphemes repeat; phonological parallelism is manifest in rhyme, rhythm, and other uses of sound. All may be regarded as instances of cohesion when they create links across clause and sentence boundaries. Such parallelism is a frequent and noticeable feature of many speeches, prayers, poems, and advertisements, though also, rather less saliently, of casual conversation (Tannen 1989). It can have a powerful emotive effect; it is also a useful *aide-mémoire*. In conversation it may create solidarity and interpersonal convergence. Thus, though often salient in literary texts, it is by no means distinctive of them.[9]

Parallelism, rather than realizing existing links, may create them.[10] Two words which rhyme, for example, may imply a link between their referents. Parallelism is also of great importance to the argument in this book for two reasons. Firstly, it is largely ignored by AI schema theories of how text is represented in the mind (see Chapter 3). Secondly, it is central to the Jakobsonian and stylistics attempts to associate literariness with formal linguistic features.

Aspects of literary cohesion: verb form sequences

Parallelism is, as it were, a luxury, available for rhetorical effect to add or create links between sentences, but in no way obligatory. A second kind of link can be effected by the constraints upon verb form determined by preceding clauses. The form of the verb in one clause can limit the choice of the verb form in the next, and we may be justified in saying that a verb form in one clause is 'unacceptable', or perhaps even 'deviant', because it does not fit with the form in another, although (as indicated in the critique above of Rumelhart's attempt at a grammar of sentences) there are always contexts in which unlikely combinations are possible. (We should also remember that many literary genres, as Fleischman (1990:175) observes of narrative, are marked categories of linguistic performance 'whose grammar differs in certain respects from that of everyday language'.)

The existence of constraints on verb form operating across clause boundaries is perhaps best illustrated by such striking deviations as, for example, these words of Jesus in the Authorised Version of St John's Gospel:

> Before Abraham was, I am.
> (John 8:58)

in which the breaking of the bonds of grammatical tense seems, perhaps, to represent the speaker's claim to independence of tense's semantic correlate, time.

Yet, again, this example belies the claim that departure from expected tense sequences is an exclusive feature of literature. (To me it seems that the Bible is not primarily a literary work, though it may have literary qualities.)

Aspects of literary cohesion: referring expressions

Pro-forms: The use of repeated pro-form referring expressions in discourse creates a 'chain', linking clauses and sentences together. Comprehensive explanation of the successful interpretation of referring expressions is notoriously difficult, and an issue to which much attention is devoted in computational linguistics (see for example Appelt 1985:8–121; Reichman 1985; Alshwani 1987; Dale 1988). Any theory capable of predicting interpretation will need to take account of far more than linguistic form, and deal with such issues as topic, focus, saliency, and schematic knowledge. This is because the interpretation of such referring expressions must be pragmatic. It demands a decription of the relevant context.[11] In my terms this means a description of the knowledge of interlocutors. Such a description can be provided in terms of schema theory. Consider the likely interpretations of the pronoun in an example given by Pitrat [1985] 1988:7):

> The teacher sent the class dunce to the headmaster because he wanted to throw pellets.

in which the reference of 'he' is achieved only by knowledge of school hierarchies, which of the three possible candidates is likely to throw pellets, and sanctions against disobedient pupils.

   Co-reference through pro-forms is ubiquitous if not universal in extended discourse, and hardly a candidate feature for a characterization of literariness. More marked co-reference through nominal group repetition and absence of reduction might seem, however, to have a certain literary quality.

Repetition: Repetition of the original nominal can create the same sort of chain as pronouns, conveying the same semantic content, though with a different stylistic effect. The use of repetition is more frequent in certain discourse types than in others. Advertisements, for example, often repeat the brand name together with other words, which—we might hypothesize—they wish to associate with it (Cook 1992:154). Legal discourse, on the other hand, tends to avoid pro-forms. It is often argued that this diminishes possible ambiguity, though in many cases that is disputable. Instruction manuals favour repetition to avoid ambiguity. Literary discourse often favours repetition over pro-forms too, as in the opening stanza of Robert Burns' poem 'A Red, Red Rose'.

> O *my luve*'s like a red, red rose
> That's newly sprung in June;
> O *my luve*'s like the melody . . .
> (my italics)

In this case, perhaps, the repetition suggests the pleasure of the appellation, present also in the lover's habit of repeating the beloved's name (Barthes [1977] 1990). Here once again, however, as the non-literary texts reveal, literature holds no monopoly.

Reduced repetition: An intermediate form between pro-form reference and repetition is the use of a reduced form of a noun phrase. Thus 'a small boy' becomes 'the boy'; 'the river Alma' becomes 'the river'; 'the door on the right' becomes 'the door' and so on. This too may be exploited for literary effect, as it is in the following extract from Raymond Chandler's novel *The Long Goodbye*:

> Back from the highway at the bottom of Sepulvada Canyon were two square yellow gateposts. A five-barred gate hung open from one of them. Over the entrance was a sign hung on wire: PRIVATE

ROAD. NO ADMITTANCE. The air was warm and quiet and full
of the tomcat smell of eucalyptus trees.

I turned in and followed *a gravelled road* round the shoulder of
the hill, up a gentle slope, over a ridge and down the other side into
a shadow valley. It was hot in the valley, ten or fifteen degrees hotter
than on the highway. I could see now that *the gravelled road* ended
in a loop round some grass edged with stones that had been
lime-washed. Off to my left there was *an empty swimming pool*.
Around three sides of it there was what remained of a lawn dotted
with redwood lounging chairs with badly faded pads on them. The
pads had been of many colours, blue, green, yellow, orange, rust-red.
Their edge bindings had come loose in spots, the buttons had popped,
and the pads were bloated where this had happened. On the fourth
side there was the high wire fence of a tennis court. The diving board
over *the empty pool* looked knee-sprung and tired. Its matting covering
hung in shreds and its metal fittings were flaked with rust.
(Raymond Chandler: *The Long Goodbye* [1953] 1959:101 my italics)

Here the marked failure to fully reduce the noun phrases 'a gravelled
road' and 'an empty swimming pool' lends the passage an air of attention
to detail which may suggest timelessness, sinister significance, heightened
sensation, and vivid memory.

An alternative to chains of anaphoric referring expresions and to
repeated or reduced nominals is the use of semantically related nominals,
such as superordinates, hyponyms, synonyms, meronyms, and even
antonyms. Links through meronyms (words referring to the parts of
something) are difficult to distinguish from links through membership of
a single schema. In later chapters, when I come to list the contents of
schemata, I shall include items which are meronymically related to the
central item (thus 'feather', for example, is an item in a schema for a
'bird'). Cohesion through meronymy is intimately connected to metonymy
(in which an entity is referred to by mention of a part of it, or of an
entity related to it), a phenomenon which, in literary theory, has often
been discussed in partnership with metaphor (see Wales 1989:297).

The role of cohesion in discourse

Some writers (for example van Dijk and Kintsch 1983) regard cohesion
as an instance of coherence. Others (Brown and Yule 1983:191–9; de
Beaugrande and Dressler 1981:48–111) regard the two as distinct, seeing
cohesion as an element of text explicable in terms akin to those of
formal linguistics, and coherence as a result of the interaction of text
and receiver, which, though it may be aided by cohesion, is distinct and

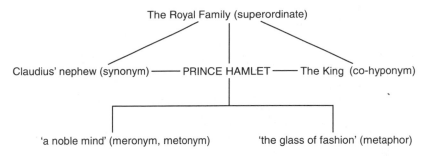

Figure 2.1: Sense relations: a literary example

independent from it. It is true that, in principle, cohesion is neither necessary nor sufficient to create coherence, yet in practice a discourse of any length will employ it. That most coherent texts are also cohesive, however, does not imply that coherence is created by cohesion. If an actual sequence of cohesive sentences is divorced from its context, an incoherent effect may result: for example this randomly selected extract from Martin Amis' novel *Other People* ([1981] 1982:89):

> She thought, I'm becoming like other people. I'm getting fear and letting the present dim. But it had to happen Mary.

Such extracted 'texts', though cohesive, are not coherent without some specific knowledge on the part of the receiver (Bransford and Johnson 1973). The important point however, as far as a literary text is concerned, is that a reader, presented with a contextless text, will assume that there *is* coherence and read on, or seek elsewhere to find it. In fact the absence of coherence is often an incentive to read further and thus deliberately courted in literary discourse, where the reader's only motivation to proceed will often be interest or pleasure. The only alternatives to this faith that there is coherence to be discovered once the necessary knowledge is acquired, is to label the sender as insane, or the text as one created by some random process. In literature, even these expectations are possible: there have been many excellent writers with psychiatric conditions, and randomness as a mode of composition has been employed in the creation of some literary works such as Tristran Tzara's Dada poems (made from words pulled out of a hat) or William Burroughs' cutting and folding of the pages of his manuscripts to create new combinations of their words (Odier 1970).

Conversely, as has often been observed, there are short discourses, especially conversational interchanges, which can be perceived as coherent, given the necessary contextual or cultural knowledge, but not cohesive.

Enter FARQUAR

Farquar   Doctor Daubeney's carriage!

Lady Hunstanton   My dear Archdeacon! It is only half past ten.

The Archdeacon   I'm afraid I must go, Lady Hunstanton. Tues-
                             day is always one of Mrs Daubeney's bad
                             nights.

Oscar Wilde (1893): *A Woman of No Importance*, Act III

Such instances have been major factors in pointing to the inadequacy of discourse analysis conducted in purely formal terms, and in instigating a search for other sources of coherence. This search has led to investigation of the role of pragmatic interpretative processes, of know-ledge of textual structures, and of knowledge of the world in general. Yet although awareness of the interaction of knowledge and text in the creation of coherence has now become a commonplace in discourse analysis, it has not yet made a substantial impact on literary theories. Yet without a sense of this interaction, any analysis of literary effect in purely formal terms is left stranded.

Cohesion is a manifestation of certain aspects of coherence, and a pointer towards it, rather than its cause or necessary result. Cohesion is never more than a partial textual realization of coherence (which is a feature of the perception of text rather than of text itself). Even in texts with a density of cohesive ties, many links of co-reference, cause, sequence, and logic, though recoverable by the reader or listener, remain unstated and have no textual manifestation whatsoever. Though an increase in cohesion may, up to a certain point, make a text clearer, less ambiguous, and more coherent, there is a point beyond which it may make it duller and less readily processible. This is, for example, particularly evident in legal texts.

In short, in any text, there is a great deal of information which is not stated—not only connections which could be indicated with cohesive devices, but also intermediate and component events, and the motives, plans, feelings, and reasoning of participants. If this were not so, any discourse would grow to an unwieldy—even perhaps infinite—length (Cook 1990a). It would also become pedantic and boring.

The omission fallacy

Though we may loosely describe these unstated connections as 'omitted', this does not necessarily imply that they were present at some stage in the formulation of the discourse. The common tendency to assume that they were might justifiably be described as 'the omission fallacy'. When com-munication takes place and discourse is perceived as coherent, missing elements can be constructed if necessary by people processing the text, just as they could have been included if necessary by the sender. This is precisely why they are not needed. But they may never be present unless such a construction is required. This is a potential problem for schema theory.

Let us consider a brief example of two consecutive sentences from a short story by G. K. Lapochkin (1992):

> The guard dog died when one of the prisoners threw it poisoned meat. The handler cried all night, though we had always thought of him as heartless.

This potentially coherent sequence contains a number of cohesive devices: pro-forms and conjunctions, and verb forms relating across clause and sentence boundaries. One might also argue for a degree of semantic relation between the words 'guard dog', 'prisoners', and 'handler', between 'poison' and 'died', or between 'cried' and 'heartless': they might well be found close together in a semantic network for example (Garnham 1987:22–5). The coherence, however, rests on more than these textually realized relations. In terms of causality, for example, neither the causal chain which links the throwing of the meat to the death of the dog, nor the death of the dog to the weeping of the handler, nor the weeping of the handler to the presupposition that he is heartless, is explicitly stated. Readers suppose that the dog ate and digested the meat; that the poison entered its cells; that this created various biological effects which led to its death; that its death was perceived by the handler; that this perception caused various emotions to arise in his mind; that these emotions caused him to cry; that this crying was perceived by the prisoners and judged by them to be a sign of compassion, disrupting their previous assessment of the handler. Needless to say, the chain of cause and effect here is further reducible to a level of detail where causes are unknown. Though we talk loosely of 'a cause of death' or 'a cause of tears', it is hard to be precise about either. Motives, too, are unstated. We do not need to know why the dog ate the meat or why the prisoners wanted it to do so. The temporal relation between the events depicted in the two main clauses can also be assumed. In the absence of contrary indications,[12] the linear development of discourse is presumed to represent iconically the sequence of events in time (Leech and Short 1981:235).

Coherence, then, while reinforced by cohesion, is also created by elements which have no textual realization, but can be provided by someone processing the text when necessary. Given the human predilection to perceive coherence wherever possible, there may well be instances where the links will be different when provided by different individuals. Such may often be the case in the literary juxtaposition of clauses or sentences. The following opening of a poem, 'Missing dates', by William

Empson (though also possibly about poisoning) may meet with less consensus than the sentences about the guard dog:

> Slowly the poison the whole bloodstream fills.
> It is not the effort nor the failure tires.

Meaning as encoding/decoding versus meaning as construction

To say that the links which create coherence are only very partially realized in the text has severe implications for any merely semiotic theory of language which views communication as the encoding and decoding of thoughts. Although this theory has very deep roots in the Western tradition, continuing from the Aristotelian to the Saussurean models of communication, it is one which has been discarded in contemporary views of language in favour of a view of meaning as actively constructed by the mind through the interplay of the text with knowledge and reasoning (Sperber and Wilson 1986: 1–64). In this post-semiotic paradigm there are a number of approaches to text, each placing different emphasis upon elements in the construction of meaning. Thus linguistics focuses upon grammar and semantics. Pragmatics, often taking this linguistic part of processing for granted, devotes most of its attention to the principles and reasoning procedures which enable speakers to infer intention, function, and facts with no overt textual realization. The AI approach to text, on the other hand, has devoted a large proportion of its attention to the nature and organization of knowledge of the world. Discourse analysis has tried eclectically to draw on all these approaches, sometimes seeking for an extension of the rules of grammar to higher units than the sentence (Harris 1952; Werlich 1976; Longacre 1983), sometimes examining the processing strategies which language users employ and the textual features which help orientation within discourse.

Pragmatic approaches and their capacity to characterize 'literariness'

As already observed, in brief spoken exchanges it is quite common to encounter sequences of utterances that are almost entirely bare of cohesion. In the view of pragmatics, such sequences are coherent through pragmatic inference, connected through the functions they perform. The theory which I wish to put forward concerns the function of literary discourses, and part of my argument is that this function is not adequately explained by the current orthodox functional theories. It is pertinent at this point, therefore, to say something about these current functional views.

It is also worth noting at this point the frequently overlooked ambiguity of the term 'function', which can mean both 'function for the receiver' and 'function for the sender', the two not necessarily being the same. The term 'function', in other words, may refer to the effect of a discourse—what it does—rather than the intention behind it—what its user does with it. Pragmatics has a tendency to concern itself very much with function in terms of the intention of the sender rather than with the effect on the receiver. Discussions of literary discourse are often concerned with function as effect rather than intention. Most functional taxonomies, such as those described below, conflate the two interpretations, considering their relationship to be unproblematic.

'Function' is often dealt with on two levels: the first concerning the broadest descriptions of the purpose of language in general, the second concerning the more specific acts performed by individual utterances. The two levels are, however, related, the micro-functions of individual acts being sub-categories of the general macro-functions of language. The micro-function of 'ordering' for example is one of several which may be subsumed under the macro-functional category of the directive. It is with macro-functions that I am concerned here.

Macro-functions

There have been many, sometimes conflicting, attempts to classify the main functions of language. Among the most frequently cited are those proposed by Bühler (1934); Jakobson (1960); Searle (1969, 1975b);[13] Popper (1972), and Hymes (1972).[14] (For the relations between these taxonomies see Figure 2.2 below). Fundamental to all functional approaches to language 'is the belief that uses of language shape the system' (Wales 1989:198). In general, and with the major exception of Jakobson's poetic function, which I discuss below, the functions these writers suggest can be grouped under four main headings: those concerned with expressing inner states, those concerned with communicating information, those concerned with creating and maintaining social relationships, and those concerned with affecting the behaviour of others. In the theories of Jakobson, Popper, and Hymes[15] there is also a fifth category: the metalinguistic function in which language describes and regulates itself.

With reason, however, we may reduce this fivefold generalization even further. If we regard the expression of inner states and the discussion of the language itself as communicating information, and if we regard attempts to affect the behaviour of others as part of the regulation of the social world, then we may say that language has, in all these theorists' views, two main functions:

1 the communication of information about the world
2 the creation and maintenance (or destruction) of social relations

This generalization echoes part of Halliday's categorization of the functions of language (Halliday 1973:22–46; 1976:19–27).[16] The two major functions above are equivalent respectively to Halliday's

1 ideational function
2 interpersonal function[17]

Together, these two major functions allow human beings to:

1 undertake the co-operative manipulation of the environment
2 create and maintain social relationships

It could be argued that the successful human manipulation of the environment is made possible by social relationships, and that therefore the second of these categories derives from the first.

Among the functional taxonomies listed in Figure 2.2, there is one function which does not fit easily into either of the two main categories. This is Jakobson's 'poetic function', in which the dominant focus is on linguistic form rather than on any other element in the communicative situation. Other classifications either include no such function or (having adopted it from Jakobson)[18] pay it less attention. This does not fit easily into either of the two general categories described above [19] and must be listed separately, adding a third purpose to human language use, which, for the moment, we must list as:

3 something unknown (the poetic function)

For although Jakobson talks of literary language as having a poetic function, he nowhere gives an explanation of what that function is in terms of what it does or is intended to do. The emotive function expresses inner states and feelings, the conative function seeks to affect the behaviour of others, and so on. These are explanations as well as descriptions. But what is it that language with a poetic function does?[20] To say that the poetic function focuses attention on the linguistic form of the message, and to describe this with great perception and detail as Jakobson does: this is description, but not explanation.

In mainstream Hallidayan linguistics, there is a somewhat unconvincing attempt to bring the poetic function within the orbit of the interpersonal and ideational functions. Hasan (1989), in her book on verbal art, is a typical exponent of this view. She copes with the blatant meaninglessness, though evident attractiveness, of children's nursery rhymes by regarding them merely as preparation for the meaningful use of such play with codes for ideational and social purposes in adult literature:

The taxonomy most relevant to my argument is Jakobson (1960). Jakobson proceeded by first identifying six elements in communication:
- the addresser: not necessarily the same as the sender
- the addressee: usually but not necessarily the same as the receiver
- the context: in his terms the referent or information
- the message: the particular linguistic form
- the contact: the medium or channel
- the code: the language or dialect.

Corresponding to each element is a particular function of language, respectively:
- the emotive: communicating the inner states and emotions of the addresser
- the conative: seeking to affect the behaviour of the addressee
- the referential: carrying information
- the poetic: in which the message (i.e. form) is dominant
- the phatic: opening the channel or checking that it is working, either for (1) practical reasons or for (2) social ones
- the metalingual (*sic*): focusing attention upon the code itself, to clarify it or renegotiate it.

Jakobson	Bühler	Searle	Popper	Halliday
referential	representational	representatives	descriptive	
metalingual			metalinguistic	IDEATIONAL
phatic		commissives		
(1) practical				
(2) social				
expressive	expressive	expressives	expressive	
conative	conative	declarations directives	signalling	INTERPERSONAL
poetic	(no equivalent)	(no equivalent)	(no equivalent)	(no equivalent)
(no equivalent)	(no equivalent)	(no equivalent)	(no equivalent)	TEXTUAL

Figure 2.2 Functional taxonomies (A similar correlation of functional taxonomies can be found in Stern 1983:224)

Exposure to nursery rhymes and other forms of verbal art is a valuable starting point. The humble nursery rhyme is a rich resource for drawing attention to essentially the same characteristic of language that is employed so effectively in literature—namely its ability to construct meanings for us [. . .] and from the arbitrariness of the sign follows its community based nature, its dependence on social contexts, its truly creative aspect—namely our social reality.
(Hasan 1989:105)

But this approach seems motivated more by the desire to preserve the hegemony of the bi-functional interpretation of all discourse as interpersonal or ideational, than by a wish to understand why linguistic patterning to no apparent purpose is as widespread and powerful as it is, not only in literature, but in many other discourse types as well (Cook 1994b). The approach to be developed here, while not entirely accepting Jakobson's equation of the poetic function with focus on form, will nevertheless propose that literary and other similar discourses have a function which cannot be fully accounted for as either interpersonal or ideational.

Significantly, the two general functions of language described above are guarded by social sanctions, from which the function of literature (whatever that function may be) is often exempt. To send false information is regarded as wrong, and in certain circumstances, illegal and punishable. To ignore the need for phatic communion, or to attempt to direct the behaviour of others without authority, is considered rude and can lead to social isolation. Literary discourse, however, is sanctified institutionally as 'art' and, as such, at least in many cultures, exempted from the restrictions imposed on discourse which is primarily interpersonal or ideational: artists are often forgiven for being 'rude', 'untrue', or breaking taboos. (In Britain, for example, the argument of 'artistic merit' can be used against charges of pornography.) The high social esteem for those functions of language which enable efficient co-operation, and those which create social relationships, is easy enough to understand. Human life and prosperity depend upon them. Yet the high social esteem for literary discourse is more mysterious. In later chapters I shall attempt to give an explanation of this.

Functional theory and literature

Pragmatics theories of conversational principles and speech acts may go some way towards explaining how the function of utterances is inferred. They show how, in the light of general knowledge of the world, the receiver can reason from the literal, referential meaning of what is said to the pragmatic meaning, and induce what the sender is intending to do with his or her words.

The co-operative principle and literariness

One of the main pragmatic principles most frequently advanced in explanation of such inference is Grice's co-operative principle. This suggests that we interpret language on the assumption that its sender is observing (or deliberately flouting) four maxims (Grice [1967] 1975:45–6):

—The Maxim of Quality ('Be true')

—The Maxim of Quantity ('Give as much information as necessary, no more or less')

—The Maxim of Relation ('Be relevant')

—The Maxim of Manner ('Be clear, by avoiding obscurity and ambiguity, and being orderly')

Thus the principle mediates between world knowledge and language knowledge and can go some way towards explaining the construction of coherence: how text becomes discourse in the mind of the receiver. This has been the usual interpretation of the principle's relevance to pragmatics and discourse analysis (Leech and Short 1981:295; Brown and Yule 1983:31–3; Widdowson 1984:109–10).

It is worth noting, however, the rather strange relationship which exists between this principle and discourse which is classed as literature. Consider, for example, the relationship of literature to the quality maxim. Writing commonly categorized as literary ranges from that presented as true (such as George Orwell's account of his Spanish Civil War experiences in *Homage to Catalonia*), to the fantastic (such as Shakespeare's *The Tempest*). In between these two extremes, there are many kinds of relationship between fiction and fact: works which interweave fact and fiction (such as Tolstoy's *War and Peace* or Solzhenitsyn's *The First Circle*) or are loosely based on fact (such as D. H. Lawrence's *Sons and Lovers*); works which are allegorically factual (Albert Camus' novel *La Peste* or George Orwell's *Animal Farm*) or which, though fictional, may be interpreted as 'the kind of thing which might have happened' (as in any work of 'realistic' fiction).

In the case of individual literary utterances, the degree of truth seems singularly irrelevant. To ask whether opening lines like 'I was born in the year 1632 in the city of York . . .' (Daniel Defoe: *Robinson Crusoe*), or 'I went to the Garden of Love' (William Blake: 'The Garden of Love') are true, is quite beside the point. It is the case, nevertheless, that even in the most fantastic literature the connections of minor constituent detail must be perceived as possible in the real world, however fabulous the overall effect (Barthes [1966] 1977:102; Eco 1979: 166; Pitrat [1985] 1988:8–9). It is also the case, as Short (1989a) argues in an analysis of drama, that the presuppositions in fictional utterances build up a world against which the truth value of subsequent utterances can be measured. Nevertheless, the operation of the quality maxim is in literature very different in kind to its operation in ordinary discourse (Searle 1975c).

Similarly, the quantity maxim is difficult to apply to literary discourse. What is the appropriate length for something which has no apparent practical or social function? By any practical criterion, all works of literature are too long. Yet, conversely, the compression of meaning is also a frequent feature of literature, and often perceived as a virtue. The kind of linguistic inventiveness so amply detailed in the literature of stylistics often effects a degree of economy, which is implicitly praised. Widdowson (1975:15), for example, cites Shakespeare's word-class conversion of the noun 'boy' to a verb in the line 'And I shall see some squeaking Cleopatra boy my greatness' (*Antony and Cleopatra* V ii 219), observing that this enables a number of ideas to be brought together simultaneously, which in paraphrase would take many more words. In fact, the implicit claim of any school of literary criticism which devotes its time to explicating the meaning of a text at much greater length than the text does itself, implies both the existence of compression and a positive assessment of that compression. This flouting of the quantity maxim in literary texts, however, creates effects quite different from the terseness it might create elsewhere. Similarly, the maxim of relevance is hard to apply to texts with no immediate practical or social effect. Lastly, the flouting of the maxim of manner, like that of the flouting of the maxim of quantity, is often regarded as a virtue in literary writing.

It is also worth noting that the co-operative principle cannot always be easily applied to belligerent interactive discourse (Lecercle 1990; Kramsch 1993:224; Shippey 1993) or to intimate discourse (Bavelas 1991; Cook 1994c). In both of these, frequent repetition infringes the quantity maxim and sudden unexpected topic switches infringe the relevance maxim. This tallies with the suggestion by Wolfson that discourse between people in a clear power relationship is often very similar to that between people on intimate terms: when we compare these behaviours in terms of the social relationships of the interlocutors, we find again and again that the two extremes of social distance— minimum and maximum—seem to call forth very similar behaviour' (Wolfson 1988:32). Between these two extremes is what Wolfson terms 'the bulge': the great majority of relationships which are neither. Grice's maxims apply most successfully to this bulge—the civil interaction of acquaintances—rather than to closer and more emotional intercourse. The similarity of literary communication to the two extremes suggests that it too suspends social niceties. The literary voice is both the voice of power and the voice of an intimate.

In non-literary discourse, however, of the kind to which Grice applied his principle, the meanings created by these floutings are often social, signalling the attitude of the sender to the receiver of the message, and the kind of relationship which exists or is developing between them. Grice viewed these attitudinal meanings as being created by departures from the co-operative principle. An alternative way of accounting for such meanings, also widely accepted in discourse analysis and pragmatics, is to posit another principle as universally present in human intercourse: the politeness principle.

The politeness principle and literariness

The politeness principle, like the co-operative principle, has been formu-lated as a series of maxims which people assume are being followed in the utterances of others (Lakoff 1973; Leech 1983:132).[21] Lakoff suggests the following:

— Don't impose
— Give options
— Make your receiver feel good

As with the co-operative principle, any flouting of these maxims will take on meaning, provided it is perceived for what it is. In pragmatics and discourse analysis, these maxims of the politeness principle explain many of those frequent utterances (excluding literary ones) in which no new information is communicated about the world.

Taken together, the co-operative and politeness principles, and the tension between them, like the various taxonomies of macro-functions discussed above, again reflect belief in a dual purpose in human intercourse: to act efficiently together with other people, and to create and maintain social relationships.

Yet, like the co-operative principle, the politeness principle seems singularly irrelevant to much literary discourse, and it would be hard to answer a question, after reading a novel or poem, as to whether the sender had been polite. Leaving aside the obligations imposed on students of literature to read for examinations, it might also be said that literary texts are typically ones which, as they serve no immediate practical purpose, may be taken or left as the receiver wishes. Despite this, they often take up a great deal of time. As such they both keep and break the maxim: 'Don't impose'. As non-reciprocal discourse, they give no options in the sense that their development cannot be affected by the reader; on the other hand, they give the receiver an option *par excellence*: to cease receiving altogether, by closing the book or walking out of the theatre. Whether literary discourse makes its receivers 'feel good' is a similarly moot point, varying wildly from text to text and reader to reader, and considerably complicated by the deliberate seeking out of literature which causes sadness and pain.

Brown and Levinson (1987) suggest that the origin of the co-operative and politeness principles is the same in all societies. All human beings need to manipulate the environment. To do this successfully, they need to co-operate, and to enter into social relationships in which they must acknowledge the 'face' of other people. Broadly speaking, people do this in two ways. They avoid intruding upon each other's territory, for example physical territory, a particular field of knowledge, or a friendship; they also seek to enlarge the territory of others, or, in Lakoff's terms, to make the other person feel good, presumably on the assumption that the same will be done to them. Yet literature, we might note, intrudes very much upon face, in the sense that it often concerns the most intimate subjects. Here again a pragmatics theory, successful in explaining a wide range of discourse types, falls down when confronted by the literary.

A third major function: of cognitive change

The co-operative and politeness principles, then, reflecting a universal need to act together and to maintain social relationships, have been seen as a source of functional interpretation, reflecting the dual purpose of human language use referred to above. My argument is, however, that on their own, they are inadequate in dealing with certain types of discourse, including literary discourse. In the second part of this book, I shall argue that some discourse (including many literary texts) is motivated by neither of these principles and demands interpretation by quite some other principle. I call this the 'cognitive change principle'. According to this, some discourse is best interpreted as though it followed a maxim 'change the receiver'—though that may not necessarily have been the intention of the sender. Such discourse fulfils the need to rearrange mental representations: a process which can be best effected in the absence of pressing practical and social constraints. Certain types of discourse may aid this rearrangement, but in so doing, they demand suspension of both the politeness and the co-operative principles.

In some discourses, in other words, language has a function not accounted for in the functional theories referred to above: the function of changing mental representations.

Speech-act theory and literariness

Another body of pragmatic theory also frequently adduced in explanation of the inference of functions with no textual realization is speech-act theory (Austin 1962; Searle 1975b). Yet, like the conversational principles of co-operation and politeness, speech-act theory encounters problems when applied to literature, and indeed to less reciprocal discourse in general.

Firstly, and most obviously, the inference of an illocution, when a related verb is not used in its expression, depends upon the sender's correct assessment of the receiver's knowledge. Yet literary texts have, along with other written texts for unspecified receivers, a degree of uncertainty about the knowledge of the receivers; they are also very frequently severely displaced in time and culture. What judgements, for example, could Homer have made about the knowledge of his readers in the twentieth century?

Secondly, although the so-called perlocutionary force (or overall intention) of a discourse is at the best of times elusive, it seems likely, in the case of literature, that there is often, in the sense that literary works lack an overt purpose, no perlocutionary force at all.

Thirdly, if interpretation relies upon mutual knowledge of relevant context, then in a fictional work it is often difficult to say what the implied elements of relevant context are. On the other hand, relevant features of the context are often explicitly stated. They may also be constructed from the inferred presuppositions of utterances (Short 1989a).

Discourse structure

A further approach to discourse analysis and the problem of coherence is to posit larger structures, often specific to particular discourse types or genres (Swales 1990). These could be characterized as realizations of discourse schemata. In this approach, coherence may arise from a match between expectation and actuality, allowing receivers to predict what will come next. A good deal of work on discourse structure followed Sinclair and Coulthard's pioneering work (1975) on classroom discourse, and confined itself to spoken discourse. Yet even if valid for the discourse types described, the general applicability of this approach is open to doubt. Those spoken discourse types to which it is most easily applied tend to have certain features in common. They are all rather formal and ritualistic, and feature one participant with the institutional power to direct the discourse.[22] Even in spoken genres, this person may well plan the development of the discourse in advance, operating within the fairly narrow limits of the social conventions for that discourse type, rarely departing from them. Such 'deviation' from the expected structure could presumably be interpreted in varying ways. When it is assumed that such a structure is known and deliberately flouted, the deviation may be interpreted as insubordination, crime, or madness—or, if judged more positively, as radical political action. If the deviation is assumed simply to arise from ignorance, then it may be put down to immaturity or perhaps to the fact that the perpetrator is from a different culture.

This approach in the discourse analysis of spoken genres has a good deal in common with much earlier structuralist descriptions of various written text types, especially narrative, such as those by Propp ([1928] 1968) and Todorov ([1971] 1977) (to which I return in Chapter 5). In many ways, descriptions of genre structure simply assign to a wider range of discourses the kind of 'story grammar' beloved of structuralist literary theory and later taken up in AI (Rumelhart 1975), (though it might be argued that these are descriptions of text rather than discourse, dwelling on propositional rather than on illocutionary structure).

But, as with the flouting of conversational principles, deviation from the expectations aroused by a discourse structure in literature seems to produce quite different effects from many other discourse types. In structuralist descriptions there is analysis both of conformity to type and departure from it. Deviations are, moreover, often judged positively. A predictive structural approach cannot cope with deviant though coherent discourse. In discourse analysis structural analyses have worked best on discourses in which a high degree of conformity is demanded. In fact the effect of genre-awareness, like the effect of some schooling, can be very much concerned with inducing conformity (Martin 1985). Notions of genre operate rather like school rules, which take no account of the individual. In the classroom of genre, there is no room for the creative misbehaviour of the artist (which demands both awareness of genres and some disrespect for them).

Discourse as process (and literature as conversation)

One valid objection to structuralist views of discourse, comparable with structuralist story 'grammars', is that they present discourse as a product rather than a process. Overall structures, it can be argued, derive from analysis after the event rather than being present in the interaction of participants. Although this criticism may seem to apply more readily to written than to spoken genres, it is equally valid for both, as I shall argue below.

An important alternative view of discourse is provided by the conversation analysis of ethnomethodology. This reveals that even conversation, which is apparently the least structured type of discourse, yields a surprising degree of patterning to analysis (Levinson 1983:284–370). Ethnomethodology also provides a fundamentally different approach to that of structuralism. Rather than trying to impose large structures on what is happening from the outset, it begins at the most local level, trying to see how participants in interaction handle conversation: how they judge who can speak, and when. Rather than wait until a discourse is finished, and then analyse it as a whole, from the outside and with the benefit of hindsight, the ethnomethodologists try to understand how it unfolds in time. They view discourse as a developing process rather than a finished product; and this, after all, corresponds with how the participants must handle it and make sense of it, without the benefit of transcription and *post hoc* theorizing. The difference is analogous to that between process grammars and product grammars (Batstone 1994). It is also analogous to the schism in literary theory between the work of the structuralists and the work of reader-response and reception theorists (discussed in Chapters 5 and 6).

Conversation, apparently so far removed from writing in its casual haphazardness, shares many features with literature. Therefore the kinds of process models used in its analysis may be highly relevant to literary theory. Conversation analysis in fact shies away from the issue of definition of 'conversation' as such (Cook 1989:51). But such definitions as there are are imprecise—as imprecise as any working definition of 'literature'. The boundary between conversation and other discourse types, like that between literary and non-literary discourse, is a fuzzy one, and there are many intermediate cases. Yet this resistance to definition is not the only feature conversation shares with literature. Literature is also unmotivated by practical need, marked by an intimate relationship between sender and receiver: the act of reading is perceived as a private experience, a direct communication with the author. Both literature and conversation are at once predictable and unpredictable. Conversation may serve the purpose of refreshing and changing schematic knowledge (Edwards and Middleton 1987) in a similar way to literature. These features may make some of the observations of conversation analysis as a discourse type pertinent to the analysis of literature.

Against this, it might be argued that the discourse of conversation is fundamentally different from that of, say, a novel or story, in that it is the creation of two or more people in interaction, and thus only partly under the control of one individual. It might also be observed that it is spoken rather than written and that these are fundamentally different parameters in discourse typology. The difference between speech and writing, however, like the related differences between monologue and dialogue, and reciprocal and non-reciprocal, are neither as clear-cut nor as fundamental as they might at first appear.

The traditional division of language into the spoken and the written mode is clearly and sensibly based on a difference in media and perception, the means of production and reception. There are many other differences too (Gregory 1967; Halliday 1985:xxiii–xv; Biber 1988; McCarthy 1993). Yet in terms of discourse structure and typology the difference may not be so central. Spoken discourse is often considered to be less planned and orderly, more open to intervention by the receiver. There are some kinds of spoken discourse, however, (like lessons, lectures, interviews, and trials) which have significant features in common with typical written discourse. These kinds of spoken discourse are also planned, and the possibilities for subordinate participants can be severely limited. It is clear that in reading a novel one cannot influence its development (and that can be the pleasure or pain of reading), but it is almost equally hard for a criminal to influence the direction of a trial, or a primary school pupil to prevent the lesson progressing as the teacher intends.

Following Ong (1982) a debate has arisen as to whether the psychology of people in oral and written cultures is fundamentally affected by the differences between writing and speech. In Ong's view it is, and the propensity of writing to separate discourse from its utterer, from the context of its creation, and from the linearity of speech, enables literate people to perceive discourse in an entirely different manner, paying attention, for example, to exact wording, overall structure, and decontextualized ideas. (For arguments against this view, see Halverson (1991) and Feldman (1991)). Whichever view prevails in this debate, it might be argued that literature, though written and read, preserves some of the features of an older oral discourse. Its narrative voice is strongly present; the experiences it recounts are contextualized rather than abstracted; it achieves local coherence through formal parallelism, and it often exploits, even when read silently, actual or potential effects of sound.

Discourse as dialogue

In recent years, the notion that written discourse may also be regarded as shaped by an interactive process has gained strength through the theories of the Russian linguist and literary theorist Bakhtin. He argues that all discourse is in a sense dialogic (Bakhtin [1929] 1978; [1929, revised 1963] 1984; [1934] 1981; [1936] 1986).

Dialogue, in the narrow sense of alternating talk between two participants, is of course only one of the forms—a very important form to be sure—of language use. But dialogue can also be understood in a broader sense, meaning not only direct, face to face, vocalized verbal communication between persons, but also written communication in which sender and receiver are not face to face (Bakhtin [1929] 1973: 95).

It is pertinent at this point in the argument to draw attention, in illustration of the dialogic nature of discourse, to two sentence-level phenomena, both of which will be of importance in the view I wish to develop later of the dynamic interaction of language form and schematic representation engendered by literary discourse. The first is quoted and reported speech, phenomena dwelt upon at length by Bakhtin ([1929] 1973: 115–239), in which the voice of one person is incorporated into the speech of another: a fact which is reflected in the grammar of quoted speech in which an entire sentence or sequence of sentences becomes a direct object within the quoting sentence.

[(He) (said) $^{Od}_{S}$ ['(I) (shall conquer) (the world)']]
(For grammatical notation conventions see Appendix A.)

In quoted speech, choices among reporting verbs allow the reporter's attitude to be evident (even while faithfully quoting), while in reported speech various degrees of merger between the original words and those of the report allow more or less access to the original words, as required (Coulmas 1986; Tannen 1986). This effect of a voice within a voice, evident at sentence level in reported speech, is a microcosm of the similar but much more complex interplay of embedded voices in literary narration: a phenomenon to which we shall turn in detail in Chapters 5 and 8.

The second aspect of dialogic discourse which will be important to the argument later is one extensively studied in linguistics, 'Functional Sentence Perspective' (FSP)—a term often attributed to Mathesius.[23] This refers to the different syntactic arrangements (sometimes necessitating lexical changes) which may realize the same conceptual content. For example:

1 Honoré Balzac was born in 1799 at Tours, the son of a civil servant.
2 In 1799, Honoré Balzac was born at Tours, the son of a civil servant.
3 It was in 1799 that Honoré Balzac, the son of a civil servant, was born at Tours.
4 It was at Tours in 1799 that Honoré Balzac was born, the son of a civil servant.
5 A son, Honoré Balzac, was born to a civil servant at Tours in 1799.
6 Mme Balzac, the wife of a civil servant, gave birth to a son called Honoré at Tours in 1799.

and so on. In a discourse consisting of a succession of sentences, each one will arise from a choice between the kind of grammatical and lexical options illustrated above.[24] The second sentence above, for example, is the opening of the short, and very factual, biographical sketch of de[25] Balzac in the frontispiece to an English edition of one of his novels.[26]

Honoré Balzac was born in 1799 at Tours, the son of a civil servant. Put out to nurse and sent later to boarding school, he had, except between the ages of four and eight, little contact with home. In 1814 the family moved to Paris, where Honoré ˜continued his boarding school education for two years, and then studied law at the Sorbonne. From 1816 to 1819 he worked in a lawyer's office, but having completed his legal training he knew he wanted to be a writer.

Similar variations in perspective to those offered above for sentence 1 could be made to each of the subsequent sentences. The strange thing about these choices, however, is that while each sentence apparently means exactly the same thing, the aptness of choices, from the reader's viewpoint, may aid or disrupt the construction of coherence. In fact, contrary to opinions expressed in reader-response literary theory, there is evidence to support the view that there is more uniformity of judgement among readers about this than might at first appear (van Peer 1986; Short and van Peer 1989; Short and Alderson 1989). This phenomenon can be explained in terms of the interaction of form and knowledge: more specifically in terms of the interaction of form with the sender's knowledge of the knowledge of the addressee.

If coherence is affected by choices of FSP, then it is possible that the choice is being dictated by the sentence before, each one having a 'knock-on' effect on the structure of the next. If this, and only this, were the explanation, then FSP might justifiably be regarded as an instance of context-independent formal connection between sentences. FSP, however, is contextual as well as formal, dictated by the addresser's assumptions about what the addressee wants to know. Apparently monologic discourse, in fact, may be viewed as a succession of answers to imagined and unspoken questions by the receiver (Widdowson 1978: 25–6). In this light, all discourse seems to proceed dialogically, even if the other voice is only present as a ghost. The order of information in each utterance may be conceived as the answer to an imagined question, in which, as a general rule, known information is fronted and unknown information forced to the end, following the principle of 'end focus' (Quirk et al. 1985:1360–2).

One widely accepted explanation of this phenomenon is that the ordering of the discourse is determined by the sender's hypotheses about what the receiver does and does not know (Halliday 1976:174–8; Halliday 1985:278–81; Quirk et al. 1985:1360). Information divides into two types: that which the sender thinks the receiver already knows, and that which the sender thinks the receiver does not already know, or 'given' and 'new' information respectively. Any unit of information may change status as the discourse proceeds, and what was new in one sentence become given in the next, precisely because it has just been said. Indeed, communication might be defined as the conversion of new information into given information, and a successful communicator as a person who correctly assesses the state of knowledge of his or her interlocutor. If the sender misjudges, and treats what is given as new, the discourse will be boring. In the reverse case, when the new is assumed to be given, the discourse becomes incomprehensible. In this sense it can be said that the structuring principle of all discourse is dialogue.

These are issues which are much discussed, in different terms, in literary theory. While formalists, structuralists, and New Critics argue for an examination of the text as an autonomous object unsullied by consideration of authorial intention or reader variation, phenomenologists, and reader-response and reception-theory critics argue for the necessity of including a description of the individual reader. Bakhtin ([1929] 1973: 83–99) argues that dialogue is one of the fundamental structuring principles of all discourse, written and spoken alike. The phenomenon of FSP gives weight to this hypothesis even at the level of the clause, and thus penetrates far into the territory of sub-sentential linguistics. Paradoxically, this domination of the 'dialogic principle' is as true in discourse—like literary discourse—which appears to be created by one person alone, as it is in discourse which is created by two or more people.

It is also arguably true that dialogue precedes monologue in both ontogenetic and phylogenetic language development, and this gives further weight to arguments for its predominance in human discourse in general.

The phenomenon of FSP illustrates potential and actual interaction of levels, showing that they are in no sense discrete, and warning against any atomistic or reductionist approach to discourse. It reveals the futility of an account of grammatical choice, or of the relationship between grammatical choice and coherence, in isolation from a description of the knowledge of a specified receiver or group of receivers. For these reasons, FSP is a key piece of evidence in the argument of this book, as it suggests a limitation to the translation of discourse into some formal non-linguistic representation advocated by AI schema theory (see Chapter 3), and suggests rather an intimate and inextricable interaction between linguistic form and knowledge representation.

In their approach to discourse, schema theory and linguistics-based literary theories have a tendency to err in opposite directions. The former seeks to account for knowledge independently of linguistic choice, and the latter to describe linguistic choice without reference to the knowledge of specified receivers. What I seek here is a means of relating the two.

The 'post-scientific' approach

Before closing this chapter on discourse analysis and entering the very different domains of AI-inspired schema theory (Chapter 2) and text-based literary theory (Chapter 3), it is necessary to make some reference to other uses of the term 'discourse analysis', especially those which are highly influential in literary theory.

The approach to discourse analysis adopted so far might broadly be characterized as that which emerged from linguistics, most particularly from the 1970s onwards.[27] The linguistics-based approaches to language in context have in common a 'scientific' approach to the study of communication. They imply that the scientist and scientific discourse can somehow stand apart from the process, observe it, and assess it. They also all subscribe to the view that meaning is constructed through the interaction of some existing mental representation can be formulated and understood. To talk of coherence as constructed through links which have no manifestation in the text implies their independent existence in the mind. These views unite these approaches, despite their differences.

There is, however, another very different use of the term 'discourse analysis' of which studies deriving from linguistics (like this one) would do well to take stock (Widdowson 1990). The term 'discourse analysis' is also used in approaches to language which derive from philosophy joining forces with literary, sociological, and psychoanalytic theory, and embracing political critiques of discourse such as feminism. Such approaches, in particular the influential discussions of discourse by Foucault, tend to work top-down, beginning with intuitively perceived categories of discourse, for example 'scientific discourse', and working downwards from them towards the details of language. Linguistics-based approaches, on the other hand, tend to work bottom-up, from the details of language and text organization towards broader categories. If a valid criticism of the latter approach points out that it is lost in detail and incapable of making broad statements, the Foucaultian approach may be characterized as being guilty of the opposite error: stressing the importance of language, but rarely considering linguistic detail. Although this book broadly accepts the 'scientific' approach, I shall regard the two approaches as essentially complementary and argue that each may gain from the insights of the other.

Three philosophical movements which have influenced such contemporary post-semiotic views of text processing, but which are not compatible with the scientific pretensions of linguistics and therefore largely ignored by it, are deconstruction, hermeneutics, and phenomenology. Each of these movements has exerted a substantial influence on 'post-scientific' discourse analysis, and on literary theories of discourse.

Deconstruction, largely associated with the work of the philosopher Jacques Derrida, has attacked, as part of a larger critique of the scientific method and western philosophy, both the Saussurean view which is the basis of twentieth-century linguistics (de Saussure [1916] 1960; Derrida [1967] 1976); and the Austinian view which is the basis of pragmatics (Derrida [1972] 1982). In the Derridian view, 'meaning', like concepts such as 'God', 'matter', 'the self', and 'nature' is yet another instance of an assumed but unproved 'centre' for belief, the questioning of whose existence leads to the collapse of the theory based upon it. At the heart of the linguistic sciences, according to Derrida, lies the division of signifier and signified, text and meaning, which whether reached through decoding or through inference, is an instance of the binary divisions which plague western thought. Picking upon minor 'marginalized' points in the arguments of Saussure and Austin, Derrida seeks to 'deconstruct' their texts and make them contradict themselves. As the attack itself can also be deconstructed, the process becomes one of infinite regression, and defers any conclusion. (This, however, only bears out Derrida's point, that there is no '*telos*'—no end and no beginning.) Language, according to Derrida, is a similar process of infinite extension: if signs mean by virtue of their difference, then each sign leads to another, and meaning is eternally both different and deferred (which is in part what Derrida means by his term '*différance*') (see Culler 1983:97). The scientific study of discourse creates its own discourse which in turn demands study, and so on. Again the process is infinite, and there can never, in Derrida's view, be a conclusion of the kind sought after by science.

In similar 'post-scientific' vein, hermeneutics, following the opinion of Heidegger that techniques of interpretation of human behaviour are necessarily different from those of the natural sciences, has been profoundly influential, largely through the works of Gadamer ([1960] 1975), in shaping the critical approaches of reception theory and reader-response. A parallel influence has been exerted by the phenomeno- logical philosophy of Husserl, who was himself an influence on Heidegger. Phenomenology, while it shares the view that meaning results from the constructive interaction of mind and text, both stresses individual variations in interpretation and 'argues that there is an ultimate limitation to the power of formalization and that the most important aspects of language lie outside its limits' (Winograd 1983:21). A similar argument is voiced by many scientific critics of AI text theory (Born 1987), and must therefore rebound upon schema theory.

Paradoxically, however, many of the views expressed by the adherents of these two approaches *are* compatible with some of the 'scientific' tenets of schema theory, and both Heidegger and Husserl regarded the achievement of meaning as a creative act involving the marriage of existing knowledge with information from the text or from the senses (Holub 1984:41). I shall return to these views, and to some of the literary theories which derive from them, in Chapters 6 and 8.

In literary studies, the deeper incompatibility of the 'scientific' approaches to language with 'post-scientific' approaches is illustrated by their failure even to engage in debate, despite attempts to bring the two sides together (Fabb, Attridge, Durant, and MacCabe 1987). The evidence for this lack of contact is an absence rather than a presence: books on either side of the divide, though mutually concerned with human interaction with texts, often simply fail to acknowledge the existence of the alternative view.

Conclusion

Current approaches to discourse analysis clearly have a crucial contribu- tion to make to an understanding of all texts, but in the case of literary texts they also have severe shortcomings. This suggests that they may not be as universally applicable to all discourse as is usually supposed. In addition, current discourse analysis, while stressing the need for knowledge in discourse interpretation, often assumes the activation and representation of that knowledge to be unproblematic. Mental representations are seen as constant and fixed, something brought to bear upon discourse interpretation rather than created and changed by it. It may be that the shortcomings of discourse analysis when applied to literature are the result of a fundamentally different relation between knowledge and text from that which pertains elsewhere.

In preparation for a development of this idea, the next chapter examines an Artificial Intelligence approach to the representation and organization of world knowledge and its role in the interpretation of text. This AI approach, for all its obvious limitations, may provide the starting point for a new way of looking at the problem.

Notes

1 Another example of the terminological confusions referred to at the end of Chapter 1.
2 I follow Clark and Holquist (1984: 146–71) in believing that Bakhtin was the author of the book *Marxism and the Philosophy of Language*, published under the name of his colleague Volosinov, and of the book *The Formal Method in Literary Scholarship*, published under the name of his colleague Medvedev. This was also the official view in the Soviet Union during the 1980s. See also Terras (1985: 34–6; Cook 1994a). For the alternative view see Matejka and Titunik (1986: vii–xiii).
3 For use of the term 'co-text' see Halliday, McIntosh, and Strevens 1964: 125; see also Wales 1989: 100. 'Context' is thus both a superordinate and a co-hyponym of 'co-text'. (There is nothing untoward about such a fact. Occurrences of the same word at two levels of generality are a common feature in word relations. 'Dog' for example can denote both a member of the genus, whether male or female, or be used to denote a male as opposed to a female: in other words as both superordinate and co-hyponym of 'bitch'.)
4 Sperber and Wilson (1986), for example, use the term in the latter sense.
5 This point is cogently argued by Widdowson (1979: 130) against Krzeszowski (1975: 41), who had claimed that the following two sentences selected from a corpus at random could not be combined into a coherent sequence:

(1) The men and women eat breakfast together.

(2) The nomads become restless in the big town.

Widdowson observes that in a particular context they could, and suggests by way of example that the event described in (2) may arise from a prohibition of the sexes eating together in the nomads' culture. Widdowson, however, stops short of the view that any pair of sentences could be combined in this way. Yet one might in fact argue that, given sufficient ingenuity and imagination, any pair of sentences could be regarded as coherent. It is worth observing, however, that the debate raised by Krzeszowski and Widdowson centres only on *pairs* of sentences. Our case for contexts which make sense of any pair might be much harder to maintain for threes, or fours, or larger groups of sentences.

6 In fact the word *'Entrez'* does not occur in *Finnegans Wake*. (Richard Brown, Leeds University: personal communication.)

7 It also takes no account of the utterance/sentence distinction employed in linguistics (Lyons 1968: 423; Crystal 1985: 277, 322).

8 The use of the term in this sense goes back to the eighteenth century when it was applied to the phenomenon in Hebrew poetry (*Shorter Oxford English Dictionary* (3rd edn): 1429). In the nineteenth century it was used in the analysis of poetry by both Matthew Arnold (ibid.) and Gerard Manley Hopkins (House and Storey 1959: 108–14).

9 Following Werth (1976), quite an industry has grown up to demonstrate this fact, based on misreadings of Jakobson's description of the poetic function (Jakobson 1960).

10 It is in fact an instance of the kind of formal, non-semantic link between sentences sought by Harris (1952).

11 Halliday and Hasan's category of exophoric co-reference (1976: 18, 31–3) would be better regarded as pragmatic.

12 In this example, the use of the past perfect 'had always thought' indicates an event prior to the event preceding it in a purely linear way.

13 I treat broad classifications of speech acts as descriptions of the major functions of language (see Wales 1989: 196). I shall use Searle's taxonomy of speech acts rather than Austin's. The best summary of the relationship of Searle's description of speech acts to that of Austin is given in Searle (1975b).

14 For summaries and comparisons of functional descriptions see Leech (1983: 46–58), Stern (1983: 221–9); Wales (1989: 195–9).

15 Hymes' (1972) taxonomy is so close to Jakobson's that it is not listed in Figure 2.2.

16 Halliday's (1975) list of the functions of language for an infant, though it is often discussed along with other functional theories, is not included here on the grounds that it is a description of child functions which are then 'mapped' on to and absorbed into the adult

functions. It is his functional taxonomy for adult language which is discussed here.

17 Halliday's third 'textual' function (1973:42; 1976:28) in which language creates cohesive text—in the ways described in Chapter 2— is quite unlike any of the functions described by the other theorists, and need not concern us here. Indeed, its inward looking, self-reflexive nature makes it seem more formal than functional, being more concerned with the internal workings of language than with the relation of language to the minds of its users or the world in which they live. As Leech (1983:57) remarks: 'there is something back to front about saying that language has the function of producing instantiations of itself'.

18 Hymes' (1972) list of functions develops and adds to Jakobson's, but he does not make the poetic function a centre of attention.

19 It is also of particular importance to my later discussion of text-based literary theories, as it is the basis of Jakobson's case for a linguistic characterization of literariness and, as such, the origin of stylistics.

20 Newman (1986), citing evidence from neurology, advances the extraordinary view that linguistic and prosodic patterning affects the brain:

> enhancing neurotransmitter synthesis among otherwise dormant neurons in both propositional and prosodic left- and right-brain linguistic areas, causing new neural circuits to be constructed, perhaps bridging the hemispheres, perhaps facilitating integration of the neocortex, perhaps facilitating evolution.

This view, as he points out, need not be as 'far fetched' as it at first appears.

21 Although Grice had suggested the existence of such a principle, he had not developed it in detail. Leech not only formulates the politeness principle in more detail than either Lakoff or Grice, but also adds to the co-operative and politeness principle an 'irony principle', and, under the heading of 'Textual rhetoric', principles of 'processibility', 'clarity', 'economy', and 'expressivity'.

22 As in, for example, the 'Birmingham School' analyses of primary school lessons (Sinclair and Coulthard 1975), medical consultations (Coulthard 1981), or TV quiz shows (Berry 1981).

23 This attribution is made, for example, by Lyons (1977:509) and Wales (1989:199). Essays by Mathesius can be found in Vachek (1964).

24 It is not my intention here to examine in all their complexity the many different analyses of this phenomenon, and in particular I shall say nothing about the interaction of phonetic focus (which is the central concern of many studies) and that achieved by syntactic

reordering. Suffice it to say that in all the varying interpretations and their different terminologies, there is agreement that the clause has a bi-partite structure, and the function of choices is to enable different information to be brought into different degrees of prominence.

25 The 'de' was a later addition to give an impression of higher social standing.

26 Oxford University Press World Classics edition of *Père Goriot*, translated by A. J. Krailsheimer.

27 From the 1930s to the 1970s a good deal of Anglo-American linguistics concerned itself with the study of language in isolation from context, and considered the sentence as the highest unit of analysis (Lyons 1968:172ff). Its data were either invented by the analyst (Lyons 1968:154); idealized (Lyons 1977:586–9), or written language which was already generally of the standard variety and divorced from any particular situation. The field of study, in other words, was phonology, grammar, and lexis with varying degrees of emphasis on semantics, and indeed this self-imposed limitation might well be considered to be many people's definition of 'linguistics'.

Although this approach was dominant during the 1940s, 50s and 60s, many other traditions of linguistics persisted in studying language in context, most notably that continuing the work of anthropological linguistics begun by Boas in North America (see Bolinger 1975:506–14); that associated with the work of J. R. Firth in Britain (see Firth 1957) and continued by the neo-Firthians (see Halliday 1973:50–1; 1978:51); the functional approach of the Prague School (see Vachek 1964; Bolinger 1975:514–24), and, in Russia, the linguistics initiated by Bakhtin, which insisted on the impossibility of divorcing a description of language from a description of its users (Bakhtin [Volosinov] [1929] 1973:86). All of these approaches have had an influence on literary theory, and have also been drawn upon by the resurgent interest in discourse analysis from the 1970s onwards.

3 A second bearing: AI text theory and its limitations

Introduction

The aim of this chapter and of the following two is to bring together—as additional resources for a discourse analysis of literature—two apparently incompatible bedfellows: AI schema theory and certain schools of literary theory. This chapter investigates the points of contact which already exist between them, indicates areas of mutual interest, and proposes a theory connecting them. The forced union of two such disparate disciplines poses a number of problems and demands some justification and discussion.

AI theory and literary theory may seem initially to be disciplines of very different kinds, epitomizing the traditional separation of the natural sciences and the humanities in academic study. The first, concerned with the replication by computers of human skills, of necessity draws heavily upon the applied natural sciences and mathematics, as well as on the 'human sciences' of psychology and linguistics. Literary theory, on the other hand, concerned with elucidating the nature of literature, has often drawn its material from the 'arts', though it too has been attracted and inspired by psychology and linguistics. These differences between the two fields may well be reinforced by the mutual ignorance, different educational backgrounds, and preconceptions of reciprocal irrelevance among those involved. AI workers may regard literary theory as a subjective aesthetics, and literary theorists dismiss AI as a mundane applied science. The very different terminologies of the two fields can only serve to make matters worse.

Yet, despite their differences, the two disciplines have one major concern in common: to understand the processing and production of texts. For AI this concern is central because the ability to produce and process texts for communication is so distinctive and substantial a feature of human intelligence that it would seem hard to classify a machine which could not replicate it in some way as having more than extremely limited intelligence. That literary theory shares this concern is self-evident, even tautological, for whatever disputes may rage about the nature of 'literature' and whether that nature can be defined, few would deny that the object of study is a sub-class of text, or a sub-class of human interaction with text.

In practice, however, the texts studied by the two fields are radically different. Those used by AI are, by human standards, very simple, restricted to a prescribed area of a natural language, of the world referred to, or of language processing skills. Literary texts, on the other hand, are typically linguistically complex and provoke complex interpretation: so much so that many theories of literature imply that textual complexity, or a concomitant complexity in processing, are definitive features of literature. AI cannot approach such complex texts and, in general, does not seek to, being only interested in texts whose processing or production can be modelled by the existing level of technology. Yet this difference in the type of text analysed, and in the approach to textual complexity, does not preclude the relevance of the two areas of study to each other. Insights into the processing and production of simple texts may provide strong clues to that of more complex examples. Conversely, there are many insights in literary theory which could add to the AI approach to the understanding of texts. AI researchers, though they cannot replicate the complexities of human text processing and production, are much given to speculation on the subject. The texts which can be handled by computer, moreover, grow ever more sophisticated.

In Chapter 1, various approaches of discourse analysis, and their applicability to the analysis of literary discourse were examined. All of these approaches point towards the need for a theory of the organization of pre-existing knowledge as a necessary addition to a successful explanation of coherence. But it is also clear that factors effecting coherence behave differently in literary discourse and, for this reason, we may expect the role of knowledge to be different too. This chapter examines some specific suggestions about the nature and organization of knowledge in discourse processing. Although these suggestions have obvious shortcomings when dealing with a discourse as complex as literature, they can, as I hope to show later, be adapted to a more satisfactory model. The chapter thus prepares the ground for subsequent discussion of the relation of knowledge and literary form.

The particular theories of knowledge organization examined in this chapter are from Artificial Intelligence (AI) of the 1970s and early 1980s. Like all AI, and a good deal of current linguistics work on language, they assume that the mind abstracts a semantic or conceptual construction of 'facts' from language.[1] Representations of single 'facts' are organized into larger knowledge structures. In examining this approach I shall concentrate upon one particular theory as representative of many others (for a summary and comparison of different systems see Garnham 1988: 24–57). Eventually, I shall seek to qualify and modify the AI view, and offer my own explanation of the relationship of knowledge and text, especially within literary discourse.

The chapter, therefore, proceeds as follows:

1 It examines in general the AI approach to language and text
2 It describes and evaluates one system for representing 'facts' in text
3 It discusses some of the problems inherent in such formal representations of the 'content' of a natural language text
4 It describes one detailed version of AI schema theory.

The computational and brain paradigms of language

Making use of Kuhn's well-known characterization of the development of scientific thought as a succession of 'paradigms' (Kuhn 1962) in which periods of 'normal science' are disrupted by 'revolutions', Winograd (1983) identifies what he considers to be a major 'paradigm shift' in the linguistic sciences during the 1970s. He terms the new paradigm 'the computational paradigm' and regards it as having replaced the 'generational paradigm' as the most widely accepted and fertile framework for research into language. AI work on text was instrumental in shaping this paradigm.

The computational paradigm, in Winograd's view, is based upon a metaphorical comparison of the mind with the operation of a computer, and as such replaces other sources of metaphors for language (for example law, chemistry, biology, or mathematics) which were the basis of earlier paradigms. ('Strong' versions of AI, which contend that the computer 'really is a mind' (see Searle [1980] 1987), reject this view of the comparison as merely metaphorical, but this dispute will not affect my description at this point.) The paradigm, in the opinion of both its supporters and its opponents, is dualist, concerning itself with the mind rather than the brain, or—in the terms of the metaphor—the software rather than the hardware (Fodor 1976:9, 17; Winograd 1983: 13; Searle [1980] 1987:39; Edelman 1992:11–12). The computational paradigm views language as 'a communicative process based on knowledge' (Winograd 1983:13). In terms of the computer metaphor, the processes may be regarded as analogous to computer programs and the knowledge as analogous to data structures (Simon 1979).

The advent of the theory of connectionism (Rumelhart and McClelland 1986a, 1986b; Johnson-Laird 1988:174–94) has led some cognitive psychologists to replace the notion of mental processes (including language processing)[2] as analogous to the workings of a computer, with the notion that they are analogous to the workings of the brain (Martindale 1991:8). It is, after all, on the physical processes of the brain that human thought depends. Neural networks, constructed by computer scientists, resemble the brain in the sense that they are composed of connected nodes (although there are also many features which networks and brains do not have in common). Unlike a conventional computer which works serially, many connections in a neural network are activated simultaneously, as they are in the brain. The strengths (or 'weightings') of connections are increased by exposure to the data which activate them. Processing is parallel and knowledge is distributed rather than localized in the connections between nodes, rather than the nodes themselves. The network thus acts 'as though it knows the rules' (Rumelhart and McClelland 1986a: 32) though those rules exist only as an abstraction by an outside analyst. What appear to be independent 'knowledge' and 'rules' are in fact by-products of paths through the connections: epiphenomena rather than phenomena. Another way of this would be to say that in a connectionist model there are no products but only procedures, and no data structures but only programs.

The notion that connectionism has replaced the 'computer paradigm' with a 'brain paradigm' need not, however, disturb the argument here. Firstly, computer design and theories of the brain perennially imitate each other. Secondly, connectionist theories are more concerned with the implementation of processing, the actual 'wiring' of a computer or brain, than with the mental strategies to which that implementation gives rise. They are concerned with the sub-symbolic rather than symbolic level (Pinker and Prince 1988; Lachter and Bever 1988; Martindale 1991:9). Representations at a higher level may remain the same, even though they are wired in differently, and a whole set of nodes can function as if they were a single node coding a unitary percept (Stone and van Orden 1989). Schema theory is thus as compatible with connectionist theories of cognition as it was with their predecessors (Rumelhart, Smolensky, McClelland, and Hinton 1986; Eysenk and Keane 1990:170; Martindale 1991:184–99).

Yet another point of view emphasizing the mind's dependence on the brain and rejecting the computational paradigm is that of 'neural Darwinism' advanced by Edelman (1989, 1992). Edelman rejects the analogy between the neural networks of connectionist computing and the brain, arguing that the brain is fundamentally different from the workings of any computer, and also that it determines the nature of the mind. Edelman claims that there is no neurologically determined equivalent of either the computer programmes of serial computing, or of the programmer instructions in parallel computing. He suggests instead that the neural structures of the brain change and adapt in accordance with biological principles similar to those of evolution. Cognitive representations, in his view, are neither genetically inherited, nor wholly conditioned by external stimuli. He introduces the notion of a third force, a value system determined by the central parts of the brain, which will stimulate the outer parts to strengthen some cognitive structures rather than others. Edelman is vituperative in his rejection of both the computational paradigm and of AI work inspired by it. His theories, however, concern the development and neurological representation of cognitive structures, rather than the structures themselves. Though they may be a blow to the computational paradigm, therefore, and to hopes of reproducing schema-driven understanding in computers, they do not undermine the notion of schemata as a psychological category, nor as a factor in discourse understanding. In fact parts of Edelman's theory seem remarkably close to schema theory (Edelman 1992:118). The ontogenetic and phylogenetic origins of schemata, their neurological representation and motivation, and the possibility or impossibility of their replication in serial or parallel processing computers, are all interesting and controversial issues. But they are not the central concern of this book.

A central difference between both the computer and the brain paradigms and their predecessors lies in the emphasis they place upon process rather than result. In contrast with the semiotic model which separates *langue* from *parole* or the generative model which separates competence from performance, they view the operation of language knowledge as their area of enquiry, believing that the 'structure of language is derived from the structure of processes' (Winograd 1983: 21). The effects of this shift in emphasis can be most clearly seen in the computational paradigm's approach to grammar. Earlier models which analysed data *post hoc* as a given whole, have been replaced by grammars such as Augmented Transition Networks (ATNs), which are concerned with the processes of classification and analysis 'on line' (see for example Wanner and Maratsos 1978; Winograd 1983:195–267; Bower and Cirillo 1985; Pitrat [1985] 1988:67–84).

A similar switch from product to process can be seen in the other two approaches to text dealt with in this first part of the book: in both process-oriented discourse analysis (see Chapter 2), and in those reader-centred literary theories which emphasize the ongoing experience of reading rather than structures derived after the event (see Chapter 6).

The AI approach to text

The AI approach to text, as I have described it above, does not view language understanding as a process of decoding, but rather one of construction. In other words, the mental representation which is at the end of the chain of processing has not been merely transferred. Any features it may share with the mental representation of the interlocutor are present by virtue of the fact that shared knowledge and shared processing strategies have interacted with text to produce similar results. As such, this view of language processing is complementary to work in pragmatics which concentrates attention upon the application of deductive and inferential rules (reasoning), and is also complementary to work in linguistics (under the traditional headings of phonology, morphology, syntax, and semantics) which concentrates attention upon text.

AI has focused on the mental representations which are the beginning (in production) and end (in comprehension) of this hierarchy. In the view of AI, however, they are not only the result of the linguistic and semantic structures perceived in the text. Existing representations (i.e. schemata) are also used. It is a two-way interaction. Schemata may be related to the assigned structures derived from text via reasoning, which is the focus of research in pragmatics, or more directly, through comparison of their contents with those derived directly from text.

Initial work in AI concentrated almost exclusively on text comprehension rather than generation, sometimes with the vague and naïve assumption that human text generation is simply comprehension in reverse (Pitrat [1985] 1988:93). In the 1980s, this imbalance was redressed slightly by a number of publications and projects on text generation (see for example Appelt 1985; McKeown 1985; Mann 1987; Danlos 1987; Patten 1988). I shall use the term 'communication' to cover both, though, as the reading of literature is my central concern, the bias here too will be towards comprehension.

Objections to AI text theory

The AI approach to text is open to challenge from a number of directions.[3] In what follows, I shall attempt to explore some AI ideas about conceptual constructions and their interaction with text, though without implying any wholesale acceptance of those ideas as theories of human psychology. I shall also examine problems overlooked in this approach. I should say at this point, however, that it seems to me counterproductive to see these views as either wholly 'right' or wholly 'wrong'. They may simply be helpful in progressing further. Certainly the strong emotional reaction to any hint of an end to the human monopoly of intelligence, or to any suggestion that research in AI may provide insights into human thought, is not helpful. I rather take the view that the AI approach may provide a starting point upon which a more complex model of human interaction with text may be built. It is not necessary to identify the kind of text-handling strategies developed in AI as either human or non-human. Human beings, as van Dijk and Kintsch point out in their complex model of discourse comprehension, may use many strategies simultaneously (van Dijk and Kintsch 1983).

For the moment, however, I shall provisionally accept the AI approach as a plausible theory of human communication. One of the strongest versions of this belief in the applicability of AI to human psychology is to be found in the work of Roger Schank and his colleagues during the 1970s and 1980s. This, together with the power of his theory, and its extraordinarily widespread influence and citation (almost every contemporary introduction to discourse analysis, psychology, and AI has a section devoted to his theories), is my reason for concentrating on his work.

The degree to which this version of schema theory, or indeed schema theory itself, continues to be used in AI need not concern us here. Versions of schema theory, once stated, have become independent of their original purposes. What we are concerned with here is their potential to form components of a discourse analysis of literature, rather than with their continuing use in AI. AI researchers will not be concerned with such an enterprise, just as discourse analysis need not be centrally concerned with AI. Schema theory belongs to both.

The constructivist principle

Two points about the AI approach to mental representation need to be made very clearly:

1 Mental representations are considered to exist in some language other than a natural language.
2 Such representations may be derived either from a natural language representation (i.e. a discourse) or from events themselves.

These tenets are referred to by van Dijk and Kintsch (1983:5) as the 'constructivist principle' of the computer paradigm. I shall adopt this term here, and refer to the derivation of a non-linguistic representation from text as 'conceptual construction' (sometimes referred to as 'mentalese'). My aim in the long term, however, is to challenge the general applicability of the constructivist principle, by suggesting that a good deal of representation is inseparable from the specific linguistic choices of the text. And certain mental representations and operations may even be carried out in language itself, making such specific linguistic choices essential. (A similar challenge can be found in Edwards and Potter 1992.)

One alternative to the constructivist principle much discussed in cognitive psychology is that experience is not represented symbolically (as posited by the constructivist principle) but analogically, in mental images (Eysenk and Keane 1990:207–37). I am not particularly concerned with this debate here, though I have no argument with the claim that many thoughts are represented analogically as images. The focus here is, rather, upon the relationship of linguistic to constructivist representation. My claim in this book will be that some mental representation is neither constructivist (using some symbolic representation other than language) nor analogical (i.e. in mental images) but exists in language itself.

The constructivist principle and memory for wording

The belief that human memory of texts does not usually include the linguistic form of the original suggests the use of non-verbal representations in memory by people. This corresponds with the orthodox view in linguistics and psychology that memory for wording fades rapidly, and that information is not encoded in long-term memory linguistically. This view tallies with intuition, in that we often seem to remember 'what' was said, rather than the words which were said. Further evidence often cited is from psychological experiments on recall in which subjects confuse sentences with different syntactic structures but similar meanings (Johnson-Laird and Stevenson 1970); they do not remember whether sentences were active or passive (Sacks 1967); they do not remember whether information was presented in one or more sentences (Bransford and Franks 1971). We should approach this standard view, however, with caution, and be careful not to overgeneralize. Belief in the replacement of wording by meaning is largely based on laboratory experiments in which the texts presented to subjects for memorization were decontextualized and of no personal significance. Moreover, subjects were deliberately confused by being shown texts of similar meaning but different encoding. Bartlett (1932)—significantly the supposed founder of schema theory—is also often cited. But Bartlett, whose focus was in any case elsewhere, deliberately selected texts which were culturally alien to his subjects.

A further body of research supporting the view that memory is always for meaning rather than wording concerned itself with pre-literate societies, disputing the widely held belief that in oral traditions there is a good deal of word-for-word learning and repetition. Often cited is Lord's (1960) study of a Yugoslav tavern keeper and singer Demo Zogic who, while honestly claiming to be repeating the same songs—some of them as long as seventeen hours—was shown by tape recordings to be changing the wording considerably. His conception of 'sameness' seemed to be quite different from that of literate people, who understand 'same' to refer to word-for-word repetition (Hunter 1985). (Similar evidence is provided by transcriptions made of genealogies by colonial authorities in West Africa, where one generation's rendering turned out to be quite different from that of its predecessors (Ong 1982:59)). Whatever the success of such research in proving the absence of verbatim memory in the non-literate, it cannot be cited as evidence of the degree of verbatim recall among the literate—especially given its concurrent claim of a radical difference in the cognitive processes of the non-literate and literate. There is, on the contrary, research on the memory of literate people in non-laboratory conditions which seems to show that people, given texts of personal significance in context, can and do remember them. Keenan, McWhinney, and Mayhew (1977) showed that a group of students recalled verbatim sarcastic, personal and witty remarks from a recorded seminar. Bates, Kintsch, Fletcher, and Guliani (1980) demonstrated verbatim recall of other less emotive 'natural discourse' such as lectures and soap operas. Memory for wording seems to vary, then, with personal significance and with discourse type. Literary language is also often remembered, as are verbatim chunks of advertisements and prayers, as well as words used at emotionally charged moments such as separation, declarations of love, and imparting news of death.

In recent years, the standard linguistics view that words are combined anew in production, or analysed down for meaning, has also received a blow from growing evidence that proficient speakers of a language use a vast number of 'ready made chunks' of language retrieved directly from memory, although the size of chunks referred to are usually of phrase, clause, or sentence length (Bolinger 1974; Cowie 1981; 1990; Pawley and Syder 1983; Ellis and Beattie 1986:248–9; Nattinger and deCarrico 1992). All this throws doubt on a constructivist principle which claims that text is *always* converted into a non-linguistic representation in memory.

The constructivist principle and 'realism'

Many current approaches to literature discount as naïve the positive evaluation of literary works for being 'true to life', in other words, reflecting the accuracy of the author's observations of the world. Literariness, we are told, resides not in holding 'the mirror up to nature',[4] but in the manipulation of form and convention. We should, I think, be wary of such confident dismissal of what is undoubtedly a widespread popular notion of excellence in literature; especially since the constructivist principle may give some backing to this popular belief. Even a limited acceptance of the constructivist principle could validate positive evaluations of fictional works for being 'true to life'. For though a narrative may be fictional as a whole, the non-linguistic representations of the units which compose it[5] may correspond to representations of non-fictional events, and may thus give a theoretical basis to evaluative judgements based on the match between the two.

Consider an example. In Paul Scott's novel *The Towers of Silence* ([1971] 1973:327) a male character, standing in front of the lavatory, decides to urinate quietly against the porcelain on the inside of the lavatory bowl, rather than noisily into the water, so that the sound of his action will not embarrass people in the next room. When I read this, it struck me (and no doubt other male readers) as a good use of detail, because it is so 'true to life'. (This rather crude example is a good one to demonstrate this point. Because of the private nature of urination, this strategy to avoid embarrassment, though known by male readers, is unlikely to have been verbalized.) In terms of the constructivist principle, we may say that a positive judgement of this detail as 'realistic' may result from comparison of the representation of the 'fact' derived from its verbal realization in the novel with its representation from non-verbal experience in the mind of the reader. Linguistic choices such as those between synonyms ('piss', 'urinate', 'pee') or different Functional Sentence Perspectives ('What he did was . . .', 'The side of the bowl was the place where . . .', etc.) (see page 49) will not affect the original non-verbal representation.

One system of conceptual construction: conceptual dependency theory (CD)

> Conceptual dependency is based on the theory that language is used to describe events that take place in the world and that these events consist of actions which can be represented as conceptualizations. The emphasis is on the content of information and not on its form. Thus the level at which actions are represented is language-independent and any two sentences which describe the same action and are therefore identical in meaning will have a single representation for that meaning.
> (McTear 1987:33)

AI schema theory is based upon the premises of the constructivist principle that concepts are represented by the mind in some formal system, and that this representation can be derived either from events in the world or from linguistic representations of those events. Linguistic representations which 'mean the same' but are different in form will also give rise to the same formal conceptual constructions. These large claims—if accepted—immediately raise two practical questions:

1 What is the nature of the formal representation?
2 How is it derived from and translated into natural language?

These crucial questions are usually glossed over in discourse analysis which invokes schema theory, and talks (sometimes rather glibly) about the interaction of knowledge and text, without clarifying what form knowledge takes if it is not itself a mental representation of text. This is one of the central questions for an evaluation of schema theory to address, and one which will lead me eventually to reject the traditional view of schemata and language as necessarily separate, and suggest ways in which each permeates the other in certain types of discourse.

Most importantly, from the point of view of discourse analysis, the theory must account for the function of variations in natural language representation: different types of cohesive tie, for example, or different

Functional Sentence Perspectives (see pages 48–51). A third question which arises from the claims outlined above is therefore:

3 What are variations in natural language representation for, if they are to be so readily discarded, and the beginning and end of communication is a formal representation in 'another language'?

It would seem strange if such intricate structures were assembled only later to be dismantled.

In order to avoid the vagueness of some other accounts of schema theory, it is necessary to go into some detail concerning one answer which has been suggested to the first two of the questions above. To consider, in other words, how exactly information might be represented in the mind if not in words.

From among various systems proposed in AI, I shall concentrate on one as being representative of the general approach.[6] This is Conceptual Dependency (henceforth in this chapter CD).[7] It is a system for which large claims have been made concerning its applicability in human psychology (Barr and Feigenbaum 1981:211), and for this reason it is more relevant to my present concerns than comparable systems whose interest is limited to purely artificial intelligence. Ultimately in later chapters the argument will be concerned to show why such 'language free' systems of mental representation (sometimes referred to as 'mentalese') do not adequately account for many aspects of human discourse understanding. But let us first examine how the system claims to represent natural language, before proceeding to some of the objections which may be raised.

CD: basic principles

A CD representation depicts information as an unbroken causal chain of primitive actions. In this sense, a CD representation may be said to have 'coherence' if the state resulting from each act is one which is, in the world (or the intelligence's perception of the world—for both text and knowledge may be wrong but internally consistent), the starting point for the next act.

CD was originally conceived as a system for representing the meaning of sentences and for deriving inferences from them. It was then developed further to describe texts. Its building blocks are events, which are seen as the results of earlier events and the causes of subsequent events. By inferring and representing explicitly events that are—or appear to be— omitted in a discourse (see pages 34–6), it can present coherence as an unbroken chain of causes and effects. Some of the events represented are events in the world, others are events in the mind, and the two are not regarded as being different in kind. Sections of the causal chain may take place 'within' the mind, with one 'mental event' causing another. The moving of information from one 'part of' the mind to another, for example, is placed on a par with moving an object from one place to another. This strange mixture of positivism and mentalism is a potential source of confusion and misunderstanding to anyone who is used to regarding these two approaches as mutually exclusive.

In its representation of individual sentences, CD reduces a word denoting an action to a series of constituent primitive acts. Most commonly, these acts will be the constituents of the meaning of a verb, but they can also be associated with other grammatical classes.[8]

In the original (1972) formulation, eleven primitive acts were postulated (see Table 3.1). Many actions denoted by a single word are thus represented by a number of acts: 'give' for example involves both **ATRANS** and **PTRANS**; 'buy' and 'purchase', whether as nouns or verbs, will involve the **ATRANS** and the **PTRANS** of both money and an entity. Each primitive act is related optionally or obligatorily to entities performing particular roles: agent, object, instrument, and so on.[9] From this representation, various inferences can be drawn and made explicit. 'Buy' for example must involve two agents (buyer and seller) and two patients (goods and currency). Each act will additionally entail other inferences. An inference to be drawn from **PTRANS**, for example, is that its object is not where it was. An inference from **INGEST** is that the patient is inside the agent. Clearly, there are enormous problems involved in associating the correct acts with the occurrence of a particular word in natural language. Even in the apparently straightforward example of 'give' and 'buy' there are many complications. There are non-literal uses of words. 'Giving advice' will involve quite different acts (**SPEAK**, **ATTEND**, **MBUILD**) from 'giving a present'. There are complex

Act	Coding
1 The transfer of abstract relationship such as possession or control	**ATRANS**
2 The transfer of the physical location of an object	**PTRANS**
3 The application of physical force to an object	**PROPEL**
4 The moving of a body part of an animal by that animal	**MOVE**
5 The grasping of an object by an actor	**GRASP**
6 The taking of an object inside an animal by that animal	**INGEST**
7 The expulsion of an object by an animal	**EXPEL**
8 The transfer of mental information between animals or within an animal	**MTRANS**
9 The construction by an animal of new information from old	**MBUILD**
10 speaking	**SPEAK**
11 the action of attending or focusing a sense organ towards a stimulus	**ATTEND**

Table 3.1: CD acts

variations on standard meanings. It is hard to say what exactly is **PTRANS**ed, to whom and by whom, when somebody buys something by credit card.

There is also a need to represent stative relations. I shall use the following abbreviations in subsequent analyses: BE (for projected complementation), IS or ARE (for actual complementation), HAS (denoting inalienable possession), SOC-CONT (denoting the state of having social control over something), KNOW (know), and WANT (want).

CD: two examples

Thus far, CD allows inferences to be made explicit, though it cannot evaluate which of those inferences will be important in discourse. The relations between actions and entities may be related diagrammatically as in the representation of a sentence in Figure 3.1. Here, various inferences have been drawn from knowledge activated by the encounter with the word 'eat' in conjunction with 'with a spoon'. (For a start the spoon is assumed to be the instrument, not a companion! (See Rich 1983: 326–8).) These inferences will include such facts as 'the spoon contains ice cream'; 'John moves the spoon backwards and forwards to his mouth', and so on. Schank (1984: 78–81) compares the information in such a diagram to that which would be necessary in explaining how to eat to someone who had never done it before.

Note, however, that different Functional Sentence Perspectives (for example 'What John did was eat ice cream with a spoon') would all be represented by the same diagram. There are many linguistic representations, in other words, to which one single mental representation

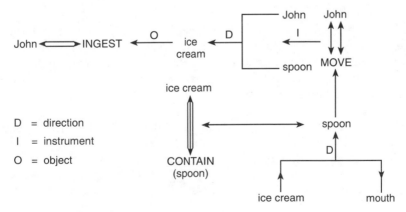

Figure 3.1: CD diagram of 'John eats ice cream with a spoon' (Barr and Feigenbaum 1981: 302)

corresponds. This raises the fundamental question of why this should be. Later on, I shall suggest that in literary discourse, differences in linguistic realization may actually disturb mental representations.

The next stage in CD, once all inferences have been made explicit, is to establish links between events in terms of cause and effect. These too are often omitted in human discourse. Very frequently, for example, as Schank and Abelson observe (1977:23), the **MBUILD** act which is the intermediate between manifestations of mental activity is omitted, because inferred. In the following, for example:

John cried because Mary said she loved Bill

the mental representation which links the two is omitted. John, in other words, did not cry as a direct result of Mary's words, but as a result of a mental construction caused by them.

Cause	Coding
1 An act results in a state[10]	↑ **r**
2 A state enables an act	↑ **E**
3 A state or act initiates a mental state	↑ **I**
4 A mental act is the reason for a physical act	↑ **R**
5 A state disables an act	↑ **dE**
When the separation of (1) and (2), and of (3) and (4) has no consequence for inferences, they may be paired together as follows:	
6 An act results in a state which enables an act	↑ **RE**
7 An act or state initiates a thought which is the reason for an act	↑ **IR**

Table 3.2: CD causes and effects, and their coding

CD: text representation

With this apparatus, texts, in principle, can be represented in terms of causality, always supposing that unstated causal connections have been inferred and made explicit. CD, in other words, depicts an unbroken chain of states and events, each of which is the result or cause of any immediate neighbour. Schank and Abelson (1977) give the example in Figure 3.2.

The linking of events is one way of describing coherence though it does not fully account for how these links are produced, if they are produced at all, by the receiver.

CD: an assessment

An obvious objection to this system is that while it may be capable of handling the highly simplified and controlled texts of AI, it will be

Consider the following story

John was thirsty. He opened a can of beer and went into the den. There he saw a new chair. He sat down in it. Suddenly the chair tilted over and John fell on the floor. His beer spilled all over the chair. When his wife heard the noise she ran into the den. She was very angry that her new chair had been ruined.

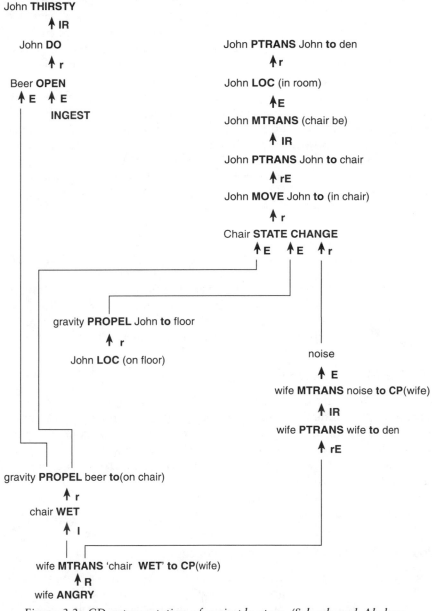

Figure 3.2: CD representation of a simple story (Schank and Abelson 1977:28–9)

baffled by the complexity of human discourse. The problem may be not merely quantitative but qualitative too. Success with machine handling of simple texts does not imply that the same strategies, amplified and expanded, will work on more complex texts, nor that they are the strategies actually used by humans. From an AI perspective, the essential question about CD representations is whether they can be executed by machine. Nothing is proved in the consideration of human text handling, however, by concocting a representation of a given discourse into which inferred acts and states have been inserted. To do this is merely to use the analysts' inferences, and not to explain them.

The status of CD as a theory of the human processing of natural discourse (as opposed to the machine processing of controlled discourse) remains as speculative as any other theory of psychology and language. This judgement, however, cuts both ways, and its status is no lower than any other speculation for being unproved.[11] AI, however, together with those who accept the computational paradigm in linguistics, does speculate that a conceptual construction (in CD or some similar form), algorithmically derived from sense data or natural language, is at the heart of human discourse understanding. In effect, CD is an image of how miniature schemata might gradually be built up for each word. Again, there are obvious qualitative as well as quantitative limitations. Not every word meaning can readily be captured by a reduction to constituent objects, acts and states, even if these include mental 'objects' and 'acts'. 'Kiss'—as Barr and Feigenbaum observe (1981:214)—is not the same as '**MOVE** lips to lips'. Clearly the complexities grow as the texts encountered approach those of natural language.

Problems for conceptual constructions

If a system of conceptual construction like CD or any other attempt to represent 'the content' of text is to play a part in a theory of discourse, it must come to terms with a number of problems concerning the relationship between the underlying representations which it proposes as an account of coherence, and their realization and use in discourse. As these may point us forward towards a development of schema theory, and also towards the insights of literary theory, I shall examine these problems here in some detail.

Problem 1: prototypes and fuzzy concepts

Though by no means prone to the extreme naïvety of equating concepts with the words of a particular language, systems like CD do treat concepts as discrete entities, like counters which can be manoeuvred and combined in clear-cut mathematical ways. In this, they are similar to the components of word meaning described by componential analysis in semantics and, as such, they are open to the same criticisms as those proposed by prototype theory (Rosch 1973, 1977; Lakoff 1987) which suggest that classification of concepts is not based on componential analysis but by resemblance to a prototype, and that therefore boundaries between categories are 'fuzzy', and category membership graded.[12] (For a fuller discussion of the relationship between CD and semantics, see Appendix B.)

Problem 2: level of detail

In any discourse, the sender will need to choose a 'level of detail': whether to say simply, for example, 'I went to Paris' or to describe the stages of the journey. The representation of discourse as a series of propositions or acts says nothing about this choice. Most processes, actions, and entities may be regarded as composed of constituent processes, actions, and entities, or conversely as themselves being constituent parts of larger ones (Sanford and Garrod 1981:30). Physical actions, for example, may be almost indefinitely reduced. Consider the action denoted by the sentence 'She drove home' as represented in Figure 3.3. The constituent movements on the right hand side of the figure could be further reduced and described in terms of the contractions of muscles. In principle the limit of such a hierarchy would only be the limits of the physical description of matter—i.e., description of some molecular, atomic, or particle level! This level, however, is only available to some people with a particular scientific training, and generally confined to particular discourse types. For most people, for whom actions such

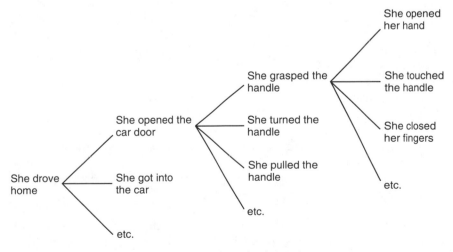

Figure 3.3: 'Level of detail'

as blinking or breathing are irreducible, the limits of reduction are reached relatively quickly.[13] Discourse analysis needs a principle to explain the level of detail. Schema theory is clearly inadequate in fully explaining this choice, as people have the option of giving more or less detail even to the same receiver, and lack of adequate explanation has been adduced in criticism of schema theory (Dresher and Hornstein 1976; Brown and Yule 1983:244).

Schema theory, however, is primarily concerned with information, whereas the reasons for the level of detail chosen may be interpersonal rather than ideational. Cooper (1986), and Tannen (1989), for example, suggest that detail may be a signal of intimacy. Addressing this problem from the viewpoint of ethnomethodological conversation analysis, Schegloff (1972) suggests that we can only choose a level of description by reference to the needs and knowledge of the addressee. Whereas the answer 'in England', for example, though possibly true, would not be a helpful riposte to the question 'Where do you live?' in a conversation between two people who both work in Nottingham, it might well be an informative answer to the same question from a fellow passenger on an intercontinental flight. This perspective is by no means incompatible with conceptual construction as an approach to discourse, but it needs to be added to it. It points to an inadequacy of any mere representation of the facts of a text. Successful communication must distinguish between what is true and what is needed.

A further complication in literary discourse is that reduction to constituent detail may obscure a general view of what is happening, and this may be used for narrative effect. There are many well-known literary narratives which emphasize this by presenting all the constituents of an act through the eyes of a character who, through some mental limitation, cannot abstract a characterization of the whole: the idiot Benjy's description of a game of golf in William Faulkner's novel *The Sound and the Fury*,[14] the Neanderthal Man Lok's perception of the firing of an arrow in William Golding's *The Inheritors*,[15] the child Maisie's limited understanding of an adult love affair in Henry James' *What Maisie Knew*,[16] a horse's perception of human affairs in Tolstoy's *Kholstomer*, are just a few examples.

An interesting exception to the general tendency to omit recoverable detail often occurs in narratives where, prior to recounting an extraordinary event, the narrator makes explicit reference to default elements of a schema—spells out, in other words, information which is already known to a receiver.

It was a day like any other. I woke up in the morning, got out of bed, washed, had breakfast and set off for work. Then something happened which changed my life forever . . .

Such introductions to the extraordinary are common in fantasy literature, and presumably serve the purpose of attaching the incredible, individual, deviant instance to a more familiar and typical series of events. This tendency is noted by Eco (1979:165–8) in his analysis of the James Bond novels of Ian Fleming. Fleming's narratives alternate between minutely accurate descriptions of 'the already known' (for example, starting a car) and the most bizarre incidents (for example, an assault on Fort Knox) (ibid.:167). This cataloguing of default elements may even have become a 'device' which signals to the reader by convention an impending strange event. It may also reflect the 'defamiliarization' of everyday experience which occurs at emotionally charged moments. People remember the routine events and familiar objects which accompany a disturbing experience. This fact is often reflected by the attention to detail in descriptions of such experiences. The following paragraph, for example, from *The Last Enemy*, a novel by Richard Hillary, occurs immediately after the narrator has helped rescue a mother and child buried in rubble during a bombing raid.

> Very carefully I screwed the top on to the brandy flask, unscrewed it once and screwed it on again, for I had caught it on the wrong thread. I put the flask into my hip-pocket and did up the button. I pulled across the buckle on my great coat and noticed that I was dripping with sweat. I pulled the cap down over my eyes and walked out into the street.
> (Hillary 1943:214)

Such descriptions, which are by no means confined to first person narratives, serve the dual purpose of indicating characters' emotions and informing the reader of the details of their life—their schemata. The same principle seems to be operating in this description of the mother, Mrs Morrell, a miner's wife, in D. H. Lawrence's *Sons and Lovers*:

> In her weariness forgetting everything, she moved about the little tasks that remained to be done, set his breakfast, rinsed his pit-bottle, put his clothes on the hearth to warm, set his pit-boots beside them, put him out a clean scarf and snap-bag and two apples, raked the fire and went to bed.
> (Lawrence [1913] 1961:37)

Interestingly, this problem of what motivates the inclusion of detail, often ignored in AI schema theory, is addressed by two literary theorists, the Russian formalist Tomashevsky ([1925] 1965) and Roland Barthes ([1966] 1977:74–124), whose theories are discussed below in Chapter 5.

Problem 3: principles for omitting connection

A related, but different problem, is the omission of connections between one action and another. Extending the example in Figure 3.3, the sentence 'She drove home' might or might not be omitted from a sequence such as:

> She left work at seven. She drove home. When she arrived home . . .

CD, as we have seen, may aid the generation of inferences which have no realization in the text. Most of the elements of these representations are likely to be absent from discourse. This applies not only to connectives indicative of causal, temporal, and logical links, but also to entire acts: the movement of the spoon to the mouth in Figure 3.1 for example; the eating of the poisoned meat by the dog (see page 35); the closing of the fingers in Figure 3.3. But discourse analysis needs a principle to explain the basis of omission and inclusion.[17] One set of answers is provided by relevance theory (Sperber and Wilson 1986:15–21), which espouses the principle that what is mentioned is what is relevant, and defines relevance as the greatest contextual[18] change for the least processing effort (ibid:46–50). This explanation, however, seems quite as incomplete as the AI approach. Discourse does far more than just communicate information, and there may be other reasons than cognitive efficiency for the inclusion or exclusion of detail.

Problem 4: failure to account for linguistic choices

The single greatest problem with the constructivist principle is its failure to give any explanation of the function of linguistic differences between utterances which will supposedly yield the same non-linguistic representation. CD, for example, purports to express meanings which can be realized in different linguistic forms. The corollary of this claim is that it omits certain variations of linguistic form, and gives no account or explanation of these variations. Such variations would include linguistic features such as:

- —Functional Sentence Perspectives which topicalize or focus
- —deictic terms and article choice which reflect the sender's orientation to the content
- —modals expressing the sender's attitude or judgement
- —choices between subordination and coordination or between synonyms
- —density of cohesive ties
- —use of discourse markers to direct the receiver.

All these are paid virtually no attention in CD, however crucial they may be in the creation and maintenance of coherence. Van Dijk and Kintsch (1983:10–18), in their global view of discourse comprehension, suggest that recourse to a conceptual construction is but one of a number of strategies open to the receiver. The others include:

—perception of rhetorical structure (or 'schema' in their terms)
—knowledge of production (i.e. text generation) strategies
—attention to stylistic cues
—attention to non-verbal elements of the message
—attention to conversational mechanisms.

Some of these, especially those relating to style, rhetorical structure, and conversational mechanisms, will be intimately involved with linguistic choice.

In general, the notion of complementary strategies operating in parallel is an attractive one and seems intuitively true. Yet it may also be possible, as I hope to suggest at a later point in my argument, that these approaches interact with each other, and that such natural language phenomena as thematization, style, rhetorical organization, and discourse type, may affect or be affected by the conceptual construction which is derived from or used to generate a given discourse.[19]

A complex AI schema theory

According to the constructivist principle, many causal links in a representation of the world are left unstated in natural language, though they are—or at least can be—filled in when required. This leaves us with the problem (often skated over) as to whether causal links *are* actually filled in at some subconscious level. But that problem notwithstanding, it is the mechanisms of this omission and retrieval, and the conditions for their activation, that schema theory claims to provide.

A rigorous and complete version of schema theory will need to have some solution to these problems: how facts are represented in non-linguistic form, how they can be omitted or retrieved, and the nature of the relationship between the linguistic and non-linguistic representations. One of the most complete and influential models worked out in the AI revival of schema theory in the 1970s is that put forward by Schank and Abelson in their book *Scripts, Plans, Goals and Understanding* (henceforth *SPGU*) in 1977. For all its weaknesses, to which I shall turn later, this seminal model has the virtue of squarely confronting these issues, and providing a strong and coherent answer to them. It is not insignificant that one of the authors of the theory, Roger Schank, was also the originator of conceptual dependency theory, and through his work on that constructivist theory, came to confront the problems of omission and recall. In *SPGU* he and Robert Abelson propose a complex version of schema theory and suggest (*SPGU*: 38–9) that the function of schemata is, in this respect, twofold: on the one hand they enable us to omit a sequence of well-known causal links, thus saving time (*SPGU*: 41); on the other hand they enable us to provide them if needed.

Although this version has undergone severe modification as a model for AI programming, not least by Schank himself,[20] it has a number of distinct advantages for my argument, which is concerned primarily with adapting a version of schema theory for the analysis of literary discourse. Firstly, it is still one of the most detailed, rigorous, well-known, and influential versions of schema theory. Secondly, it is primarily concerned with text production and processing rather than intelligence in general. Thirdly, it concerns itself with human intelligence, not with artificial intelligence alone.[21] Lastly, the version is self-contained, and makes scant reference to others, so by specifying this theory I shall avoid terminological and conceptual confusion.

Moreover, even if the details of the model are inaccurate as representations of human intelligence, its basic claim may still stand, and be of importance in discourse analysis. I take this basic claim to be that human understanding (and in *SPGU* specifically text understanding) can be represented as a hierarchy of levels of schemata in which failure to understand on one level can be referred to the level above. In production the opposite is true, and what cannot be generated by one level, must originate in the level above.

This does not, of course, deny the possibility that, in more automatized instances, the higher levels need not be involved at all. In fact the function of low-level schemata is precisely to bypass higher level processing. The implications of this principle for a theory of coherence are clear. Failure of connection at a lower level may be referred to a higher one.[22]

The levels postulated in *SPGU* are as follows:

THEMES
GOALS
SUB-GOALS
PLANS
SCRIPTS

In order to explore some of the particular problems which even a complex schema theory encounters when employed in the analysis of literary texts, and also to avoid the vagueness inherent in many descriptions of the role of schemata in discourse interpretation, it will be necessary to give more detail of this hierarchy than is usually provided. I shall do this, working through the categories, as Schank and Abelson do, 'bottom up'.

Scripts

Scripts are structures 'that describe appropriate sequences of events in a particular context ... a predetermined, stereotyped sequence of actions that defines a well-known situation' (Schank and Abelson 1977:41). They fall into three main categories:

—situational scripts (for example, restaurant, bus, jail)
—personal scripts (for example, being a flatterer, pickpocket, spy, jealous spouse)
—instrumental scripts (for example, lighting a cigarette, starting a car, frying an egg)

As such, they are the closest of *SPGU*'s categories to the general description of schemata given in Chapter 1. A script may have a number of 'tracks', which are different but related instances of the same general category. In one of *SPGU*'s examples, the restaurant script, the tracks are such instances as Fast Food Restaurant, Coffee Shop, Italian Restaurant, etc. Each script is represented from the point of view of one of the participants and his or her role in it—in the case of the restaurant script, such roles as customer, or waitress, or owner. Each script has an 'essential precondition' and 'a main consequence'. The essential precondition for a customer's restaurant script is 'wanting to eat', and the main consequence is 'having eaten'. In addition, each script has a number of 'slots' (similar to the 'default elements' described in Chapter 1) whose realization can be assumed unless there is information to the contrary. The slots in a script are:

—a number of props
—the roles of participants
—the entry conditions
—results
—scenes and their sequence.

The distinguishing feature of scripts, as a type of schema, is that these slots are instantiated by quite specific entities and events. If we imagine, for example, a 'trial' script from the point of view of a judge, then the props will be a wig, a gavel, and so on; the roles will be defendant, lawyers, witnesses, etc.; the entry condition will be 'being appointed to hear the case'; the result will be punishment or exoneration of the defendant; the scenes will be indictment, plea, defence case, etc.[23] The script is therefore an example of specific rather than general knowledge and, though connected to general plans and goals, may run without reference to them. A script is dependent on personal experience, either of situations or reports of them, and will thus vary both between individuals and within individuals.

A script, it is claimed, is activated by any one of a number of 'headers' concerning the preconditions (for example, 'wishing to please someone' may activate a 'buying a present' script); the instrumental function of actions (taking the subway may activate a 'shopping' or 'work' script); a location habitually associated with the script ('The Loon Fung restaurant'), or explicit mention of the occupant of a slot in the script ('that friendly waiter in the Loon Fung'). In text understanding, script activation enables details to be bypassed, or provided by the default elements of the script, as required.

There are, of course, a number of problems connected with the smooth running of a script in text processing, and the description given in the paragraphs above is perhaps misleading as, in practice, scripts which run without obstacles, errors, or deviations are unlikely to be worth talking or writing about. A theory of script-based text understanding, though it may take the above description as an unmarked instance, will need to take into account a number of marked cases, for example:

—the incidental mention of potential 'headers' for other scripts
—the concurrent activation of rival scripts which will then compete to be the one used in understanding
—the concurrent running of more than one script, or of one script as part of another
—'headers' which may create 'scriptal ambiguity' (*SPGU*: 59) as to which of a number of scripts that share them is the one to activate
—obstacles to the course of events which may necessitate either a loop back to an earlier point, or script abandonment
—unexpected events which may lead to scripts being abandoned or held in abeyance until the event has run its course
—movement from one script to another.

SPGU regards the contents of scripts as stored in some form of conceptual construction, such as CD. As such, representations may be derived equally from texts representing events and from events themselves. The account is often ambivalent as to whether it is referring to text or event, and in effect no distinction is made. My own example, above, of the judge's trial script, would apply equally to the event and to a text relating the event from the judge's viewpoint. The description of script-based understanding says nothing about different linguistic realizations of the same conceptual content and the effect these may have upon the selection and running of a relevant script or scripts. This is a major issue at the heart of the theory to be advanced in Chapter 7.

One further problem is that, although knowledge about the sequencing of scenes is often cited as a crucial feature distinguishing scripts from other postulated schemata such as 'frames', 'scenarios', etc., it seems likely that certain scripts, while they may specify scenes, cannot specify an invariable order for them. Let us suppose, for example, that individuals in the modern world have some sort of 'hospital' script (from a patient's viewpoint), which contains many other dependent scripts (for example, a 'medical examination' script), and that this hospital script contains such scenes as: doctor's visit, meal time, visiting time, admission of new patient, etc. There would be variations in the ordering of these scenes. A doctor's visit, for example, may, and indeed often does, occur at any point. In later analysis, it will be seen that not all scripts can include rigid scene-sequencing constraints. *SPGU*'s insistence on this aspect of script composition results from the limited types of text with which it deals.

Plans

Although much verbal and non-verbal experience is repetitive enough to be dealt with by scripts, there are also experiences which are sufficiently novel and unpredictable as to demand interpretation with reference to a structure which is not so specific as to its constituent elements. Such a structure is postulated in *SPGU* as a 'plan'. This structure is a schema, in the sense that it consists of ordered 'slots', but is far less explicitly connected to specified places, individuals, or locations. In terms of behaviour, a plan is used to deal with situations for which the agent has no existing script. In terms of text understanding, assumptions about the plans of agents described in the text may create coherence when no relevant script is available in the understander's memory. In the case of texts, such as descriptions of landscape or objects, in which no agents are referred to, the function of plans in providing coherence is less apparent and, significantly, such texts are conspicuously absent from AI work, though they are common enough in literature. It may be, however, that in such cases a reader's hypotheses about the plans of the author, or hypotheses about the author's attempt to influence the reader's plans, may contribute to coherence.

Plans, according to *SPGU*, realize goals, which may themselves be subordinate to higher goals. It is the recognition of the goal, or sub-goal, and the stages of the plan realizing it, which establish coherence. I shall adapt one of the examples in *SPGU* by way of illustration. If the goal or sub-goal is to be in a state of having social control of an object and there is no script available for doing this, then there may be a number of 'named' plans. *SPGU* hypothesizes that the named plans to achieve this goal are: 'ask for';[24] 'invoke topic';[25] 'inform reason';[26] 'bargain object'; 'bargain favour'; 'threaten'; 'overpower'; 'steal'. Each of these plans for achieving the goal of gaining social control of an object is realized by a 'planbox'. All planboxes consist of:

key action + controllable precondition + uncontrollable precondition + mediating precondition + result

The agents, things, places and information are not specified as in a script, but can be adapted to variables. The constituents of the planbox for 'ask for', for example, can be represented in conceptual dependency as follows:

Planbox: 'ask for' (realizing sub-goal SOC-CONT)
  key action   = PTRANS O to X
  + controllable precondition   = X BE (Prox(Y))
  + uncontrollable precondition   = Y SOC-CONT O
  + mediating precondition   = Y WANTS to PTRANS O to X
  + result   = O BE (PLOC X)

where O, Y, and X are variables, standing for, respectively, the object, the owner and the asker, LOC means 'location' and PROX means 'near'. The planbox can be used in a situation whose constituent elements are utterly new. It can be adapted to very different situations. One might equally well use this planbox to ask someone for a coin for the phone, or for a silver cross to ward off vampires. The difference between scripts and plans thus suggests two very different types of schemata: those in which slots are specific entities, people and events, and those which are more widely applicable to a greater variety of situations.

Recognition of planning by characters in a discourse may provide coherence to sequences or sentences. *SPGU* gives the following example:

1 John was lost. He pulled his car up to a farmer who was standing by the road. (*SPGU*: 75)

This is coherent because John's action can be seen as executing the controllable precondition of a planbox 'ask for' to obtain information. (This interpretation also makes use of 'scriptlike' knowledge that farmers are likely to be people who know the area.) The following sequence, on the other hand:

2 John was lost. He noticed a chicken. He tried to catch it. (ibid.: 76)

is incoherent[27]—unless we know of some way in which the catching of a chicken may execute a relevant planbox, such as 'find out', or unless we assume that the plan (suggested by our knowledge that people who are lost try to find out where they are), has been abandoned in favour of another plan. (John might be a pagan priest trained in augury through entrails, a Ph.D student writing a thesis on chickens, the driver of a lorry from which chickens often escape, or just very hungry.)

What this leaves out of account, however, is an overriding belief human readers have, often exploited in literature, that the texts they read are coherent if only they can find the key. The simple reason for this belief is that the producers of texts do set out to communicate with somebody. It seems, therefore, more likely that when such sequences as (2) are encountered in actual discourse, people will read on as though the text *is* coherent, assuming that actions are parts of plans that execute goals, even when the goals are unknown. (This will be illustrated in an analysis of a passage from *Crime and Punishment* in the next chapter.) Tolerance of suspended goal revelation, however, is accompanied by a growing demand for knowledge of the goal, which must be satisfied at some later point, if the text is not to be viewed as finally incoherent or the character as mad. (Surrealist texts form an interesting exception to this rule for in their case, paradoxically, the unifying goal is that of the artist attempting to eschew goals altogether.)

The essential point about plans for text processing is that in cases where we cannot process by reference to a script and create coherence by assuming the default elements of that script, we may do so by reference to a plan, fitting the more specific elements of the text to the generalized goal-related elements of the planbox. Interpretation with reference to a plan will involve more effort and more time. Repeated exposure to the same situation (more than one encounter with vampires, frequent overpowering of people to take their possessions) will lead to the replacement of plan-based interpretation by script-based interpretation.

It is important to notice at this point that the theory of scripts and plans makes no claim for their cultural homogeneity or universality. One may speculate about the degree to which the contents of scripts and plans coincide in members of the same culture. It might even be possible to define cultural identity for a given individual in this way. Yet these lines of inquiry are not pursued in *SPGU*, which, on the contrary, stresses variations, even within a single community. Thus, the specific contents of scripts and plans, and even whether a particular eventuality is dealt with by a script or by a plan, will vary between individuals and social groups. For an ambulance driver, for example, an accident will be dealt with by a script, while for someone less frequently involved in accidents, it may be dealt with by a planbox. Even for two people dealing with an accident by script, the details will be different, according to whether they are, for example, a priest, a doctor, or someone who faints at the sight of blood. Within the individual, moreover, the contents of plans and scripts will change. (If a prime minister, for example, has a 'meeting-important-people' script, it will have changed as he or she rose to power, and will change again on his or her retirement.) Therefore, some people will process a given text predominantly with reference to scripts, while others will activate a higher proportion of plans. This may

well create different ways of understanding the same text. Jackie Collins'
novel *Hollywood Wives*, about Hollywood love affairs, may be interpreted
through scripts by a Hollywood star, but only with reference to plans
by somebody else.

In literary analysis, individual differences in scripts and plans, and the
consequent differences in the projection of scripts and plans onto
characters, are highly relevant. This may be illustrated by the following
account of differences in interpretation. A poem frequently analysed in
British literary critical and stylistics classes is Wilfred Owen's 'Futility',
which reflects upon a soldier's death from hypothermia in the trenches
during the First World War.

Futility

Move him into the sun, —
Gently its touch awoke him once,
At home, whispering of fields unsown.
Always it woke him, even in France,
Until this morning and this snow.   5
If anything might rouse him now
The kind old sun will know.

Think how it wakes the seeds, —
Woke, once, the clays of a cold star.
Are limbs, so dear-achieved, are sides,   10
Full-nerved—still warm—too hard to stir?
Was it for this the clays grew tall?
—O what made fatuous sunbeams toil
To break earth's sleep at all?

The opening line of the poem is often explained as a futile or perhaps
symbolic attempt to revive the soldier, a refusal to accept the death of
the young. This is to interpret the imperative in terms of a plan involving
a vain attempt to execute the goal of preserving life or dealing with death.
I once encountered, however, a rival explanation which, significantly, was
advanced by a First World War veteran with experience of the trenches.
This elderly survivor explained how, in the absence of burial facilities,
the bodies of soldiers who had died of cold overnight were immediately
removed from the trench, partly to avoid risk of infection, partly to
satisfy some need for action, partly to maintain morale. In this reading,
the opening command becomes the rough, routine order of the officer
in charge. This is to interpret the opening in terms of a script, no doubt
one which was familiar to many people at the time. Of these two
readings, I feel the latter is the more horrifying. Dealing with death is
routine.

In this reading, however, we may glimpse a phenomenon which is of crucial importance in the development of a theory linking schematic effects to particular linguistic choices. In the veteran's interpretation of the opening line, the sun is mentioned, almost accidentally, as a synonym for 'the open air'; the subsequent musing on the sun takes this mention as a point of departure. A conceptual construction of this command would, however, regard the choice between synonyms as insignificant; in this context, both would 'mean the same'. Yet it is only this lexical choice which links the script invoked by the opening line—let us call it a 'removing corpse script'—to the script in the next lines: a 'waking up at home script' (from the viewpoint of a young farmer). The anaphoric referent 'it', creating cohesion with a noun phrase which was not the topic of the preceding sentence, emphasizes the tenuous nature of the link. The conceptual links developed as the poem progresses, derive from the linguistic choice of 'sun'.

Another important and potentially confusing point about plans, whose relevance to literary analysis will be considered in the next chapter, is that they may form parts of each other, or even of scripts. In this sense, the hierarchical relation of *SPGU*'s schema types to each other is recursive, and analogous to that of the ranks of grammar. (A clause, for example, although higher in the rank structure than a phrase, may yet be a constituent of a phrase.) Such structures as those in Figure 3.4 are therefore possible, where instances lower down the tree are part of schemata higher up. A holiday script, for example, may contain a scene slot filled by 'going home' which may be realized through an airport script, although if the airport is unexpectedly closed, this may activate a plan. An important difference between the tree (in Figure 3.4) and grammatical trees, however, is that the vertical connections represent alternative rather than consecutive realizations. The plan or script at the highest node is realized through the plans or scripts lower down. This

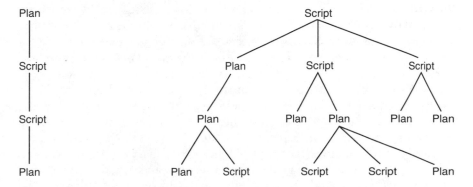

Figure 3.4: Hierarchical relationship of plans and scripts

vertical movement downwards is pursued as far as necessary. If this strategy fails, another line is followed.

Goals and sub-goals

Just as unconnected actions in CD representation can be explained at the level of scripts and plans, so scripts and plans need explanation at a higher level too. This next level, in *SPGU*, is that of goals, and these may be divided into two: main goals and sub-goals. If we assume that agents in a discourse have plans, although we cannot recognize what they are, we may nevertheless be able to reconstruct them by reference to sub-goals and, similarly, unknown sub-goals may be interpreted with reference to goals. The five main goals proposed in *SPGU* are:

Satisfaction	of hunger, sex, sleep, addiction
Enjoyment	of travel, entertainments, exercise,competition
Achievement	of possessions, power, job, social relationships, skills
Preservation	of health, safety, offspring, people, property
Crisis handling	of accident, fire, storm, etc.

Consider a literary example. Lady Macbeth urges Macbeth to wash his hands of blood to avoid detection. Why? She wants him to avoid detection to preserve his life; perhaps she wishes him to preserve his life to further her own status. In this interpretation, her goal is to further her own status. This is executed by the sub-goal of advancing her husband's status. This activates a plan to preserve his life, which in turn gives rise to the plan of avoiding detection. This last plan is executed by, among other things, an (instrumental) 'washing hands script' (although the usual slot filler 'dirt' has been replaced by 'blood'). Such an interpretation reveals a number of problems. It highlights the fuzziness of the dividing line between goals and plans. It also reveals a growing uncertainty in interpretations at higher levels. Scripts are relatively transparent, as are plans. The goals behind them are at once both more mysterious and more interesting. (It is the ambiguity of Lady Macbeth's goals which attracts the greatest interest.) On the other hand, there are certain 'basic' goals of which we may be fairly sure for most people: the goals to survive, to protect offspring, to seek sexual satisfaction. It is the intermediate area between these most fundamental goals and the plans and sub-goals which execute them which are both most interesting and most frequently concealed.

Very often, literature concerns itself with departure from expected goals. In Lady Macbeth's case, she significantly and 'unnaturally' denies the goal of protecting her own offspring, which would otherwise be attributed to her 'by default':

I have given suck, and know
How tender 'tis to love the babe that milks me:
I would, while it was smiling in my face,
Have plucked my nipple from his boneless gums,
And dashed the brains out, had I so sworn as you
Have done to this.

(*Macbeth*, I. vii. 54–9)

There are also, in *SPGU*'s hierarchy, sub-goals employed in the execution of these main goals. The main goal of preserving one's own children, for example, might be realized through, among others, the sub-goal of ascertaining the identity of a baby-sitter, and the sub-goal of using that baby-sitter. The second of these will then be initiated by a planbox 'ask', which, if it fails, will create a recursive loop, leading to asking another baby-sitter, or a change of plan, perhaps to stay at home. Clearly, there are complex interrelations and preference rules between both goals and sub-goals, and those which operate with enough frequency and predictability will be handled by plans and scripts. Sub-goals, moreover, may have their own sub-goals, and no limit is set to this recursion. We may regard main goals as types of schemata whose default elements are actual or potential sub-goals, and sub-goals as schemata whose default elements are other sub-goals and/or plans.

At this level, as at that of scripts and plans, there is much room for debate as to the degree to which goals are universal or specific to cultures, social groups, or individuals. This of course may be the source of interest in reading texts concerned with other people's goals. Many of *SPGU*'s categories are specific to the culture and social class of its authors, and it might be unkindly observed that there are many ways in which the list reflects the goals of a male, middle-aged North American academic—though, to be fair, the authors often show humorous recognition of this. It is easy enough to speculate on different classifications and identities of goals and, in sociology, psychology, and anthropology, there are in fact many such attempts (for a discussion see Atkinson, Atkinson, Smith, and Hilgard 1987:315–46). However, the accuracy or inaccuracy of *SPGU*'s specific suggestions concerning main goals in no way invalidates the theory that goals of some sort control the lower levels of both discourse and action.

Themes

Just as plans and scripts demand goals, so goals need explanation too. In text comprehension, if a goal is not recognized, or is unfamiliar, recourse may be made to some higher level. Whether or not there is a degree of universality in goals, it is indisputable that the priority given in conflicts between goals varies both within individuals, from individual to individual, and from group to group. Why will one person risk their job for sexual satisfaction and another sacrifice sexual satisfaction to their job? Why will one individual stop work to watch television and another stop watching television to work? And why, for that matter, do such preferences change within the behaviour of one individual? Once again reference to a higher level is demanded, and *SPGU* proposes the category of themes, divided into three, as follows:

Role themes	'being a lawyer', 'being a garbage collector', etc.
Interpersonal themes	rated on scales of positive/negative, intimate/distant, dominant/submissive; realized in relationships such as 'lover:lover', 'father:son', 'boss:employee'.
Life themes	under headings such as personal qualities, ambition, life-style, political attitude, approval, physical sensations; realized in such manifestations as 'being a communist', 'liking luxury living', 'wanting to become rich'; 'being honest'.

(*SPGU*: 131–50)

This process of explanation at higher and higher levels is potentially endless, but the explanation of themes, as *SPGU* point out, is beyond the scope of the investigation of text understanding. Further speculation would need to consider such issues as the interaction of the nature of intelligence with the neurophysiology of the brain, and the degree to which an intelligence is 'programmed' genetically or environmentally. Indeed, the notion of themes correlates well with the neural Darwinist notion of an innate, individually variable, value system dictating the development of cognitive structures (Edelman 1992).

Conclusion

This chapter has looked at a sophisticated and seminal version of schema theory, more or less accepting it at face value and without much criticism. The texts on which the theory has been applied in AI are all strikingly simple: a necessary limitation for work which sought to model the system on computer. What needs to be done now is to see how it stands up in the analysis of complex discourse. In the next chapter, I shall make a more speculative application of the theory, as a step towards my own modification of schema theory and its peculiar relationship to literary discourse.

Notes

1 The terms 'conceptual' and 'semantic' are often used interchangeably. For further discussion see Garnham 1987:29–40.
2 There is debate about the degree to which language knowledge may be stored in this way (Lachter and Bever 1988; Pinker and Prince 1988).
3 Not only is it incompatible with approaches such as deconstruction and hermeneutics which challenge the scientific approach in general, it has also been hotly disputed by philosophers and psychologists who *do* share AI's scientific assumptions (Searle [1980] 1987; Dreyfus and Dreyfus 1986; Born 1987; Boden 1987, 1989). AI simulation, it is argued, has not succeeded in approaching human capacities for text handling (Shanker 1987), and even if it had, similar results would not necessarily indicate similar processes (Searle [1980] 1987). Successful symbol manipulation, argue AI's opponents, does not entail understanding or intentionality, and human beings may employ quite different, more intuitive and heuristic, strategies (Dreyfus and Dreyfus 1986). It is not the machine which thinks but the programmer with the aid of the machine (Neumaier 1987; Kobsa 1987). False premises, incorrect knowledge, mistaken inferences, and inbuilt bias may make an artificial intelligence unreliable (Boden 1989) (though these, of course, are failings of human intelligence, too). AI strengthens the mechanist metaphor and ignores the moral significance of language (Harris 1987). There is, in short, in the view of some scholars, inadequate evidence for making the leap from the partial abilities of AI programs to conclusions about the human mind.(For an AI answer to these kinds of objections to its claims, see Schank 1986:1–24.)
4 *Hamlet*, III.ii.26.
5 Ironically, such units are well described in formalist analyses. They resemble Propp's 'functions' or Tomashevsky's 'motifs': see Chapter 5.
6 Comparable systems of representation are 'semantic networks' (Quillian 1968), 'propositional textbases' (Kintsch 1974), and 'mental models' (Johnson-Laird 1983). All share the belief that the 'content' of text can be represented in a way which will correspond to different linguistic realizations.
7 Developed by Schank (1972), and described in Schank (1975:268–71); Schank and Abelson (1977:11–17; 30–32); Barr and Feigenbaum (1981:300–5); Winograd (1983:402); McTear (1987:33–9); Pitrat [1985] 1988:26–9), and many other places. CD has been widely

used in AI and is frequently referred to in text linguistics and discourse analysis (de Beaugrande and Dressler 1981:44; Brown and Yule 1983:241ff; Sperber and Wilson 1986:259) as a partial explanation of coherence.

8 The relevant acts entailed in a particular word are part of the knowledge about that word. The theory is thus potentially useful in lexicology. There is, in fact, a good deal in common between this approach to word meaning, and that of the lexicologist Melchuk (see especially Melchuk 1988).

9 These terms are similar to those for case roles in case grammar (Fillmore 1968). For discussions of adaptations and uses of case grammar in computational linguistics see Winograd (1983:311–28).

10 Schank and Abelson suggest a set of terms for describing states. To this is appended a set of scales concerning attributes of states marked numerically from −10 to +10. These are used 'only suggestively' (Schank and Abelson 1977:15) and the set is an open one. Examples of scales are:

Health	dead, diseased, under the weather, tolerable, in the pink
Anticipation	terrified, nervous, hoping, confident
Mental state	broken, depressed, all right, happy, ecstatic
Physical state	end of existence, damaged, OK, perfect
Awareness	dead, unconscious, asleep, awake, keen

In each of these scales the left hand term would be marked−10 and the right hand term +10, with intermediate terms having intermediate numerical value.

11 It is doubtful, in any case, what such proof might consist of. Even the total simulation of human text handling to a degree that would pass the Turing test for intelligence (Turing 1950), accompanied by a full statement of procedures used, could still be dismissed as proof, as it is for example by Dreyfus (1987) and Searle ([1980] 1987). Turing suggests that a machine could be classed as intelligent if it is impossible to tell in interaction whether one is communicating with a person or a machine (for further discussion see Schank 1986:1– 15).

12 Conceptual dependency is both in harmony and in disharmony with prototype theory. On the one hand, it is extended in schema theory to build up elaborate prototypes, not of single concepts but of frequent or typical combinations of them. On the other hand, the components of schemata are discrete concepts which admit no 'fuzziness'. Prototype theory is compatible with the Wittgensteinian notion of 'family resemblance'. Rosch borrows the term and takes the idea as a starting point (Rosch and Mervis 1975). This underlines

a view that belief in conceptual representation and a Wittgensteinian approach are at odds (see Fodor 1976:69–73). In this sense, schema theory can be made to contradict itself, and is ripe for deconstruction.

13 It may also be that schemata, in non-scientific practice, operate on a finite number of levels, perhaps something like the five levels of generality in lexico-semantics (e.g. 'creature'—'mammal'—'dog'—'collie'—'Welsh collie' (Brown 1958; Cruse 1986:145). If so, it is still true that schema theory needs to account in some way for selection of level; but to say this is to argue for an addition to the existing theory rather than for its abandonment.

14 Discussed by Cluysenaar 1976:90ff. and Leech and Short 1981:202–7.

15 Discussed by Halliday 1973:103–38.

16 *The Inheritors* and *What Maisie Knew* are written in the third person, but maintain the limitations of the character's perception.

17 So does AI work on text generation, as opposed to text interpretation. Reasons for the choice of level of detail, which can be taken as given in text processing, must be considered more exactly. The shift of emphasis towards text generation focuses the attention of AI on this problem.

18 For Sperber and Wilson, 'context' is a set of propositions in the mind.

19 There are discussions of the interaction of conceptual structure with discoursal choice. De Beaugrande and Dressler (1981:99) suggest, for example, that a concept which lies at the node connecting other concepts in a semantic network is likely to be foregrounded in some way in discourse. This kind of principle is receiving more attention in recent AI literature on text generation (see for example Mann 1984, 1987).

20 Schank's subsequent books *Dynamic Memory* (1982a) and *Explanation Patterns* (1986) are developments of *SPGU* rather than completely new departures. Their main contribution is the suggestion that schemata may be broken down in memory and then reassembled for processing, with each new experience modifying existing schemata. Their descriptive categories are, however, less satisfactory for analysis than those of *SPGU*. *Dynamic Memory* pays scant attention to the plans of characters in discourse (which are a major factor in *SPGU*). Plans are, as I hope to show below, a particularly useful category in interpreting coherence, and are widely used (see, for example, Appelt 1985:13–21; Reiser, Black and Abelson 1985; Litman and Allen 1987; Rist 1989). *Explanation Patterns*, though it does reinstate an emphasis on planning, is primarily concerned with the ability to explain events as an index of intelligence.

21 All Schank's major work purports to describe both human intelligence and an actual and potential artificial intelligence. The subtitle of

SPGU is 'An inquiry into human knowledge structures'; of *Dynamic Memory* 'A theory of reminding and learning in computers and people', and of *Explanation Patterns* 'Understanding mechanically and creatively'. Clearly, if they are implemented in computer programs, then they are *de facto* descriptions of those programs, but that is not my major concern.

22 As in any rank structure in which one rank consists of elements from the rank below and is to be explained in terms of the rank above, there is, of course, the problem of where to go when one reaches the top or the bottom of the model. The alternatives would seem to be either to extend the rank hierarchy indefinitely and thus simply postpone explanation, or to hand over the burden of explanation to some other academic discipline when the upper and lower limits of the hierarchy are reached. *SPGU* suggests that explanation of the highest level in text processing must be sought in the neurophysiology of the brain (*SPGU*: 148). There is, however, in Schank's work no reductionist or materialist claim that mental processes can be explained in physical or biological terms (Schank 1986: 12).

23 As a trial is largely a linguistic phenomenon, these may be seen as aspects of text structure too.

24 *SPGU*'s term here is **ASK**, but I have changed the term to ASK FOR to avoid confusion with 'ask' in the sense of 'ask a question'.

25 *SPGU*'s name for this plan is actually INVOKE THEME, but there is some confusion here as the word 'theme' is used in a specialized sense later in *SPGU* (see later in this chapter). On the assumption that it is the general sense of 'theme' which is intended here, I have changed the word to 'topic' to avoid confusion.

26 INVOKE TOPIC and INFORM REASON as a way of asking for something presumably—though *SPGU* does not mention this—rely upon pragmatic inference to interpret mention of the topic, or of the reason for wanting the object, as having the illocutionary force of a request or demand.

27 Although both sequences are cohesive—through the anaphoric referents 'he' and 'it'—this is not sufficient to create coherence in (2).

4 Testing the AI approach. Two analyses: a 'literary' and a 'non-literary' text

Introduction

Although schema theory is often invoked in discourse analysis as an explanation of the process of understanding, the details of the relation between schema and text are often left rather vague. This chapter, in order to test the validity of schema theory as an instrument for describing text understanding, attempts to use the schema types described in the last chapter in the analyses of two complex pieces of discourse: the opening of a novel, and an advertisement. It specifies types and contents of schemata for the texts, how these schemata relate to each other, and how they relate to particular sections of text.

The texts and examples used in AI schema theory, and in related work attempting to implement it,[1] are necessarily simple, in order that they may be processed or produced with the rigour needed in computer modelling, according to the capacities of AI. This simplicity of AI texts may be characterized as follows. They tend to be narratives, following a strict chronological sequence. The clause structure is simple and Functional Sentence Perspective unmarked. Vocabulary is limited and lexical cohesion is effected through denotation rather than connotation. The texts concern events within a limited world, initiated by a fixed number of actors with known goals. Coherence is achieved with reference to a fixed number of known schemata. Narrative stance is uncomplicated. There is no adaptation of a narrative persona with a consequent apparent limitation on authorial knowledge. As a result, there are no complex changes of viewpoint between the points of view of author, narrator, and characters; nor are there gradual changes from one to the other.[2] Perhaps most importantly of all, these texts are invented for the purpose of demonstration and analysis, rather than being taken from a corpus of naturally occurring texts (Sinclair 1991:6). It is the texts which are adapted to the theory, rather than the theory to the texts. Hence their simplicity.

The texts analysed in this chapter, by contrast, are intricate. Events do not follow a chronological order. Clause structure is complex and sentence perspective often marked. Cohesion is complex. The interpretative schemata which I shall suggest for the texts are consequently both uncertain and open-ended. It is not always possible to distinguish with any certainty between scripts, plans, goals, or themes. Uncertainty arises because interpretation may refer to readers' schemata, which will vary between individuals and groups, and also to speculation about the characters', narrator's, and author's schemata, which are tentatively constructed by the reader as the discourse progresses. Open-endedness arises from the activation of potentially huge scripts—a 'city script', for example, or a 'holiday script'. There is an inevitable selectiveness and arbitrariness in decisions concerning the boundaries of schemata: whether, for example, knowledge of kitchens is part of knowledge of houses, or a separate domain of its own.

The aim, therefore, cannot be to achieve the precision of AI text analysis, and it certainly cannot be to produce an analysis rigorous enough to be used in any processing algorithm. The aim is rather to suggest a possible network of a reader's schemata, activated or added to by the text, and of a reader's hypotheses about characters' schemata. Though speculative, however, the analysis is a preliminary reconnaissance, and points towards ways in which schema theory may contribute to the analysis and characterization of literary discourse. Inevitably, it must be to some extent an analysis for one reader (me, the author), though the coherence of these passages for many other readers, and the perceived 'normality' of such textual clues to script activation as the use of definite articles for default elements (see pages 12–14), suggest that within a discourse community, individual and group variation is not as significant as is sometimes supposed in reader-response literary theory:[3] a view which is strongly expressed by Short, when he writes of 'the major fact that, though we are all different, we agree to a remarkable extent over the interpretation of texts. Indeed, if it were not the case, it would be difficult to see how communication could ever take place' (1989c: 3).

Summarizing schemata

In assigning schemata, I shall use the following symbols:

$ = script
Π = plan
Γ = goal (sub-Γ = sub-goal)
Θ = theme

These symbols may be followed by a 'type' (for scripts and themes only), a 'viewpoint', and a 'name'. The following abbreviations are used for script types:

SIT   = situational
PERS = personal
INST = instrumental

and for theme types:

ROLE   = ROLE
INTERP = INTERPERSONAL
LIFE   = LIFE

The following abbreviations are used for viewpoints:

R   = reader
C (or name of character)   = character
R/C   = reader and character

(I have included this last group although in a sense, of course, all schemata are readers' schemata. Their autonomous existence for characters is illusory.)

The name of the schema refers to its contents. Thus $ SIT LANDLADY CITY means 'a situational script about a city from the landlady's viewpoint'. Plans and goals have no type, but only a viewpoint and a name. Π LANDLADY GET RENT means 'the landlady's plan to get the rent'.

The two texts

The first text analysed is a translation of the opening paragraphs of Dostoevsky's *Crime and Punishment*, and the second is a magazine advertisement for Gore-Tex outdoor clothing. Both may seem odd choices in an argument concerned with the relationship between schemata and literary language: the first because, being a translation, the language has been changed; the second because advertisements are not normally regarded as literary at all, although their use of language often uses literary devices (for further discussion see Cook 1992).

It is, however, precisely the problematic and peripheral relation of these two text types to literary language which makes analysis of them particularly revealing. Both provide evidence against the view that 'literariness' arises from specific linguistic choice. The contrast between them will therefore be useful in the later argument concerning the stylistics approach to literariness (in Chapter 6).

In a translation, by definition, none of the linguistic choices of the original appear. This raises considerable problems for any characterization of literature as a particular use of language. The assumption that the literariness of a source text somehow survives in translation must rest upon one of two premises. On the one hand it may be claimed that the translator has sought and found equivalent linguistic choices to those in the original which create a literary effect, or that he or she has added new ones with no equivalent in the original. In this first view, the translation may be 'literary', but this literariness is its own property, created by the translator, rather than deriving from the original. On the other hand, it may be claimed that the literariness of the original is not dependent on linguistic choice, but derives from the nature of the fictional world (its events, contents, characters, etc.) In this second view, the fictional world can be preserved, because although the words are different, the semantic referent is the same. The 'same story' will survive linguistic change. This may be intra-lingual as in paraphrase, inter-lingual as in translation, or involve a change of medium, as in the conversion of literary narratives into films, ballets, cartoons, or operas. This latter view fits well with the constructivist principle (described on pages 65–8) which claims that linguistic representation is converted into some other form of representation in the mind. Translation and source are regarded as equivalent because they give rise to similar schemata.[4]

In any actual translation there is likely to be evidence for both these views. Literariness will reside at times in unique linguistic choice, at times in the fictional world. Thus, in practice, some literary features are lost in translation; others survive through well-chosen equivalents; others are unique to the translation; others are in the story itself. Dostoevsky, whose writing is used here, is an interesting case in point. The staccato, apparently rushed and chaotic nature of his Russian prose (with frequent contradictions, ambiguities, changes of direction and syntactic breaks) has often been 'tidied up' by English translators in the belief that these features were stylistic faults which need correction. The result has been some weakening of the disturbing effects of the original (induced by very specific linguistic choice). Nevertheless, Dostoevsky's reputation has remained high with English readers, presumably because the literariness of his work resides in his plots and characters as much as in his language.

This complex relation of source and translation creates problems for the analysis of the translation used here. In general, the analysis assumes the constructivist principle and refers to events and entities as though they were the same for the reader of Russian and the reader of English. Where there is mention of specific linguistic choices these must, of necessity, refer to those in the English translation and assume that they are equivalent to a choice in the original Russian (though this may not in fact be the case).

Translation, then, provides evidence of literariness which is not dependent upon unique linguistic choice. Many advertisements, by contrast, present the opposite phenomenon. Though non-literary, their essence may depend upon language which can be neither translated nor paraphrased. Whereas, in literary works, a measure of greatness may survive when shorn of this original language, many advertisements may possess nothing but the language.

Text One: The opening of *Crime and Punishment* (translation)[55]

On a very hot evening at the beginning of July, a young man left his garret in S——— Lane, went out into the street, and, as though unable to make up his mind, walked slowly in the direction of K——— Bridge. He succeeded in avoiding a meeting with his landlady on the stairs. His garret, right under the roof of a tall five-storey building, was more like a cupboard than an apartment. His landlady, who sub-let the room to him, together with meals and the services of a maid, lived in a separate flat on the floor below. Every time he went out, he had to walk past her kitchen, the door of which was almost always wide open; and every time he walked past that door, the young man experienced a painful and cowardly sensation which made him wince and feel ashamed. He was up to his neck in debt to his landlady and was afraid of meeting her.

It was not as though he were cowardly or submissive. Quite the opposite. But recently he had been in an irritable, tense state—like hypochondria. He had withdrawn into himself and cut himself off from everybody so completely, that he was afraid of meeting anybody, not only his landlady. He was crushed by poverty, but even his impoverished circumstances had recently ceased to be a burden to him. He had lost all interest in daily affairs and could no longer be bothered with them. Actually he was not afraid of his landlady at all, whatever plots she might be hatching against him. But to have to stop on the stairs and listen to a lot of silly practical nonsense which was of no interest, to all those nagging demands for payment, to all those threats and complaints, and then to have to wriggle out of it and think up excuses and tell lies ... no thank you! A thousand times better slip downstairs like a cat and escape without anybody noticing.

Suggested schemata

This text might be interpreted in terms of the following schemata:

Scripts	Plans
$ SIT R SUMMER	Π YOUNG MAN GO OUT
$ SIT R CITY	Π YOUNG MAN GO SOMEWHERE
$ SIT R HOUSE	Π YOUNG MAN AVOID LANDLADY
$ PERS YOUNG MAN BEING A LODGER	Π LANDLADY INVOKE TOPIC
$ INST YOUNG MAN GO OUT	Π LANDLADY DEMAND RENT

$ PERS R/C ARGUMENT

Π LANDLADY THREATEN
Π LANDLADY COMPLAIN
Π YOUNG MAN EXCUSE
Π YOUNG MAN LIE
Π YOUNG MAN AVOID
　LANDLADY

Goals

Γ YOUNG MAN UNKNOWN

Γ LANDLADY STAY SOLVENT

Γ YOUNG MAN STAY SOLVENT

sub-Γ YOUNG MAN AVOID
　RENT
sub-Γ LANDLADY GET RENT

Themes

Θ INTERP YOUNG MAN
　BEING LODGER
Θ ROLE YOUNG MAN BEING
　COWARD
Θ LIFE YOUNG MAN
　UNSOCIABLENESS
Θ LIFE YOUNG MAN BEING
　POOR
Θ LIFE YOUNG MAN NERV-
　OUS TENSION

The 'contents' of some of these schemata might be as follows (square brackets [ ] indicate default elements mentioned by the text; angle brackets < > indicate suggestions for further default elements not mentioned):

$ SIT R HOUSE

Type: situational
Viewpoint: reader
Content: house
Headers in text: 'his garret'

Slots:
—a number of props: [little room], [several storeys], [S_____ Lane]
—the roles of the participants: [lodger], [landlady]
—entry conditions: $ CITY ?
—scenes: [being in], [meeting other occupants], <having visitors>, <sleeping>, <waking>, [eating], [going out], [being out].

$ SIT R CITY

Type: situational
Viewpoint: reader
Content: city (Possible track: nineteenth-century St Petersburg)
Header in text: 'S_____ Lane'; 'K_____ Bridge'

Slots:
—a number of props: [houses], [streets], [bridges], parks, etc.

—the roles of the participants: <police>, <shopkeepers>, <students> etc.
—scenes: [walking], <working>, [being at home].

$ PERS YOUNG MAN BEING A LODGER

Type: Personal
Viewpoint: Young man
Content: Being a lodger
Header in text: 'his garret right under the roof', 'his landlady'

Slots:
—a number of props: [room], [rent], [meals]
—the roles of the participants: [lodger], [landlady], <other lodgers>
—the entry conditions: possibly [Θ BEING POOR] or [Θ BEING A STUDENT]
—results: [possibly $ ARGUMENT]
—scenes and their sequence: [being in], [$ GO OUT], [$ MEET LANDLADY]

$ INST YOUNG MAN GO OUT

Type: Instrumental
Viewpoint: Young man
Content: Going out
Header in text: 'left his little room'

Slots:
—a number of props: [stairs], <front door>
—the roles of the participants: [landlady]
—the entry conditions: [possibly $ SUMMER], or [$ ROOM], or [Θ UNSOCIABILITY], or [Π AVOID RENT]
—results: [being in the street]
—scenes and their sequence: [going downstairs], [passing kitchen], [meeting or not meeting landlady].

There are numerous possible readers' scripts which may affect interpretation, e.g. $ SIT R DOSTOEVSKY NOVEL; $ SIT R YOUNG MEN, etc.

The list is speculative. There is not, and perhaps cannot be, any claim to 'correctness' or 'completeness'. The above suggestions, moreover, could be broken down into a larger number of small 'sub-scripts', for example, $ KITCHEN, $ STREET. There is also arbitrariness in deciding whether schemata are themes, goals, plans, or scripts. YOUNG MAN GO OUT and YOUNG MAN AVOID LANDLADY for example might initially be regarded as plans, though on the evidence of the passage as a whole, it seems that they are so habitual for this character that they are better described as scripts. (Thus YOUNG MAN GO OUT is listed above as both a script and a plan.) The 'contents' of some of these schemata might include the following:

Analysis

The following analysis attempts to link the proposed schemata to the unfolding of the text. Names of schemata are written in three lines above the text, the top line containing themes and goals, the second plans, and the third scripts. This presentation does not deal with the problem of when and how a schema ceases to be relevant, and, in general a schema, once activated, is treated as continuing. I do, however, repeat the name of a schema where I consider it to be brought back into prominence by the text. Inevitably, for reasons of space, not every potential minor schema which may be temporarily activated can be included. A schema is named when it seems to contribute significantly to understanding.

———————————————— Γ YOUNG MAN UNKNOWN ————

———————————————————— Π YOUNG MAN GO OUT

———— $ R SUMMER ————————————————

On a very hot evening at the beginning of July, a young man left

———— $ R HOUSE ———————— $ R CITY ————

his garret in S———— Lane, went out into the street, and, as

Γ YOUNG MAN UNKNOWN ————————————

———— Π YOUNG MAN GO SOMEWHERE ————————

though unable to make up his mind, walked slowly in the

Γ YOUNG MAN UNKNOWN ————————————

direction of K———— Bridge. He succeeded in avoiding a

Θ ROLE YOUNG MAN BEING A LODGER _____

Π YOUNG MAN AVOID LANDLADY _____

$ PERS YOUNG MAN BEING A LODGER _____ $ R HOUSE _____

meeting with his landlady on the stairs. His garret, right under

_____ Θ LIFE YOUNG MAN BEING POOR

_____

_____

the roof of a tall five-storey building, was more like a cupboard

_____ Γ YOUNG MAN STAY SOLVENT _____

_____

_____ $ PERS YOUNG MAN BEING A LODGER

than an apartment. His landlady, who sub-let the room to

_____

_____

_____

him, together with meals and the services of a maid, lived in a

_____

_____ Π YOUNG MAN GO OUT _____

$ R HOUSE _____ $ INST YOUNG MAN GO OUT

separate flat on the floor below. Every time he went out, he

_____

_____ Π YOUNG MAN AVOID LANDLADY _____

_____ $ R HOUSE _____

had to walk past her kitchen, the door of which was almost always

_____

_____

_____

wide open; and every time he walked past that door, the young man

_____ Θ ROLE YOUNG MAN BEING A COWARD _____

experienced a painful and cowardly sensation which made him

Θ INTERP YOUNG MAN NERVOUS TENSION__

wince and feel ashamed. He was up to

Θ LIFE YOUNG MAN BEING POOR Θ ROLE YOUNG MAN BEING
A COWARD

his neck in debt to his landlady and was afraid of meeting her

_____ Θ ROLE YOUNG MAN BEING A COWARD _____

It was not as though he were cowardly or submissive. Quite the

_____ Θ INTERP YOUNG MAN NERVOUS TENSION

opposite. But recently he had been in an irritable, tense state

_____ Θ LIFE YOUNG MAN UNSOCIABLENESS

—like hypochondria. He had withdrawn into himself and cut

_____ Θ ROLE YOUNG MAN BEING A COWARD _____

himself off from everybody so completely, that he was afraid of

———————— Π YOUNG MAN AVOID LANDLADY ————

meeting anybody, not only his landlady. He was crushed by

Θ   LIFE YOUNG MAN BEING POOR   ————————

poverty, but even his impoverished circumstances had recently

———————————   Θ LIFE YOUNG MAN UNSOCIABLENESS

ceased to be a burden to him. He had lost all interest in daily

affairs and could no longer be bothered with them. Actually he

Θ ROLE YOUNG MAN BEING A COWARD   —————
Π YOUNG MAN AVOID LANDLADY — SUB-Γ LANDLADY GET
RENT

was not afraid of his landlady at all, whatever plots she might

Γ LANDLADY STAY SOLVENT   ————————
SUB-Γ LANDLADY GET RENT   ————————
——————————— $ R HOUSE ————
be hatching against him. But to have to stop on the stairs and

Π LANDLADY INVOKE TOPIC   ————————

listen to a lot of silly practical nonsense which was of no

Π LANDLADY DEMAND ———————————————————————
$ R/C ARGUMENT   ———————————————————————
interest, to all those nagging demands for payment, to all those

---

Π LANDLADY THREATEN Π LANDLADY COMPLAIN ————————

---

threats and complaints, and then to have to wriggle out of it and

---

Π YOUNG MAN EXCUSE Π YOUNG MAN LIE Π YOUNG MAN
AVOID LANDLADY

---

think up excuses and tell lies . . . no thank you! A thousand times

Θ YOUNG MAN NERVOUS TENSION ————————————————
Π YOUNG MAN GO OUT Π YOUNG MAN GO SOMEWHERE ———
———————————— $ INST YOUNG MAN GO OUT ————————
better slip downstairs like a cat and escape without anybody

———————
———————

———————

noticing.

Discussion of analysis

Naming, classifying, and assigning schemata in this way is highly
speculative and highly problematic. Yet the problems encountered are
illuminating. One major problem concerns the viewpoint in each schema.
In processing, a reader will make use of existing schemata and build
new ones. Some of these reader's schemata will contain characters'
schemata, narrator's schemata, and author's schemata. (For the author,
one might speculate, the situation is reversed: author's schemata contain
reader's schemata.) Any section of narrative can be described from one
or more of these viewpoints. In addition there is variation between
readers. This can easily be illustrated with reference to the second schema
postulated here, $ SIT R CITY, which, while it may be an accurate

description for, say, most contemporary British readers, will be something more like $ SIT R NINETEENTH CENTURY ST PETERSBURG for, say, readers who know in advance (from a $ R DOSTOEVSKY NOVELS) where and when the action takes place. And, even within broad groups of readers no $ CITY or $ ST PETERSBURG will be exactly the same. (Readers with direct or vicarious experience of the beginning of July in St Petersburg will know that the events narrated here take place during the 'White Nights', a time of year in this Northern latitude when virtually continuous daylight makes people restless and wakeful. The author may well have assumed that Russian readers will supply this detail as a default element from their $ SUMMER and $ ST PETERSBURG.)[6]

Movement between the characters' viewpoints, and interweaving of author's, narrator's, characters', and reader's schemata is well illustrated in the meeting on the stairs. It is part of both Π LANDLADY GET RENT, and a failure of Π YOUNG MAN GO OUT. It also, we might surmise, realizes a plan of the author's: something like Π AUTHOR CREATE INTEREST THROUGH CONFLICT which in turn executes a goal, perhaps Γ AUTHOR WRITE A SUCCESSFUL NOVEL. Narrator's schemata are perhaps the hardest to characterize, existing in the interface between reader's, author's, and characters'. The reader, meanwhile, is presumably adding each event to the scripts he or she is building about the character of the young man, the house, and the landlady.

My choice among these possibilities is thus a considerable simplification. I have tended to emphasize reader's schemata and those of one character, the young man. This seems justified by the predominance of reference to the young man, his goals and plans. The absence of information or suggestion about the higher goals and themes of the landlady also reinforces this impression. It is difficult to suggest a higher level schema for her than STAY SOLVENT and GET RENT, both of which are likely to be defaults in an $ R LANDLADY. The narrative moreover frequently adopts the young man's view: 'he was lucky to avoid a meeting with his landlady'; 'all this silly practical nonsense'. In terms of Functional Sentence Perspective, the anaphoric 'he' is very often in the given (or topic) position.[7] 'Landlady' by contrast is not, and needs repetition, despite the absence of any other female character to cause ambiguity of reference. It is also possible that readers activate a schema about novels, in which a young man is more likely to occupy the central character slot than a landlady!

A further major problem is to differentiate scripts, goals, and themes. Key factors are the degree of habit on the part of a character, the permanence of a particular state of affairs, and whether one action is subsidiary to another. Being a lodger may be a temporary script for some people, and a life theme for others. A reader's judgements must await further information, and may change as more details are provided. Much of the coherence and interest of this text is provided by the absence of motivation in the young man's initial exit from the house, and the lack of enough detail to reveal whether this action results from a plan or a script (readers will assume, of course, that the conscious actions of a human agent derive from *some* plan or goal). That the situation is initially seen from a reader's viewpoint is clearly indicated by the indefinite article in the phrase 'a young man'—he is neither named nor assumed to be known. Various possible goals and plans may be suggested by the interaction of a reader's schemata and the text, ranging from the desire to go out on a hot summer's evening (from $ R SUMMER), to the desire to escape a small uncomfortable room (from $ R HOUSE), to the plan to avoid the landlady (from $ R BEING A LODGER). Further explanations are then suggested in terms of personality or—in our terms—themes. Unsociableness, nervousness, depression, and being poor may all motivate the exit, and indeed each other. Finally, the young man's action is represented as one which is often repeated, hence the suggestion of the script $ INST YOUNG MAN GO OUT as well as Π YOUNG MAN GO OUT; the origin of the goal of avoiding the landlady, however, remains unclear, and may be caused by any—or any combination of—the suggested themes. Nor does the possibility of some other purpose disappear. That the young man has some darker intention—though not its exact nature—is revealed in the two paragraphs which follow this extract. Though I have not here postulated a $ SIT R YOUNG MAN, one might argue that the building of this script by the reader is potentially (provided he remains as 'central character') one of the major causes of coherence for the whole novel.

A further complication in the assignment and description of schemata arises from the apparent contradiction in the text between 'he . . . was afraid of meeting anybody, not only his landlady' and 'Actually, he was not afraid of his landlady at all.' Dostoevsky's writing is characterized by rapid and contradictory changes of viewpoint, a technique which led Bakhtin to describe his novels as 'polyphonic' and 'dialogic' (Bakhtin [1929, 1963] 1984: 5–47, 251–70; Bakhtin [1934] 1981). This is a case in point. What we have here is the invocation of two contradictory themes, in the first of which the young man is a coward, in the second of which he is not. This causes the straightforward approach of the opening lines, in which narrator informs reader, to be disrupted in a shift of viewpoint, an apparent abdication of narrative control which is quite alien to the simple text types of AI. Here the cohesion affected by the colloquial 'actually'[8] perhaps provides the clue, and the second version, we may presume, is the young man's own. There are thus two sets of schemata: the first being the narrative view, the second the young man's own: his schema of his own schemata. This is a problem not dealt with in AI schema theory. Themes, though they are the ultimate source of scripts, are also a part of them. A script about a character, and a character's script of himself/herself, contains themes.

Schemata and coherence

Coherence is created, at least in part, when a reader perceives connections between schemata. These connections may be causal (Θ LIFE YOUNG MAN BEING POOR may cause SUB-Γ YOUNG MAN AVOID RENT) or because one schema is contained in another ($ SIT R HOUSE is part of $ SIT R CITY). Connections can be represented diagrammatically. I shall do this in two ways.

The first diagram (Figure 4.1) is a hierarchical representation of connections between schemata. This may be regarded as as product view of the discourse (see pages 46–8). The second diagram (Figure 4.2) represents relationships between schemata as boxes, enclosing and excluding each other.[9] This may be regarded as a process view of the discourse. In this diagram, numbers and arrows indicate the linear sequencing of schemata. Pervasive schemata which unify the passage as a whole are represented as enclosing boxes. These are Γ YOUNG MAN UNKNOWN and Π YOUNG MAN GO OUT. Reference to these begins and ends the extract and all other schemata are related to them. When they are invoked again at the end of the text they have changed considerably. The unknown goal is now to some extent clarified. What was initially perceived as a plan has become more like a script.

Both diagrams are speculative. They are two among many other possibilities. One reason for this is that almost any schema may be both the container and the contained in relationship to another. Thus, for example, the city is part of the young man's life, but equally the young man is a part of the city.

Text Two: 'Every Cloud has a Silver Lining' (advertisement)

Two relatively superficial differences between the two texts need some comment. Firstly, Text One is an extract, the first of several hundred pages, while Text Two is complete.[10] Treating parts of a text in isolation can have a distorting effect upon perception of both cohesion and coherence (Cook 1986). I assume, however, that this hazard is less serious when an extract is the opening of a text, as a degree of coherence will exist at each point in the reading process, and some absence of connection will be tolerated on the assumption that it will be resolved by later information.

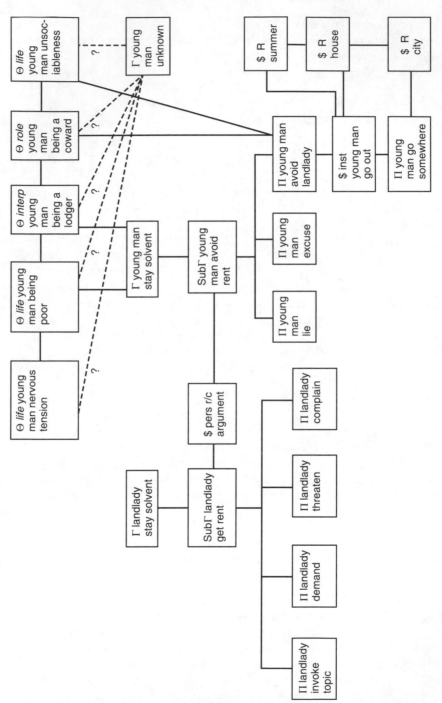

Figure 4.1: Diagram of schema relations in Text One (1)

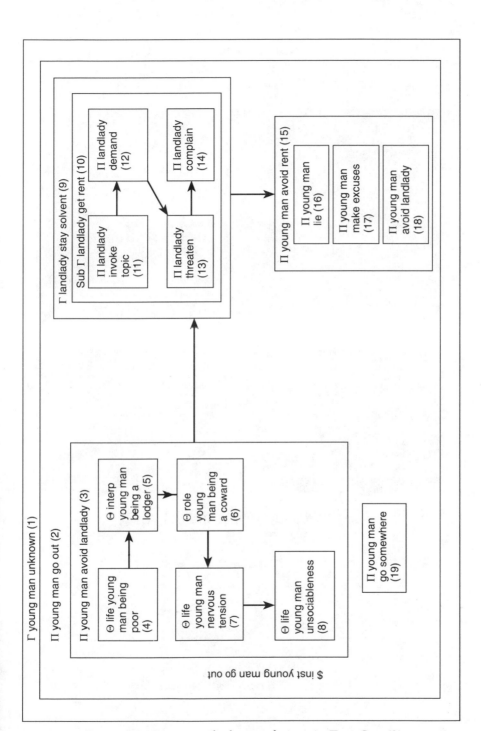

Figure 4.2: Diagram of schema relations in Text One (2)

Every cloud has a silver lining.

Rannoch Moor. Scotland. The wind is howling down the tracks and the last train has gone the same way; be grateful you're wrapped up in GORE-TEX® fabric.

It's not only totally waterproof, it's also impenetrable to stiff breezes, gales and even hurricanes. In fact, the harder the wind blows, the more noticeable the insulation effect becomes.

And if you've worked up a good sweat trying to match the timetable, you'll still be comfortable. Because of the unique membrane structure of Gore-Tex fabric, perspiration can escape freely, keeping you feeling fine. It's the most breathable weatherproof fabric ever invented, and is guaranteed for three years to stay that way.

And these days, Gore-Tex fabric is one of the most stylish as well. It comes in a choice of fashion colours and features in top ranges of leisure and sports wear.

All of which makes it just the ticket for travelling first class, however you plan to get home.

Gore-Tex fabric consists of an outer fabric, a lining material and a skin-like membrane that has no fewer than 9 billion pores per square inch, each pore is 20,000 times smaller than a raindrop but 700 times larger than a molecule of perspiration. That's why rain cannot pass through, but sweat escapes easily.

GORE-TEX® fabrics

GORE
Creative Technologies Worldwide

®GORE-TEX is a registered trademark of W L Gore & Associates Inc. W L Gore & Associates (UK) Ltd, Kirkton Campus, Livingston, West Lothian, Scotland. Tel: 0506-412525. Telex: 727236.

Figure 4.3: Advertisement for Gore-Tex

Secondly, Text One is words only, while Text Two is accompanied by a picture (see Figure 4.3) showing a healthy, young, handsome, stylishly dressed man wearing a Gore-Tex coat and—because of the camera angle—dominating the view of the small windswept station where he is sitting.[11] Clearly, in such advertisements, there is interplay between text and image, and such features as the meaning of anaphoric referring expressions (such as 'he') and of exophoric referring expressions (such as 'you') may be determined by the picture (Cook 1988, 1992: 155–8). Slots for evoked schemata may well be provided pictorially.

Although there is clearly much more to say about the relation of text and image in this advertisement, I shall from now on deal with it as writing only. This is because the main concern of the argument in this book is with unillustrated prose: this text (and the advertisement discussed later in Chapter 6) are introduced for the insight they may provide into literary discourse rather than in their own right, and it is thus their use of language, rather than the dimension of additional meaning provided by pictures, which is most relevant. (For further extended discussion of the interaction of language and pictures in advertisements, however, see Cook 1992: 37–93.)

I shall now repeat the same stages of analysis as in that of Text One.

Suggested schemata

The text is here interpreted in terms of the following schemata:

Scripts	*Plans*	*Goals*
$ SIT R/C HIGHLAND SCOTLAND	Π R/C RETURN HOME	Γ R/C SAVE MONEY
$ SIT R/C BE ON HOLIDAY	Π R/C CATCH TRAIN	Γ R/C BE MODERN
$ INST C WEARING GORE-TEX	Π R/C STAY WARM	Γ R/C STAY COMFORTABLE
	Π R/C STAY DRY	Γ R/C BE STYLISH
	Π R/C BUY TICKET	Γ R/C MAINTAIN STATUS
	Π R/C GORE-TEX	

The conventions here are the same as for the passage from *Crime and Punishment*. In general, the contents are much easier to specify than in Text One. They might include the following.

$ SIT R/C HIGHLAND SCOTLAND

Type: situational
Viewpoint: reader/character

Header in text: 'Rannoch Moor, Scotland'
Slots:
— props: [the tracks], [the last train], [the wind], (Gore-tex), <sheep>, <streams>
— roles: <tourists>, <residents>
— entry conditions: <desire, money, and time to travel>
— results: [need to return home]
— scenes and their sequence: <arriving>, [being there], [being on holiday], [leaving].

$ SIT R/C BEING ON HOLIDAY

Type: situational
Viewpoint: reader/character
Header in text: 'Rannoch Moor, Scotland'
Slots:
— props: [sensible clothing], [tickets], [train], [railway], <restaurant>
— roles: [holiday maker], <waiters>, <hotel owners> etc.
— entry conditions: <time>, <money>
— results: [being comfortable/uncomfortable]
— scenes: [travelling], <staying somewhere>, <swimming>.

(Like $ CITY in Text One, these first two scripts are huge, and subsume many others, e.g. $ RAILWAY, $ TOURIST ACCOMMODATION.)

$ INST C WEARING GORE-TEX

Type: instrumental
Viewpoint: character
Header in text: 'you're wrapped up in Gore-Tex fabric'
Slots:
— props: [wind], [stations], [moorland]
— roles: [traveller]
— entry conditions: Π C BUY GORE-TEX
— results: [being warm], [dry], [comfortable], [stylish], [having high status]
— scenes: [walking], [running], [waiting].

Analysis

'Every Cloud has a Silver Lining'

———————————————————————————————————

———————————————————————— Π R/C RETURN HOME

$ SIT R/C HIGHLAND SCOTLAND $ SIT R/C BE ON HOLIDAY

Rannoch Moor, Scotland. The wind is howling down the tracks and

—————————————————— Γ R/C STAY COMFORTABLE ————————

Π R/C CATCH TRAIN ——————————————— Π R/C STAY WARM

the last train has gone that way; be grateful you're wrapped up

—————————————————— Π R/C STAY DRY ——————————

$ INST C WEARING GORE-TEX ————————————————————

in GORE-TEX fabric. It's not only totally waterproof, it's also

———— Π R/C STAY WARM ——————————————————

—————————————————— $ SIT R/C HIGHLAND SCOTLAND ————————

impenetrable to stiff breezes, gales and even hurricanes. In

——————————————————————— $ INST C WEARING GORE-TEX

fact, the harder the wind blows, the more noticeable the

insulation effect becomes.

—————————————— Γ R/C STAY COMFORTABLE ————————————

Π R/C RETURN HOME Π R/C STAY DRY Π R/C CATCH TRAIN

And if you've worked up a good sweat trying to match the

———— Γ R/C STAY COMFORTABLE ——————————————————

—————————————————————— $ INST C WEARING GORE-TEX

timetable, you'll still be comfortable. Because of the unique

—————————————————— Π R/C STAY DRY ————————

—————————————— $ INST C WEARING GORE-TEX ——————————

membrane structure of Gore-Tex fabric, perspiration can escape freely, keeping you feeling fine. It's the most breathable

_____ Γ R/C BE MODERN _____ Γ R/C SAVE MONEY _____
_____ Π R BUY GORE-TEX _____

fabric ever invented, and is guaranteed for three years to stay

_____ Γ R/C BE MODERN _____

that way. And these days, Gore-Tex fabric is one of

Γ R/C BE STYLISH _____

the most stylish as well. It comes in a choice of fashion

_____ Γ R/C MAINTAIN STATUS _____

colours and features in top ranges of leisure and sports wear.

_____ Γ R/C MAINTAIN STATUS _____
_____ Π R BUY GORE-TEX _____ Π R/C BUY TICKET _____

All of which makes it just the ticket for travelling first class,

_   Π R/C CATCH TRAIN.   _

however you plan to get home.

Discussion of analysis

I have attributed most schemata to both the reader and the character (the young man in the photograph) on the assumption that the male reader is invited to identify with him, or seek to imitate him. (The situation for women readers is discussed below.) The exophoric referent 'you' thus apostrophizes both the character and the reader. Interestingly, if we assume, as the advertiser does, that the reader does not yet own a Gore-Tex coat, then the only script which does not reflect the viewpoint of both the character and the reader is $ INST C WEARING GORE-TEX. The only other schema which is not shared is Π R BUY GORE-TEX. This cannot be one of the character's present plans, as he is already wearing Gore-Tex, and has thus, presumably, already executed the plan in the past. The effect of the reader instigating Π R BUY GORE-TEX will be to eliminate it and create a new script $ INST R/C WEARING GORE-TEX, thus achieving complete identity between the schemata of character and reader.

A complicating factor in all this is that, despite the apparent apostrophization of the reader, the advertisement may also be read by someone who will buy the coat for a partner. (As advertisements almost exclusively aim at, and depict people in, heterosexual relationships, I shall assume that such a reader is a woman.) In this case the process of identification is more complex, and the potential buyer must first empathize with the recipient of her purchase and then identify on his behalf with the character. Alternatively, she may be directly attracted to the character, and seek to make the recipient of her gift more like the character—by buying him a Gore-Tex coat.

As in the first analysis, there is a degree of arbitrariness about decisions concerning the distinction between scripts, plans, and goals. A person who frequently returns home from this station might well handle events with a script—though if so they would be less likely to miss the train! In the absence of any information to the contrary, we may assume that this is not a regular activity. The fact that there is only one character, with whom the reader is blatantly invited to identify, makes the assignment of viewpoint extremely straightforward, and there is an absence of any direct reference to anything theme-like. There must be themes which motivate goals, such as Θ BEING ATTRACTIVE or Θ BEING SUCCESSFUL. But the text assumes that these are the same for reader and character: present by default and thus unmentioned.

An assumption which I have made about this text is that the young man (and 'you') must be in Scotland on holiday. Readers do not assume that he lives or works in the vicinity of Rannoch Moor and is simply on his way home, perhaps to a station a couple of stops down the line. This impression is partly created by the picture, in which the character is wearing hiking boots and sitting on a rucksack. But it also suggests that for many (non-Highland Scottish) people a default element in their script $ HIGHLAND SCOTLAND is that it is a place for holidays. This is why I have suggested 'need to return home' in the results slot, and 'arriving, being there, and leaving' in the scenes and their sequence slot. If this hypothesis is true, we have a good example of a phenomenon I shall term 'double inclusion'. For many people, Highland Scotland is part of their $ BEING ON HOLIDAY, and being on holiday is also part of their $ HIGHLAND SCOTLAND. Another example of double inclusion is the relationship of $ WEARING GORE-TEX, which may contain holidays as one of its scenes, to $ BEING ON HOLIDAY, which may contain Gore-Tex as one of its props. Similar relations have already been noted in Text One.

Schemata and coherence

The interconnection of the proposed schemata are represented diagrammatically in Figures 4.4 and 4.5, using the same methods of representation as in Figures 4.1 and 4.2. Note, however, that the symmetry achieved by beginning and ending with a pun cannot be represented in CD. The link here is purely linguistic, like that effected by the phrase 'the sun' in 'Futility' (see page 87).

Conclusions from analyses

The above analyses give rise to a number of conclusions concerning:
1 The usefulness of schema theory—and of Schankian schema theory in particular—in discourse analysis
2 Differences between the two texts as being possibly indicative of differences between two discourse types
3 Categories of schema.

I shall deal with each of these in turn.

1 Schemata in discourse analysis

The evoked schemata in a coherent discourse are perceived as connected. In this sense, describing such connections is an integral part of discourse analysis, whether of literary or non-literary discourse. One schema, moreover, is crucial to coherence, as all other schemata are related to it. In Text One, this schema is the young man's goal. In Text Two, it is the reader's plan to buy Gore-Tex. There is a danger, of course, that the inevitable subjectivity in decisions concerning the contents and type of schemata could attract the valid criticism that connections, and the identification of a central schema, are the product of the analysis rather than the texts. Against this, I would argue that discourse itself is the product of analysis. There is no such thing as coherent text but only text which is coherent for given readers—i.e. discourse. Thus, if I have

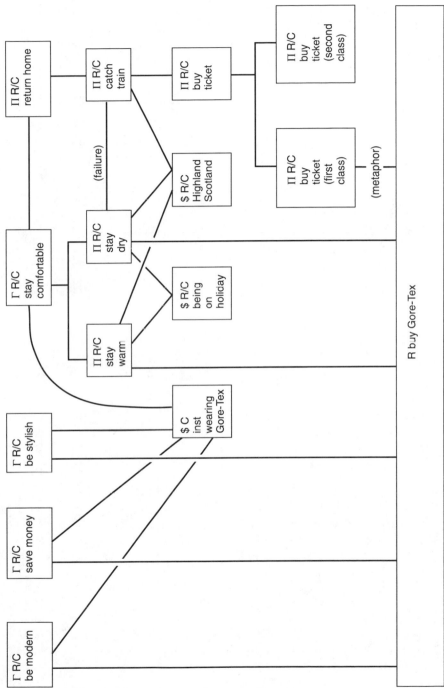

Figure 4.4: Diagram of schema relations in Text Two (1)

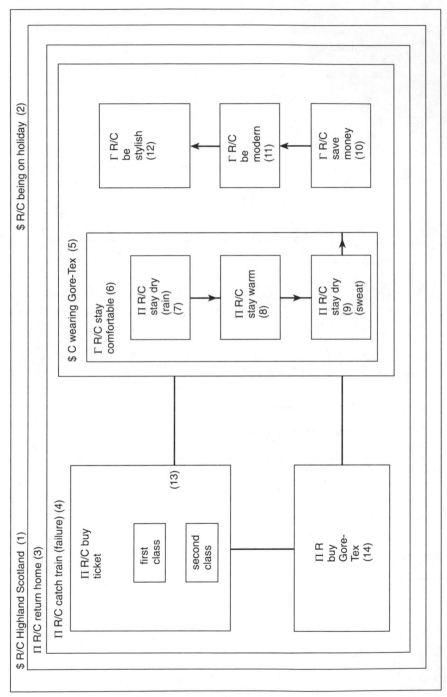

Figure 4.5: Diagram of schema relations in Text Two (2)

succeeded in accurately describing my own perception of coherence, I have described one variant of coherence itself.[12] Description can only be made more global by adding to this one reader's viewpoint the viewpoints of others.

2 Schemata and discourse type

There are important differences between the roles of schemata in the two texts, which suggest possible differences between the two discourse types they represent. Contrary to the Jakobsonian approach to literariness (discussed in Chapter 6) these are not differences in the use of linguistic form. In my view, the literariness of Text One survives translation, which is a change of such form. The advertisement, on the other hand, though it makes use of word-play which is beyond paraphrase or translation, would not, in most people's estimation, be considered literary.

On the other hand, the schemata evoked by the two texts, and the kinds of connections which exist between them, are very different. In the advert, goals and plans are both assumed, unquestioned and, therefore, presumably reinforced. The focus is upon their fulfilment through the purchase and use of the product, which is a slot filler in several scripts. In Text One, on the other hand, goals and plans are disputable and themselves sources of interest. Viewpoints in Text One are shifting and unclear, and this is tolerated. In Text Two viewpoints are more uniform, and where there is a difference, the communicative purpose is to remove it. In Text One, there is a conflict between the plans of one character and those of another; in the advertisement there is no such conflict. In Text One, 'slot fillers' in scripts serve to illuminate goals and plans; in the advertisement the focus is upon scripts for their own sake, and upon one slot filler in particular—the product.

3 Categories of schemata: a modification

This analysis has revealed a number of weaknesses and complications in the *SPGU* categories of schemata when used in the analysis of complex discourse:

- —It is not possible to specify a sequence of scenes in all scripts.
- —It is not possible to specify entry conditions or results.
- —At any point in a narrative, in establishing coherence, reference may be made to the schemata of the reader, the author, or the characters. (The narrative stance can perhaps be characterized as an interweaving and juxtaposition of these viewpoints.) This considerably complicates attempts to represent connections and multiplies the number of possible interpretations.

—A schema may both contain and be contained by another schema. This applies both where the two schemata are of the same type (i.e. two scripts) and also across levels (a script and a plan, a script and a theme, etc.). This phenomenon of 'double inclusion' means that, even given a limited number of schemata, the possible permutations in representing connections are enormous.

—A representation of schemata does not reveal connections which are text-structural or which exist only through linguistic choice. The symmetry given to Text Two by the opening and closing puns is a case in point.

—Distinguishing plans from scripts, on the one hand, and sub-goals from plans, on the other, is not always possible.

For these reasons I shall make the following modifications to the basic categories in further analyses:

1 I shall recognize only three levels of schemata.[13] The first, corresponding broadly to scripts, I shall term 'scriptlike schemata' (symbol $S). I shall define these as schemata whose contents, whether in terms of objects, people, or events, are specific. Such a schema will not need to specify results, or a sequence of scenes. Consequently, in future, when listing contents of schemata only a selection of the contents (defaults) of scriptlike schemata will be given, indicating the relationship of each default element to the whole. In listing contents of scriptlike schemata, the terms used such as 'props', 'roles', and 'results' will be used in a freer and more selective manner. The principle of double inclusion will enable the listing of plans and themes as default elements of scriptlike schemata.

2 I shall make no distinction between plans and sub-goals, but have a single level called 'plans'.

3 Similarly, I shall subsume the *SPGU* categories of goals and themes under a single heading for which I shall retain the name 'themes'.

4 Most importantly, in future analyses, it will be necessary to emphasize connections established through linguistic and text-structural choices which are not taken into account by AI schema theory.

Notes

1 Such as the 'Sam', and 'Talespin' programs described in Schank (1984), and the 'Moptrans' and 'Frump' programs (Schank 1986: 10).

2 Described by Leech and Short as 'slipping' (1981:340).

3 As already observed on pages 49–50, this view is borne out by empirical investigations. Van Peer (1986), for example, has correlated

formal foregrounding and psychological saliency for a wide variety of readers.

4 It might be said that the degree to which a schematic analysis is equally applicable to the original and the translation is a measure of 'equivalence' and could be used to evaluate different translations of the same original (Cook 1984:61–75; Cook and Poptsova-Cook 1989).

5 The translation of this passage is by Guy Cook and Elena Poptsova-Cook.

6 Magarshak's translation (Penguin 1956) gives the name of a bridge (Kokushkin Bridge) and a street (Carpenter Street) although Dostoevsky had only written K———— and S————. One might suppose that in Russia in 1866, for a novel set in an unnamed city, the name 'St Petersburg' would be provided by default.

7 This is true of the Russian original too.

8 The Russian equivalent, *v sushchnosti*, is perhaps not so colloquial.

9 This means of representing connections is used by Reichman (1985) in her description of conversational 'context spaces' (related series of claims and counter claims made by participants which, in Reichman's theory, are 'units' of conversation).

10 Except for the further description of Gore-Tex fabric in the triangular box.

11 I happened to visit Rannoch Moor station while writing this, and discovered that it is not the scene of the photograph!

12 A weakness of this claim is that it assumes that my intuitions about the schemata activated correspond to those which I actually used.

13 In *Dynamic Memory* (Schank 1982a) the number of levels is also reduced to three but not in the way proposed here. In *Explanation Patterns* (Schank 1986:71) scripts are treated as 'fossilized plans'; 'themes' are replaced by 'beliefs'.

5 A third bearing: literary theories from formalism to stylistics

Introduction

The argument so far has critically examined discourse analysis and schema theory as tools for the analysis of literary text. Schema theory can contribute to discourse analysis by showing how, where coherence is not signalled by cohesion, induced from conformity to text structure, or pragmatically inferred, it can nevertheless be constructed through schemata. The types of schema described in the previous chapter are hierarchical, and coherence can be established by referring to as high a level as necessary. Failure to account for coherence at one level can be overcome by reference to the level above. Failure at the highest level will often lead to the attribution of incoherence or madness (though this is as likely to reflect a failure of comprehension as of production).

So far, however, the approach has inevitably presented only a partial framework. It has been far more concerned with conformity to expectations than with deviation from them. Nevertheless, it does have the potential to classify an instance of deviation from expectations by identifying it with one of the given levels. A further shortcoming of the approach so far is that it has viewed the construction of coherence as the interaction of a single isolated text with knowledge of the world; it has taken little account of knowledge of other texts, and of the complex effects which intertextual resonances may have on the overall effect. It has also neglected discourse as a mode of action affecting—or attempting to affect—the lives of others, and the consequent effects of different narrative stances. Related to both these omissions is the crucial role of choices between linguistic and text structures: the many ways in which the same conceptual content can have different functional or temporal arrangements, the number and nature of overt signals of this arrangement, the demands of knowledge of similar structures in other texts, the level of detail, and sub-sentential linguistic choices. Indeed, the conceptual content itself may be affected or dictated by structure.

The aim in this chapter will be to elaborate the approach in ways which will enable it to cope more fully with literary discourse, and to develop its potential as a description of readers' experience of deviation. As a preliminary to this expansion, I shall examine ideas from a body of knowledge which, despite its heterogeneous nature, is now widely characterized as 'modern literary theory', seeking for additional insights and contributions. This examination is essential for a number of reasons if schema theory is to contribute to a theory of how cognitive change is effected through literary discourse.

These reasons may be summarized as follows. Firstly, there are literary theories which voice objections to some of the premises of schema theory, and these objections must be answered. In particular, schema theory, which stresses knowledge and interpretation as to some degree separate from form, is at odds with theories which stress linguistic and textual form as all-important. Secondly, there are theories which, though couched in different terminologies, derived from different sources and applied in different fields, are nevertheless compatible with schema theory, and which, in fact, develop it and amplify it. (In a way, sophisticated versions of schema theory exist, under different names and unacknowledged by AI, in the writings of avant-garde literary theorists of earlier decades.) Thirdly, there is a considerable body of literary-theoretical literature on the nature and function of linguistic and text-structural deviation, which may both benefit from and add to schema theory. Fourthly, there is a comparatively small body of literary-theoretical writing which is explicitly aware of, and uses, AI text theory (Abelson 1987; de Beaugrande 1987; Ryan 1991).[1]

My aim, then, is to try to draw relevant insights from literary theory and AI text theory together, and to use them in a theory of the function of literary discourse. The first task, however, is to say something about the nature of modern literary theory in general.

The rise of 'modern literary theory'

One of the commonplaces of post-modernism is its exploitation of Nietzsche's observation that, contrary to common sense, cause follows rather than precedes effect (Nietzsche (ed. Schlechta) 1966:804). When we sit on a pin we feel the pain first and then seek the source afterwards; only when we perceive the pin as the source does the source, as source, exist. The idea is fertile and iconoclastic. Thus, Derrida reasons that, contrary to the orthodox view of linguistics, writing precedes speech both ontogenetically and phylogenetically, for the concept of speech can only be grasped through writing, and only in writing can people begin to understand that the source of writing is speech (Derrida [1967] 1976). So too, Hayden White reasons that historical events come into being through the descriptions which they have, apparently, caused (White 1973). The same argument may be applied to 'product' views of grammar, text, and discourse such as those described on pages 45–6 above.

Aptly, the concept of 'modern literary theory' might be characterized as a similar *post factum* creation. In recent years, a multiplicity of university courses, anthologies, and introductions (for example Jefferson and Robey [1982] 1986; Eagleton 1983; Davis 1986; Rylance 1987; Lodge 1988; Rice and Waugh 1989) have brought together, under this single title, an imbroglio of diverse writings, categorized them, related them one to another, and generally 'closed them down'. To say, therefore, that 'modern literary theory' ignores or is unaware of AI text theory, merely reflects the arbitrary choices and categories of the latter-day creators of the discipline. AI text theory could easily be included within the field. Its lack of specific attention to literature need not exclude it, as anthologies and courses frequently include writings (for example, by Marx, Freud, Saussure, and Derrida) which though considered relevant to literature, do not often address it directly.

Despite the rather arbitrary and *post factum* nature of the field, and notwithstanding the diversity and incompatibility of approaches which the term subsumes, modern literary theory may broadly be characterized as writing about literature which does not merely accept and comment upon a literary canon, but rather seeks to understand the rationale behind the canon. Its aim is to understand, not particular literary texts *per se*, but the nature and function of literature in general. In so doing, however, it may, and frequently does, employ analyses of individual texts and provide considerable insights into them.

Within this general framework, particular theories and groups of theories may be identified by their concentration upon one element, or upon combinations of elements in the model of communication presented in Figure 5.1. Other theories and groups of theories may be characterized by their rejection of the terms of such a model, arguing for example that the reader only exists through the text (Bakhtin [Volosinov] [1929] 1973; Barthes [1970] 1974), or that the author is a culturally determined and thus dispensable concept (Barthes [1968] 1977; Foucault [1969] 1979). The hanging of theorists and their writings onto the pegs of this model—or something similar to it—yields a finite number of labels which are then conveniently used for the chapters of introductory texts, the sections of anthologies, the weeks of courses, the titles of books in series. In the anthologies and introductions referred to above, the following categories are the most favoured: formalism, structuralism, linguistics, psychoanalysis, Marxism, feminism, reader-response, and post-structuralism. The attachment of each of these 'movements' to an element of Figure 5.1 may be listed as in Table 5.1 (overleaf).

We may detect, in this categorization, a nascent rigidity and uniformity in which individual theorists who do not profess allegiance to one 'school' or another are nevertheless lumped together under the nearest heading. Others, such as Bakhtin, whose stature has only recently been

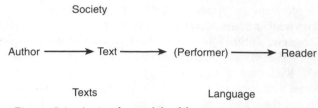

Figure 5.1: *A simple model of literary communication*

Author	literary scholarship and biography (rejected)
Performer	acting theory (not included)
Society	Marxism, feminism
Text	formalism, linguistics, stylistics
Texts	structuralism, post-structuralism, deconstruction
Language	linguistics, stylistics
Reader	feminism, psychoanalysis, reader response, reception theory, post-structuralism
Theories which contest these categories:	Bakhtinian criticism, post-structuralism, post-modernist feminism, Lacanian psychoanalysis, deconstruction

Table 5.1 *A typical correlation of 'schools' and elements in literary theory courses and anthologies*

acknowledged in the West (see Clark and Holquist 1984; Terras 1985: 34–6; Lodge 1987; Cazden 1989; Hymes 1989; Cook 1994a), are left stranded, while theorists like Barthes, whose thoughts have developed idiosyncratically through temporary attachment to different philosophies, have their work fragmented and misrepresented. In addition, certain elements of communication receive short shrift. There is little attention to the author, other than a negative critique of literary biography and scholarship. The intermediate role of the performer in drama and recitation is almost entirely ignored (a fact which is underlined by the almost universal reference to the 'reader' in preference to the 'audience'). The perception of linguistics is limited to Saussurean semiotics, Jakobsonian functionalism, and an occasional reference to Chomsky; there is little awareness of developments of text theory in discourse analysis or of the computational (including the AI) paradigm. Related to this—as some branches of linguistics have now taken decisive steps towards cognitive psychology—is the absence of theories of the cognitive role of literature.[2] The presence of psychology in the literary theoretical canon (for a canon is what—ironically—it has become) is limited to psychoanalysis and phenomenology.

In the following discussion of literary theory, despite these shortcomings, I shall provisionally adopt these widely disseminated categories.

My aim, however, is not simply to add another heading to the list: 'AI text theory', which could then be appended to future anthologies or inserted into new editions. I seek, rather, to maintain an awareness of the dangers of this rigid categorization, while also using it as a guide to this enormous and complex area. I hope to conclude, however, that ideas which can contribute to a discourse analysis of literature occur in the writings of many different and apparently incompatible schools, and that compartmentalization disguises similar and mutually fertile ideas. Above all, I hope to show that schema theory has a considerable contribution to make to attempts to describe literariness as deviation.

In the terms of the communication model in Figure 5.1, my primary interest is in the relationship of author, reader, text, related texts and language, and in the issue of whether these categories are valid. For this reason, and for reasons of space, I shall exclude those schools whose emphasis is primarily on the relation of the literary text to its social, political, and historical context. I shall not, then, pursue feminist, Marxist or psychoanalytic theories further. My exclusion of these approaches does not imply that they have no contribution to make to a theory of the effect of literary discourse on schemata. Nor does it imply that the categories of Table 5.1 are any more than a descriptive convenience: no author, reader, or text can be rigorously separated from the social and historical context in which, and through which, they exist.

My first concern will be to trace theories which characterize literariness as a deviant or patterned use of language—as, in other words, a particular type of text. From the ultimate failure or incompleteness of these theories I shall progress to some of the literary theories which regard literariness as a relationship between texts and readers, and are thus more readily compatible with schema theory.

Theories of pattern and deviation

From this ravelled skein of complex and often contradictory writings, it is possible to pick out a single thread of thought which sees in literature a tendency to deviate from expectation.[3] In so doing, there is also a parallel strand which attempts to describe the nature of the expectations which are overturned, for talk of deviation must remain impressionistic and intuitive if it cannot describe the plain backcloth of normality against which the brighter stitches of deviation stand out. (For discussion of a psychological rather than formal approach to the terms see page 11 above.) 'Normality' and 'deviance' are an instance of a mutually defining binary pair, in which neither term can 'mean' without the other (Cixous and Clément 1975: 115). Although post-modernists (like Cixous) regard such pairs as a means of ideological control, and seek ways of escaping or at least of reversing the value judgements they encapsulate,

I shall adopt this particular pair as a useful tool for the moment. It may be that in literature, the deviant is elevated to the normal, and that one of the functions of literariness in discourse is to reverse the perceptual placing, in a move akin to deconstructionist readings of binary distinctions in established philosophical and scientific writings.

In attempting to trace these theories of deviance, I shall pick out, from among the categories of theory described above, a developing tradition which runs from Russian formalism, through structuralism and Jakobsonian functionalism, to stylistics, reader-response, and reception theory. I shall highlight theories within this tradition which echo or foreshadow schema theory and can contribute to it; but I shall also heed the arguments advanced against the tenets of these approaches by post-structuralists, while bearing in mind that I may, in the manner referred to in the opening paragraph of this chapter, be imposing my own conceptual structure after the event. Nevertheless, in so far as earlier theorists explicitly occupied themselves with the nature of deviance and normality in discourse, their area of enquiry inevitably touches that of schema theory, for schemata are expectations, and the essence of schema theory is that discourse proceeds, and achieves coherence, by successfully locating the unexpected within a framework of expectation.

The formalist theory of defamiliarization

Although the term formalist may be generally applied in literary theory (as it is, for example, by Davis (1986:45) and Rylance (1987:31)) to any who seek to study the literary text as an autonomous object divorced from the specific circumstances of its creation and creator, and from the historical and social context of its reception, the term is most generally associated with the 'Russian formalists', a group of critics who were active in Moscow and St Petersburg in the years immediately prior to and after the Bolshevik revolution. It was a 'school' which recognized itself as such, willingly accepted the label 'formalist' (though it was initially applied as an insult) and indeed met as a group in the shape of the 'Opoyaz' and 'Moscow Linguistics' circles (Bennet 1979:18; Eikhenbaum [1926] 1978:32; Terras 1985:151–4). It also came to a relatively neat historical end, for despite its initial sympathy with the Bolshevik revolution and with Marxism, it soon fell foul of the growing dogmatism of Soviet ideas of literature. It was criticized both by Lunacharsky, the first commissar for the arts, and by Trotsky who referred to the formalists as 'followers of St John' (Terras 1985:134), implying (ironically with an analogy later taken up by deconstruction) that the formalists, like the fourth evangelist, were believers in the 'logos', a metaphysical root of language. Though Shklovsky, one of the school's founding members, lived and worked in Moscow until the 1980s (Clark and Holquist 1984:340–3; Terras 1985:407), the activities of the group ceased fairly abruptly after his forced recantation of the formalist approach in 1930.[4] The movement can be defined in terms of its personnel (the most prominent figures are Eikhenbaum, Jakobson, Tomashevsky, Tynyanov, Shklovsky, and Brik) or more fittingly (in keeping with the formalists' own rejection of the concept of the author) in terms of its ideas. As these ideas contain the seeds of the major theories of subsequent movements which I wish to integrate with schema theory and discourse analysis, I shall describe them here in some detail.

Like many movements, formalism began, and defined itself initially, in terms of its polemical and iconoclastic rejection of the critical status quo. Firstly, it scorned the biography and scholarship which dominated the study of literature at the time: 'a history of generals', as Tynyanov ([1929] 1978:66) mockingly characterized it, preoccupied with such petty biographical questions as 'did Pushkin smoke?' (Brik [1923] 1977:90). Provocatively, it declared the author's individual circumstances irrelevant (Tomashevsky [1923] 1978). Even if Pushkin had not lived, it was suggested, his poetry would still have been written (Tynyanov [1929] 1978). 'There are no poets or literary figures; there is poetry and literature' (Brik [1923] 1977:90). Secondly, it rejected the current symbolist definition of art as 'thinking in images' (Eikhenbaum [1926] 1978:11), and the perennial Aristotelian view of art as mimesis: a view which was cruelly to reappear and wreak revenge on the formalists in the doctrine of socialist realism. Opposition to the notion of art as reflection cost many their freedom, health, or lives.

From the initial wild attacks on the critical establishment emerged a new and radical aesthetic, the cornerstone of which is the notion of *ostranenie*: a neologism created by nominalizing the Russian adjective for 'strange' and prefixing it with a morpheme denoting a process. This term is most frequently translated into English as 'defamiliarization' or 'making strange', expressing the idea that the function of literature is to restore freshness to perception which has become habitual and automated: to make things strange, to make us see them anew.

> This new attitude to objects in which, in the last analysis, the object becomes perceptible, is that artificiality which, in my opinion, creates art. A phenomenon, perceived many times, and no longer perceivable, or rather, the method of such dimmed perception, is what I call 'recognition' as opposed to 'seeing'. The aim of imagery, the aim of creating new art, is to return the object from 'recognition' to 'seeing'. (Shklovsky [1940] 1974:114)

> the fate of the works of bygone artists of the word, is the same as the fate of the word itself: both shed light on the path from poetry to prose; both become coated with the glass armour of the familiar. (ibid.:68)

This 'making strange', however, was not conceived as taking place at the level of content, as it would be in a theory regarding literary language as a transparent or reflective medium through which 'reality' may be perceived. It is, rather, at the level of form, that 'the glass armour of the familiar' is shattered. Shklovsky unequivocally rejected the reigning critical view that 'new form comes about to express new content', replacing it with the assertion that 'new form comes about not in order to express new content but in order to replace an old form that has already lost its artistic viability' (Shklovsky, quoted by Eikhenbaum [1926] 1978:29). With this radical new view of 'form conceived as content itself' (ibid.), the centre of critical attention shifted away from the relationship of the literary text with the world or with its creator, and towards internal formal relationships, either within one literary work or between literary works. Defamiliarization in literature is viewed as operating either intertextually or intratextually ('syn-functionally' or 'auto-functionally' in formalist terms (Tynyanov [1929] 1978:68)). It is achieved through formal 'devices', and it is the study and classification of devices to which the bulk of detailed formalist analysis is devoted. This, the formalists believed, would help to define 'literariness', the object of their study, and pave the way to their ultimate goal, the establishment of a science of literature (Bennett 1979:48). This goal, together with their early historical position, places them firmly, in spirit if not always in execution, at the beginning of the 'scientific' tradition of text theory (Chapter 2, note 27). At the risk of repeating well-documented material, I shall, in the following pages, describe in detail some of the formalist devices of defamiliarization so that I may better discuss their relationship to the more recent approaches to discourse in discourse analysis and AI schema theory.

Impeded form

Shklovsky proposed that a characteristic feature of literary writing is 'impeded form', or difficulty for its own sake. This 'increases the difficulty and length of perception, because the process of perception is an aesthetic end in itself and must be prolonged' (Shklovsky [1917] 1965:12). The attention and slowing down which this entails will in itself prevent automatized perception. Characteristically, little distinction is drawn between the levels at which this impediment may take place; Shklovsky's own examples concentrate upon discourse organization. I will assume for the moment that it may take place at any of the levels suggested by discourse analysis or AI schema theory: at the text-structural level certainly, but also at the level of world knowledge, and at the sub-sentential level (including even at the graphological or phonological level). I will not assume, however, that impediment at one level necessarily entails an impediment at higher levels. Many advertisements, for example, impede processing at the sub-sentential level (through puns, ambiguities, word-class conversions, and so on) while remaining conspicuously simple at the levels of text structure and world knowledge. Handwriting which is difficult to read does not imply interesting content. It may be, however, that an impediment at world-knowledge or text-structural levels may sometimes entail an impediment at the sub-sentential level. These are points to which I shall return.

The notion of the device of impeded form encapsulates a common-sense psychological principle expressed in sayings and proverbs such as 'the grass is always greener on the other side'. What is hard to come by attracts both interest and value. There is always room for disappointment after attainment, however. There are literary experiences, such as—in many people's estimation—*Finnegans Wake*, where the effort seems disproportionate to the reward.

Bared form

In some senses, no fiction is more 'real' than another. Yet 'realism' and its illusion of verisimilitude, may be defined as that which successfully distracts the reader's attention from its own devices (Jakobson [1921] 1978; Tomashevsky [1925] 1965:80). In opposition to the criterion of realism, which praises art for the success of this distraction, much formalist analysis concentrates upon writing which deliberately draws attention to its own fictionality and the processes, conventions, and illusions of its own genre. This is referred to as 'bared form' (Tomashevsky [1925] 1965:84; Eikhenbaum [1926] 1978:20). The classic analysis is Shklovsky's commentary ([1921] 1965) on (the classic example of bared form) *Tristram Shandy*. It is a rich approach of wide applicability to any instance where the reader's or audience's attention is drawn to the artistry rather than the illusory subject matter. Nor is its relevance confined to works which are as 'modern' in spirit as *Tristram Shandy*. Consider, for example, the effects of Shakespeare's plays within plays, or Chaucer's tales within tales, on any nascent 'suspension of disbelief' (a prerequisite of realism) in their perceiver.[5]

Canonization of the junior branch

The literary work, according to the formalists, inherits the characteristics of its uncles, aunts, and grandparents, but rarely of its parents. Literary traditions proceed oedipally, each new work establishing its ascendancy by destroying the assumptions of the generation before, incidentally often taking on the characteristics of the generation before that.[6] In this sense defamiliarization is achieved intertextually: expectations created by an established group of writers are overturned by rising stars. Clearly, here, the formalist desire to treat the text as autonomous and independent of history and authors runs into trouble, for the corollary of this theory is that defamiliarization is not a feature of text, but of the interaction of text with context.

One of the means by which this rejection of the earlier generation is achieved is, according to the formalists, the elevation of a genre accorded low status by the previous generation to a vehicle for the highest art. This they termed the 'canonization of the junior branch' (Shklovsky, quoted by Eikhenbaum ([1927] 1978:32)). Thus, for example, Dostoevsky elevated the detective story in *Crime and Punishment* (ibid.). Like the theory of impeded form, this idea, once perceived, is ubiquitously borne out. Thus Wordsworth and Coleridge elevated the ballad, Blake the children's song, Capote the newspaper 'human interest story', Orwell the children's story, Bob Dylan the country and western song, and so on. The rise of vernacular literature in the Renaissance, or of the novel in the nineteenth century, may be seen as wider instances of the same process. Perhaps the institutional nature of literary study, and its innate conservatism, blocks the perception of similarly far-reaching canonizations in our own time. The status of the poem and the novel has fallen, while that of the song, television programme, and film has risen. And within literary studies, writers like John le Carré and Raymond Chandler are still often excluded because of the apparently junior status of their branch of the novel.

Syuzhet and *fabula*

One of the best-known and longest lasting devices identified by the formalist is the *syuzhet*. This word describes the narrative ordering of the plot and is opposed to the *fabula*, the sequence of events as they happened—or rather, if we are talking of fiction—apparently happened. Where *syuzhet* and *fabula* coincide, there is a straightforward chronological narrative, which we might regard as the unmarked form of story-telling: the kind of narratives most easily handled in AI. *Syuzhet* is, in many ways, the text-structural equivalent of the sub-sentential phenomenon of Functional Sentence Perspective.

Again the theory is extraordinarily productive, and is useful for describing such literary narrative devices as 'cliffhangers' (commonly used by Dickens for example), 'flashbacks' (as in George Eliot's *Silas Marner*, where the main character's early life is recounted in the later part of the book), 'interleaving' (as in Flaubert's *Madame Bovary*, where the narrative at one point jumps backwards and forwards from the lovers on a balcony to the busy market place below, or in Peter Carey's novel *Oscar and Lucinda*, which alternates between two settings), description of the same event from another narrator's point of view (as in Faulkner's *The Sound and the Fury*, where events are seen through the eyes of three different characters and then a narrator), or apparently random jumping backwards and forwards in time to create thematic juxtaposition or connection (as in Aldous Huxley's novel *Eyeless in Gaza*). It may also be used to characterize a whole genre, as it is in Todorov's structuralist analysis of the detective story (Todorov [1966a] 1988). Here Todorov[7] describes the genre's typical 'double' narrative in which the *fabula* is completely reversed, so that the initial event is described last, while the order of events in the investigation moves backwards into the events of the crime.

The distinction of *syuzhet* and *fabula* is conspicuously absent from AI text theory, both in the work on comprehension described in Chapter 2, and in more recent work on text generation (McKeown 1985; Danlos 1987; Patten 1988). A typical AI *syuzhet* slavishly follows its *fabula*. An AI program, asked to write a 'whodunit', might well begin by telling the reader exactly that!

Skaz

Skaz is perhaps the most general of all the formalist devices. Though there is some disagreement over the use of the term by the formalists, and the relation of their use to other meanings (Terras 1985:420), I shall take it to mean the manner of narration, the apparent attitude of the narrator: 'Possibly the nearest equivalent of *skaz* is *yarn*. Technically, a *skaz* is a story in which the manner of telling ... is as important to the effect as the story itself' (Lemon and Reis 1965:67 footnote). As such, it overlaps with the other devices described above, but it may also be used as an element in distinguishing what contemporary theory would describe as different discourse or text types (Gregory 1967; Brown and Yule 1983:61–2; Dimter 1985; Cook 1989:95–9), speech events (Hymes [1964] 1977), or genres (Bakhtin [1929] 1978; [1936] 1986; Swales 1990). A police report, a poem, and a personal anecdote may all describe the same incident, but their *skaz* will be radically different. Again, the concept is productive in literary analysis. If discourse is partly classified by identification of the sender, consider what defamiliarizing effects are achieved when a fictional narrator is quite outside a reader's previous experience. Shklovsky ([1917] 1965) drew attention to the defamiliarizing effect of the narrative by a horse, who perceives familiar human events as extraordinary in Tolstoy's story 'Kholstomer'; Tomashevsky ([1925] 1965) to the description by a child of an adult council of war in a chapter of *War and Peace*. Such odd points of view are by no means unusual: Benjy the 'idiot' in *The Sound and the Fury*; the unborn foetus in Louis McNeice's poem 'Prayer before Birth' (or the Jimi Hendrix song 'Belly button window'); the Neanderthal man in William Golding's novel *The Inheritors*,[8] or the dying man in his *Pincher Martin*; the corpses in Dostoevsky's 'Bobok'; a child too young to understand adult intrigues in Henry James' *What Maisie Knew*; an amnesiac in Martin Amis' novel *Other People*. A related means of defamiliarization is to use a narrator who would normally be excluded from the social milieu of the reader: Jean Genet's prostitutes and petty criminals, William Burroughs' junkies, Dostoevsky's convicts in parts of *Notes from the Dead House*, Mark Twain's Huckleberry Finn. The list is potentially endless.

Bakhtin, though not a formalist, was to take the idea further and to describe the novel, as distinct from other discourse types, as having a 'polyphony' of voices in 'dialogue' with each other (Bakhtin [1934] 1981, [1929, revised 1963] 1984:251–70). The voices may be those of different characters, or indeed the 'voices' of other discourse types. In this way, parody is born. In Fielding's *Tom Jones*, for example, there are both the voice of the moralizing sermon and the voice of the ribald tale; in Alexander Pope's *The Rape of the Lock* the voice of the epic and the voice of gossip; in *Don Quixote* the voice of realism and the voice of romance. I have already illustrated the presence of more than one voice in the analysis of the opening of *Crime and Punishment*, and contrasted it with the single voice of the advertisement in which narrator, character, and reader are all assumed to have the same goals and knowledge.

The notion of *skaz* is, in fact, so all embracing that it covers almost every aspect of discourse. It also has a good deal in common with the approach to discourse which incorporates speech-act theory, in which understanding of what the sender seeks to do with an utterance is all important to the construction of coherence. Yet again, however, an understanding of *skaz* is rather painfully absent from AI text theory, even text-generation theory, whose variation of the relationship between discoursal choice and events is limited to the omission of knowledge assumed to be already known. This is not the same thing at all.

Theme and motif

There are other endeavours, however, in which the interests of formalist analysis do seem to foreshadow those of AI text theory. Tomashevsky's theory of 'thematics' investigates what he terms the 'theme' of a literary work: 'the idea that summarizes and unifies the verbal material' (Tomashevsky [1925] 1965:67). Each work as a whole, and at the same time each part, will have a theme. The themes of a work may thus be hierarchically described. There is, however, a limit to this reduction: 'parts that are irreducible, the smallest particles of thematic material:

"evening comes", "Raskolnikov kills the old woman", "the hero dies", "the letter is received" and so on' (ibid.). These he termed 'motifs'. From this starting point, he proceeded to examine the motivation for the inclusion or exclusion of 'motifs'. If we summarize a story, for example, we will exclude some and include others depending on the length of the summary. In Tomashevsky's view, 'motifs' may be subdivided into two types: 'bound' and 'free', or, to put it another way, those which are essential to the narrative (Macbeth killed the king)[9] and those which are optional (house martins nested on Macbeth's castle). A further division is between 'dynamic' and 'static' motifs, in other words those which change the situation (Hamlet's mother Gertrude drinks the poisoned wine) and those which do not (Hamlet picks up the skull). Clearly, bound motifs and dynamic motifs are less readily omitted than free motifs and static motifs: in a tree of motifs and themes, those at the higher nodes must always survive those lower down. The theme at the highest node is the 'dominant' or unifying theme (Jakobson [1935] 1978). The problem, however, is to explain the 'motivation' for the inclusion of 'free' and 'static' motifs in the first place, and for the ordering of motifs and themes in general. Three categories of motivation are suggested:[10]

1 'Realistic motivation' which yields motifs fulfilling expectations of life in the real world, thus fostering an illusion of verisimilitude
2 'Compositional motivation' which yields motifs creating a particular discourse structure (an interlude between periods of action, for example)
3 'Artistic motivation' which yields motifs contributing to defamiliarization.

In the terms of contemporary discourse analysis, if a motif is not motivated, the text becomes incoherent.

From the above description, the coincidence of approach between thematics and the version of schema theory described in Chapter 2 should be quite apparent. Both are concerned primarily with narrative, which they arrange into a hierarchy of units; both talk of irreducible unit (motifs or CD events) as the building blocks of this structure. Tomashevsky is in fact dealing with the principle for the exclusion and inclusion of events, with the problem of the level of detail as I described it on pages 75–7. Schema theory explains omission and inclusion in terms of slot filling in schemata: a point which is absent from the theory of thematics, as Tomashevsky did not realize that an event may be essential to the plot but not mentioned because it can be inferred. On the other hand, a schema theory approach to discourse would be greatly enriched by Tomashevsky's theory.

Formalism as a theory of deviation

In retrospect, it is easy to point out that there is a good deal that is confused, omitted, or inconsistent in formalist theory. The formalist concept of defamiliarization, and the various devices which realize it, concern departure from expectation and constitute a theory of literature as deviation from a norm. Yet it fails to identify the norm by which that deviation is defined. This is largely because it focused its attention almost entirely upon literary discourse in isolation, rather than alongside non-literary discourse. It is odd that formalism, which was in many ways so revolutionary and iconoclastic, never sought to question the existing literary canon, or the concept of literature as a distinct form of discourse, but accepted both uncritically. The theory would be hard pressed to account for the defamiliarization which occurs in many other discourse types. It might avoid this problem by labelling such occurrences as instances of literariness within non-literary discourse, but with this line of argument the definition of literariness becomes hopelessly circular and diffuse.

Another central weakness is the failure to distinguish between three areas of defamiliarization: sensory perception, text structure, and linguistic form. It is strange, considering formalism's rejection of imagist, mimetic, realist, and reflection theories of art, that it should so easily make the jump from defamiliarization in the sense perception of objects to defamiliarization in text structure and language. One might argue that the former is a metaphorical description of the latter. Alternatively, the theory may simply be confused. Undoubtedly, the cause of this confusion is the absence of a rigorous linguistic theory. Saussure's work was known in Russia in the early 1920s (Kholodovich 1977), but it had not made a great impact, and was rejected by Bakhtin (Volosinov [1929] 1973: 57–63). Bakhtin himself, whose theory might have become as influential as Saussure's, did not publish his first major work on linguistic theory until 1929, under the name of Volosinov (Volosinov [1929] 1973). Bakhtin was in any case a stalwart critic of formalism for its attempts to isolate language from its senders and receivers, a view strongly expressed in a book he published under the name of Medvedev (Medvedev [1928] 1978). He may further have antagonized the formalists by the superficial compatibility of some of his theories with the orthodox Soviet Marxism of the late 1920s—though with his faith in the Russian Orthodox Church and his hatred of regimentation, he was anything but a Marxist-Leninist.[11]

The absence of a linguistic theory perhaps accounts for the creativity of the formalists' work on text structure and the sparseness of their work on language (with the exception of prosody, which I have not mentioned here). The result is a granary of fertile ideas, but the foundation is weak. In particular, the claim to deal with texts as autonomous objects does not fit with the notion of defamiliarization which, far from being a fixed feature of an isolated text, is a variable which cannot be separated from the psychology of the reader or from the particular and changing social and historical context which conditions it. Bakhtin, in his critiques of formalism, wrote that it is not possible to divorce language wholly from its senders and receivers. Language is, in his words, 'like an electric spark' which can only exist between two terminals (Bakhtin [Volosinov] [1929] 1973:103). Quite how the formalist thinkers might have reacted to this problem, or to what extent they could have made use of Bakhtin's theories of language and discourse, must remain a matter for speculation. By the end of the 1920s they were scattered and silenced. Bakhtin, too, was arrested, exiled, and forced into relative obscurity. Jakobson, in Prague and later in the USA, turned his attention to the formal linguistic aspects of literature (see below). The work which the formalists and Bakhtin had begun on the deviant discoursal features of literature thus lay dormant, buried under an exclusive attention to the formal system of language, until the revival of interest in discourse in the 1970s. 'Scientific' approaches to literature had split into two directions: the rigorous attention to sub-sentential form by Jakobson and stylistics, and the search for conformities to text structural patterns—rather than deviations from them—of the structuralists (which I discuss in the next section).

Yet the formalists, despite the weaknesses of their work and its abrupt end, had introduced a number of important theoretical concepts which are often overlooked in a schema theory approach to text. Though it may seem odd to ask high-technology scientists to return to the works of 1920s literary scholars, AI would have done well to reach back across the intervening decades to these theories. The formalists had described a type of discourse (which they, perhaps wrongly, wholly identified with literature) whose salient characteristic is deviance from expectation, but whose deviance is neither solely linguistic nor a function of the relationship of a text to events in the world. To explain this phenomenon, they had introduced the important concepts of intertextuality, internal discourse structure, discourse type, and narrative attitude, all of which have become major concerns in discourse analysis, and should have been major concerns in AI. What they did not do was try to describe the norm against which deviation is defined, or say quite why it is that readers find such deviation so attractive and important, often according literary texts a higher status than any others produced by a society. My claim will be that an answer to these questions may be provided by bringing together the insights of schema theory with the fundamental concept of formalism: defamiliarization. Firstly, however, I shall look at further development of theories of literature as deviation.

In western Europe, after (and sometimes unaware of) Russian formalism, the 'scientific' approach to literary discourse divided into two. Both approaches were profoundly affected by the growing influence of the Saussurean description of language (de Saussure [1916], 1960), but the uses which they made of this description were very different. The French structuralists, taking the categories of Saussurean description almost metaphorically, largely ignored the sub-sentential linguistic system, and searched instead for 'grammars' and structures at the higher levels of narrative and text organization, presaging the interest in 'story grammars' in AI and discourse analysis (see van Dijk and Kintsch 1983:55–9). Jakobson, on the other hand, and later Anglo-American stylistics turned back to the linguistic code, searching for 'literariness' at the sub-sentential level. These two approaches may both throw light on, and benefit from, schema theory as an aid to literary analysis. They may also elucidate the difficult problems involved in describing the intuitive categories of 'norm', 'pattern', and 'deviation'. I shall turn my attention now to each approach in turn.

Patterns in discourse: structures and structuralism

> Another interesting fact from an evolutionary point of view is the following. A work is correlated with a particular literary system depending on its deviation, its 'difference' compared with the literary system with which it is confronted.
> (Tynyanov [1929] 1978:73)

In its description of devices like *syuzhet* and *fabula*, *skaz*, motif, and theme, Russian formalism had touched upon something which is conspicuously absent in any comparatively sophisticated form from the AI schema theory described in Chapter 2. This is the point that the same conceptual information may be represented in different text-structural and linguistic forms, and that these different natural language representations, far from being marginal and relatively unimportant, may, in fact, dominate the conceptual content in the perception of the reader. (If I watch a television comedy about a particular battle, for example, and then read a lyric poem about the same battle, the genre may be more salient than events, which are, in the world schemata derived from these two representations, the same. Similarly the *syuzhet* of the account of a murder may dominate the world schema derived from it, helping to distinguish, for example, a police report and a detective story.) Different ways of presenting the same conceptual content exist at both sub-sentential level, where there are choices between various Functional Sentence Perspectives, discourse markers, and cohesive ties, and at the super-sentential level where there are choices in the arrangement of (in

Tomashevsky's terms) motifs and themes. As well as world schemata, there are also text schemata and language schemata. The relationship between the three is undoubtedly complex, but cannot be avoided. We should not assume that the influence of one upon the other is unidirectional. Choices among sentence and text schemata may directly affect world schemata.

The identification and classification of text schemata is a similar endeavour to the structuralist approach to literature. Any theory of literary discourse as a particular kind of discourse deviation or patterning will need to take account of the substantial body of theory this approach has produced. (That is the reason for considering it here.) Structuralist critics sought, by analogy with the methods of Saussurean linguistics, to identify the underlying structure (analogous to the *langue*) of a genre or group of texts, expressed—sometimes only partially—in particular texts (analogous to *parole*). Within this structure, again by extension from Saussure, they have tried to reveal how elements take on meaning through opposition, paradigmatic substitution, syntactic ordering, deletion, insertion, and transposition (see, for example, Barthes [1966] 1977: 79–125; Culler 1973, 1975a, 1975b:4–54; Lyons 1973; Robey 1973; Lentricchia 1980:102–56; Genette [1982] 1988). In this they have drawn heavily on structural anthropology, which had sought to discover the underlying *langue* of myths (Lévi-Strauss [1955] 1972, 1960) and kinship systems (Lévi-Strauss [1949] 1962), and Barthes' structuralist sociology, whose aim was to unmask the grammars of contemporary cultural artefacts such as fashion (Barthes 1967) and a whole range of contemporary 'myths', such as those concerning meat eating, washing powders, striptease, wrestling, and so on (Barthes [1957] 1973).

The terminologies, units, and objects of study in structural analyses of literature may vary, but fundamentally the procedure (the underlying structure of structuralism itself!) remains the same: to identify the minimal parts of a genre (almost always, in practice, a narrative genre) and to elaborate rules of paradigmatic substitution and syntagmatic combination. So Propp ([1928] 1968), in a seminal work significantly called *The Morphology of the Folk Tale*, worked out formulae which showed that the 'functions' (as he called the minimal units of the 449 tales he studied) are finite in number and sequences. Lévi-Struss broke down myths from a variety of sources into 'mythemes' and, by describing their various combinations, arrived at a typology of myths (Culler 1975b: 40–54). Todorov ([1969] 1987) did the same for his 'minimal schemata' of the *Decameron* and the detective story, drawing up a 'grammar' which enabled him to define the difference between this genre, the 'thriller', and the suspense novel. Greimas, whose minimal units 'semes' combine into 'classemes' which combine into 'isotopies', has done similar work on a wide range of texts from Mallarmé and Baudelaire to bar-room jokes (Greimas 1966:53; see Culler 1975b:75–95). Eco (1979) has analysed Superman comics and the James Bond novels, then reversed the process by using his semiotic analyses to generate a work of fiction (*The Name of the Rose*) which he has then analysed himself (*Reflections on 'The Name of the Rose'*) (Eco 1989). The list of extant analyses is vast.

Two examples of structuralist text analysis

Rather than repeat the details of one of these well-known narrative grammars, I shall briefly present two of my own, hoping to illustrate some of the problems and the weaknesses of the approach.

Example 1: Adventure stories

The first group of texts is one which intuitively appears to be homogeneous: six adventure stories from the late nineteenth and early twentieth centuries with boy heroes: Robert Louis Stevenson's *Treasure Island* and *Kidnapped*, J. Meade Falkner's *Moonfleet*, Mark Twain's *Huckleberry Finn*, Rudyard Kipling's *Kim*, and Thomas Hughes' *Tom Brown's Schooldays*. Analysing the plots of these six novels we might hypothesize the following elements:

1 a 'boy' lives peacefully at home
2 his father dies
3 an event disrupts this peace
4 he leaves home with an older male
5 she seeks for a precious object
6 he learns a new language
7 he is imprisoned in an enclosed space
8 he finds the object
9 he returns home as a 'man'

and a syntagmatic structure as follows:

1 2 (or 2 1) 3 4 (5 6 7, in any order) 8 9

These (in the formalist terms of Tomashevsky) are the 'motifs'; the unifying 'theme' (or 'dominant') is initiation. From the specific plots we might make paradigmatic substitutions of particular events. Thus, the older male (4) in *Treasure Island* is Long John Silver, the precious object (5) is the treasure, the language (6) is swearing, the enclosed space (7) is the apple barrel where the boy hero Jim is hiding when he learns of Silver's treachery. In *Kidnapped* the older male (4) is Alan Breck, the precious object (5) the title deeds to David Balfour's inheritance, the language (6) the dialect of the Jacobite rebels, the enclosed space (7) the ruined tower to which David is sent under false pretences by his uncle. In *Huckleberry Finn*, the older male (4) is the escaped slave Jim, the precious object (5) is Jim's freedom, the language (6) is Jim's 'nigger talk', but (7) occurs only in the earlier tale *Tom Sawyer* (where the boys are lost in a cave). In *Moonfleet* the older male (4) is Elzevir, the precious object (5) is the diamond, the language (6) is the smugglers' argot, the enclosed space (7) is the crypt which leads to the caves, and then again a prison cell.

Against this proposed regularity, whose occurrence identifies each book as one 'speaking the same language', we might identify 'deviations'—in terms of the linguistic analogy, marked patterns. Thus in *Kim* for example, though there is one dark space (Lurgan's shop) many of the other features of our 'grammar' are multiplied. Thus there is not one older man but three: the Moslem horse dealer Mahbub Ali, the Buddhist lama, and the British agent Creighton. And each of these men teaches Kim a new language: horse-dealing slang, the mystic rules of Buddhism, and the jargon of espionage respectively. There are two precious objects (the Russian plans sought by Creighton and the healing stream sought by the lama) and Kim must choose between them at the end. In *Tom Brown's Schooldays* there is a different kind of 'deviation'. The hero is himself the older male who guides the younger one through his initiation, and here the journey and the enclosed space are dreamed rather than physical, the language and the precious object spiritual rather than material.

This *langue*, moreover, like many 'uncovered' by structuralism, is not only confined to literary texts. Similar events are key features of many tribal initiation ceremonies (van Gennep [1908] 1960:65–115; Frazer [1922] 1949:692–3; Kirk 1970:71). A boy is taken into the care of an older male; he leaves home and goes into a dangerous place; he learns a new language; he is confined in an enclosed space; he finds the object; he returns home. A similar initiation ritual, for that matter, may be found closer to home in modern industrial society. University examinations (though their personnel are no longer exclusively male) have all the features of this ritual!

Example 2: Concentric narratives

Another recognizable narrative structure is that of a narrative within a narrative within a narrative—and so on. We shall term such narratives 'concentric'. Six literary works which seem, intuitively, to have this structure are: Chaucer's *The Canterbury Tales*, Joseph Conrad's *Heart of Darkness*, Emily Brontë's *Wuthering Heights*, Dostoevsky's *Notes from the Dead House* and Henry James' *The Turn of the Screw*. In *Wuthering Heights* and *Heart of Darkness* for example, a narrator gives an account of a tale told by someone else, and within this tale there are further narratives. The movement 'inwards' at the beginning is complemented by a movement outwards at the end, a return to the original narrative relationship. We might regard this as the 'unmarked' structure, in much the same way, and with as little reason, as one might describe the sentence:

Honoré Balzac was born in 1799 at Tours, the son of a civil servant

as the unmarked version among the range of sentence perspectives given on pages 49–51. A formula for the structure is set out below:

(Narrator 1 addresses reader 1 [= the reader] (narrator 2 addresses reader 2 [= narrator 1 + the reader] (narrator 3 addresses reader 3 [= the reader + narrator 1 + narrator 2] (narrator 4 addresses reader 4 [= the reader + narrator 1 + narrator 2 + narrator 3] (. . .) narrator 4 addresses reader 4 [= the reader + narrator 1 + narrator 2 + narrator 3]) narrator 3 addresses reader 3 [= the reader + narrator 1 + narrator 2]) narrator 2 addresses reader 2 [= narrator 1 + the reader] Narrator 1 addresses reader 1 [= the reader])

Or more simply, giving each level of narrative a number:

(1 (2 (3 (4 (. . .) 4) 3) 2) 1)

In addition we say that each narrator is a character in the narration of the narrative outside it, narrator 1 being a character in the discourse of the author, thus:

Narrator x = character $(x-1)$.

Moreover, the readers (i.e. receivers, though not necessarily addressees) at each level will include those at all outer levels, thus:

readers x = reader/s x + reader/s $(x-1)$ + reader/s $(x-2)$, etc. (providing no result < 1)

Many concentric narratives are variations upon this theme. *The Canterbury Tales*, for example, proceeds, generally speaking as follows:

(1	(2	(3	(4		) 3) 2 (3 (4) 3) 2 (3 (4) 3
Chaucer	Sir	Pilgrim	characters		
	Topas		in tale		

though there are also rapid transitions embedding the whole formula in miniature within one tale (i.e. level 4), as when, for example, the Friar interrupts 'The Summoner's Tale',[12] yielding the following;

(1 (2	(3		(4		(3)	(4		)))
	Summoner		characters		Friar	characters		
			in tale			in tale		

Dostoevsky's novel *Notes from the Dead House* provides another variation on the theme. The narrator reports how, on moving to Siberia, he met a reclusive ex-convict, Goryanchikov, working as a tutor to local children, and how, after this man died, the narrator was given his notebooks. The inner narrative is the story, told in the notebooks, of Goryanchikov's four years' imprisonment. Within this narrative there are further narratives: stories told by the other prisoners. Yet, despite one brief interjection by the narrator of the outer narrative, there is no return to this layer of narrative at the end, leaving the structure open as follows:

(1	(2	(3	) 2)	1	(2
outer narrative	notebooks	prisoners' stories		interjection	notebooks

This device of leaving the progression literally open-ended is arguably commoner than its opposite; it is also present in *The Canterbury Tales* and *The Turn of the Screw* (discussed in detail in Chapter 8). It has also, if we accept the process of returning stage by stage back through the levels to that of the first narration as the norm, an analogue in sentence grammar: embedded subordinate clauses, in which the reader loses his or her way, forgetting to expect a main verb and a complete main clause. Blake's poem 'Ah! Sunflower' is a single vocative noun phrase postmodified by embedded and co-ordinated relative clauses. There is no main verb. It is as though the reader is drawn further and further into a series of embedded worlds, each deriving from the one before.

Ah $_{VOC\ NP}$(Sunflower weary of time

[Who countest the steps of the sun]
$_{RCl}$

[Seeking after that fair golden clime
$_{RCl}$

[Where the traveller's journey is done]
$_{RCl}$

[Where < (the youth [pined away with desire])
$_{RCl}$

And (the pale virgin [shrouded with snow])>
< (Arise) (from their graves) and (aspire)
[Where my sunflower wishes [to go]]>]>])
$_{RCl}$

(For grammatical notation conventions, see Appendix A.)

So powerful are the inner units, however, that the absence of a main verb may pass unnoticed. Similarly, in the riveting complex of stories within stories in *Notes from the Dead House*, the reader may simply forget the outer structure of which they are a part.

In the strong structuralist view, the meaning of each exemplar of a structure cannot be found in isolation, within one text, nor in the relationship of one text to the world. The argument is that each story takes on meaning, like the Saussurean sign, through its difference from or similarity to others. Meaning is, to use one of Lévi-Strauss's explanatory images, like an orchestral score where there is not only the horizontal melody of an individual realization, but also the vertical harmonies and disharmonies of comparison (Lévi-Strauss [1955] 1972: 176). Alternatively, it is like a card index, in which a pin can be passed through the patterns on one card to see how they correspond with those on the others (ibid.: 182).

Weaknesses of the structuralist approach

The failures and weaknesses of the structuralist approach have been often rehearsed. Indeed, twenty-five years after the heyday of structuralism, they may seem rather painfully obvious. Notably, despite pretensions to a cold empirical objectivity, there is often a marked arbitrariness in the choice of an object of study—a set of texts for example—as well as in the definition of units, the rules of combination, and the selection of significant features. There is certainly none of the rigour of the sub-sentential grammars to which structures are supposed to be analogous. Barthes in his later post-structuralist work candidly acknowledged this shortcoming, defining his new minimal unit, the 'lexia', as a category arbitrarily imposed according to the insight of one reader—himself (Barthes [1970] 1974, 1973] 1981).

There is also often considerable confusion as to the nature of the structures defined. It is not clear, for example, whether a structure is to be found in one manifestation (a kind of prototypical instance analogous to those posited by Rosch in lexico-semantics (see pages 74–5)) or whether it is an abstraction applying equally to all instances (analogous to components of meaning in semantics). If the latter is the case, it is not clear how many examples are needed before the abstraction can be made, and whether this abstraction corresponds to some psychologically real processing structure or has come into being through the analysis. It is true that similar problems exist for Saussurean linguistics in the definition of *langue* and *parole*, but the structuralist objects of study, being often trans-cultural and trans-linguistic, are even more slippery than natural languages.

Above all, the closed introverted nature of the systems of strong structuralist hypotheses, in which meaning is conceived wholly in terms of systemic variation, makes it hard to see quite what the significance of the structure, or variations within it, may be. If a given structure is not related to another system outside itself—language, or thought, or history—then it seems to have no meaning other than itself, and the activity becomes a dead end. In many analyses, it is not clear whether structures are regarded as culturally and historically determined, or the reflection of universal mental structures independent of history and culture. In a study such as Propp's ([1928] 1968), where the data is from one fairly homogeneous cultural source, there are grounds for the first hypothesis; but in the work of Lévi-Strauss, which ranges freely across cultures, there seems little option but to accept the second. In fact, Lévi-Strauss, adopting a similar argument to that propounded by Chomsky (1965) in explanation of universal 'deep' syntactic structures, suggests that myths reveal universal structures of the mind. At times he even suggests that they may reflect structures of the brain (Lévi-Strauss [1960] 1972:212, 222) as does Chomsky when he writes of the 'mind–brain' (Chomsky 1988:7) commenting that 'When we speak of the mind we are speaking at some level of abstraction of yet unknown physical mechanisms of the brain'. Yet without some explicit means of linking these vaguely defined mental structures to those revealed by analysis of behaviour, there seems little point in such hypothesizing.[13]

Furthermore, as structuralism proceeds by analogy with Saussurean semiotics, Derrida's deconstructionist objections apply equally to both activities. Meaning is achieved by difference, but as each sign evokes another from which it differs, meaning is endlessly deferred. The writing of structural analyses, moreover, creates a new set of texts which may themselves be structurally analysed, initiating a process which is potentially infinite. In this interpretation, the attempt to establish a single structure unifying and giving meaning to a discrete and finite number of instances is yet another attempt to bring this endless 'play' of meaning to a halt. Proposed abstract structures are merely 'centres' (Derrida [1967] 1978:109), through which an attempt is made to 'close down' the irreducible and ungraspable interconnections. Explaining the deep structures of language or myth, as Chomsky and Lévi-Strauss do, as universal, genetically inherited mental structures, creates another kind of centre, to which all meaning relates, and beyond which interpretation cannot proceed: a centre analogous to a fundamentalist's 'God' or 'creation'. Though we may crave the stability such centres bring, it is perhaps more rewarding to let 'meaning' remain in flux. It is interesting to note the resemblance between these philosophical objections to structuralism and Bakhtin's much earlier theory of the novel (Bakhtin [1929, revised 1963] 1984). In this view, the novel is polyphonic, an intertwining of points of view from which no controlling single authorial voice can be disentangled (see also Barthes [1968] 1977:142). No single voice has a higher status than others. In the same way, perhaps, though there are structures in a set of texts, there is no single structure.

In practice, moreover, as a theory of literature, a structuralist analysis is often disappointing. Despite elaborate terminologies and procedures, the analyses themselves remain often quite simplistic, and are only convincing when applied to the most stereotypical texts. Eco (1979), echoing Barthes' ([1970] 1974:10) distinction between 'writerly' and 'readerly' texts, makes a distinction between texts which conform to structures (his own examples are the James Bond novels and Superman stories) and those which depart from them. These he terms, respectively, 'closed' and 'open' texts. The pleasure to be derived from the first category lies precisely in their safe and predictable nature. The pleasure of the second lies in their novelty—though they are never entirely novel, but rather deviations from the closed structure. Total novelty would presumably be incomprehensible (de Beaugrande and Dressler 1981:139–62). The new must always attach itself to the known in order to mean. This applies at the linguistic level, in the bipartite structure of the clause revealed in studies of functional sentence perspective (see pages 48–51), and at the level of world schemata.

The problem is that description of text structures is a powerful tool in the analysis of closed texts, yet far less powerful in the analysis of open ones. Similar problems exist in analyses which view discourse as a product; they work for socially rigid 'closed' discourse types, but not for open ones like conversation. Yet texts regarded as literary are often of the open type. Moreover, as closed structures are not only found in literature, but also in behaviour (for example initiation rites and examinations), and in non-literary texts as well, it is clear that the recognizable presence of the structure is unlikely to reveal those features which have led to an open text being elevated to literary status. Deviation from the norm may be noted, but the significance of its details remains unexplored.

Take, for example, some simple elements of the structure of a story—that there should be an end and a beginning, central and peripheral characters. Then take instances of stories which, in these terms, are deviant. In Buñuel's film *The Discreet Charm of the Bourgeoisie* there is no central character whose fate provides a unifying theme or dominant; the narrating camera, apparently randomly, picks out a peripheral character in one scene and follows his or her fate in the next, making connections seem arbitrary and unstructured. Similarly, in Julio Cortazar's novel *Rayuela* ('Hopscotch') there is no fixed sequence of chapters: they are to be read in different orders to produce different stories. The French *nouveau roman* eschews endings. What can be said of these aberrations except that they do not conform to structural expectations? There seems no way to explore their detail for its own sake, except by positing them as prototypes of a new structure.

What, for example, are we to make of concentric narratives deviating from the formula set out on page 144, providing of course that we accept that formula as the norm in the first place? It seems that the 'meaning' of such deviations lies not merely, introspectively, in their difference from expectation, but also, looking outward, in connections which the reader may build between this perceived difference and other value systems. Thus we might judge the 'meaning' of *The Discreet Charm of the Bourgeoisie* (though Buñuel would no doubt have objected)[14] to be a rejection of hierarchies of characters in traditional stories and of hierarchies of people in general, as well as a rejection of coherence. The *nouveau roman* may be judged to 'mean' that events do not come to neat endings. *Notes from the Dead House* may lay bare (in formalist terms) the automatic trust we place on a narrative first person, by denying us the narrator's final judgement, defamiliarizing the convention of trust in narrative authority. (A similar point may be made about Agatha Christie's novel *The Murder of Roger Ackroyd* in which the first-person narrator is the murderer, but does not confide this to the reader until the very end.) *Kim* may reveal that choice of adult models is not always imposed and may be a fusion of several. The meaning of the 'open' text, in other words, is often perceived to lie not only in its difference from the pattern of the closed text, but also in the specific nature of that difference, and its connection outwards to other systems of meaning. Such interpretations demand more than a catalogue of closed structures and deviations from them.

Textual structures, then, are undoubtedly significant, but their full significance can only be realized when they are related outwards, to linguistic systems on the one hand, and to conceptual representations (schemata) on the other. It is true that, in a sense, this is only to place one kind of structure inside another. The interrelation of world knowledge, text schemata, and language may simply form another, bigger, but equally closed structure. As such, this larger structure might seem to be not an escape from structure, but one step in another Derridean system of infinite postponement and play. Yet arguably, this larger structure encapsulates the totality of human experience of discourse, and its study will bring us closer to understanding discourse than the study of any of its components in isolation.

Text structures and text schemata

This section on structuralist text analysis began by observing that the notion of a recurrent structure is very similar to the notion of a text schema. It is true that various elements of a structuralist approach have been assimilated into schema theory (see, for example, Sanford and Garrod 1981: 34; McKeown 1985: 53). An important difference, however, is that while the ontological status of a structure is rather unclear, that of a text schema is far more specific and adaptable. Whereas structures, if they exist at all, belong in some vague neo-Platonic or quasi-Jungian landscape of immutable cultural, mental, or even cerebral universals, text schemata are the constructions of a given individual used very practically in text processing.[15] As such, they may be born and perish with individuals; they may be wrong, idiosyncratic, distorting. Their important feature in communication is not their 'truth' but the degree to which they are shared, and to which that shared nature is successfully exploited. In Derridean terms they are not an absolute centre, but a centre of convenience. In practice this difference may seem of little relevance, and a 'structure' posited by a 'hard' structuralist may be converted to a 'text schema' for the saying so. Yet the difference plays an important role in making schema theory essentially compatible with the literary theories of reader response and reception theory, to which we shall turn in the next chapter, as well as making schema theory more psychologically plausible in general terms. One other important difference is that, while structuralism was contented with aspects of the question of how literary meaning is achieved through structures and through deviations from them, it makes no attempt to ask why recurrence or deviation, as evidenced in literary texts, should attract the high social and personal evaluation that it does. My theory of literary discourse effecting cognitive change, as I hope to show in Part II, can at least attempt an answer to both the 'how' and the 'why' of pattern and deviation.

Roland Barthes' 'Introduction to the structural study of narratives'

In this section I have caricatured structuralist analysis as ignoring the details of language on the one hand and of conceptual representation of the world on the other. I have presented it, in other words, as a contributory but limited endeavour within discourse theory. This caricature might with justice be regarded as unfair. There are structuralist analyses which attempt to make connections, both between structures and language on the one hand, and between structures and conceptual representations on the other. Notable among such attempts is Barthes' 'Introduction to the structural study of narratives' ([1966] 1977): an analysis which is remarkable both for the breadth of its view of discourse, and for its attempt to integrate approaches which are in danger of remaining separate.

Barthes proposes a hierarchy of discourse levels for narrative, situated between the levels of linguistic description and the systems of the extra-linguistic world. Thus, he describes the structural analysis of narrative not as an activity of intrinsic and self-contained worth, but as a means of linking the levels of description below it to those above.

> Narration can only receive its meaning from the world which makes use of it: beyond the narrational level begins the world, other systems (social, economic, ideological) whose terms are no longer simply narratives but elements of a different substance (historical facts, determinations, behaviours, etc.) Just as linguistics stops at the sentence, so narrative analysis stops at discourse—from there it is necessary to shift to another semiotics.
> (Barthes [1966] 1977: 115)

Showing full awareness of formal linguistics approaches to discourse (for example, Harris 1952), he sees structural analysis of narrative as taking over where linguistics description leaves off. Sentences, the highest units of linguistic description, realize 'functions' and 'actions', the lowest units of his description of narrative.[16] Functions[17] are the minimal components of actions. The action of 'lighting a cigarette', for example, consists of the functions 'striking a match', 'putting a cigarette in the mouth', etc. Functions combine into actions, and actions into the narration. (It is thus a system which, like Tomashevsky's, can deal with the problem of the level of detail (see pages 75–8) which remains unsolved by schema theory.) Once the narration has been described, it may be linked to a system of narrative (or structure). After this, there are two directions for analysis beyond the description of the discourse in question: one to discover the *langue*, or system behind individual narrations, the other to step outside of language altogether and to examine non-linguistic systems. Barthes' hierarchy is shown in Figure 5.2.

(The world)

(The system of narrative)

Narration

Actions

Functions

(Sentence)

Figure 5.2: Barthes' levels of discourse

Here, structural description is not seen as an end in itself, but as a mediator between language and representations of the world. Such a view is deeply compatible with schema theory, adding to it a level of description between successions of sentences and conceptual representations.

Roman Jakobson's poetics

I have criticized structuralist approaches to literature for concentrating upon text schemata to the detriment of language and world schemata, and to the detriment of any theory of the interaction of these three areas. The literary theory of Roman Jakobson, which is the basis of stylistics, exhibits a complementary, but equally limited, concentration upon language, to the exclusion of the other two. The potential application of the formalist theory of defamiliarization to all three levels of discourse was thus not realized by this approach either.[18]

In this dividing of the ways, the relevance of non-linguistic knowledge representation in discourse processing was to all intents and purposes ignored, and even denied. This echoed developments in philosophy, psychology, and linguistics during the central decades of this century; it coincides with the fall from favour of theories of conceptual representation, such as Bartlett's, which are the basis of schema theory (see pages 15–18) and of phenomenological literary theories such as those of Roman Ingarden. One famous refutation of the validity of postulating a conceptual level independent of language is Wittgenstein's argument against the existence of private languages (Wittgenstein [1953] 1968: 94–6).[19] The view is also implicit in behaviourism, and though Chomsky's theories restored the notion of psychological structures underlying language behaviour, they did so only for the sub-sentential formal level and not for discourse. Only with the reinstatement of a belief in conceptual representation systems existing independently of natural languages did a holistic approach to discourse and to literature again become possible. Precisely such a reinstatement followed from the work in psychology, linguistics, and AI of the 1970s and 1980s. Jakobson's poetics, on the other hand, is work in a tradition which isolates language both from the larger issues of discourse structure and from the psychology (conceptual representations) of its users.

Among the formalists, Jakobson's interests had always been more markedly linguistic than discoursal. It was he who had coined the term 'literariness' and defined it as 'the organized coercion of *language* by poetic form' (quoted in Erlich [1955] 1980:219 (my italics)). In 1920, he left Moscow for Prague, where he worked as a translator and Soviet Cultural attaché for the Red Cross. In 1926, he was one of the founding members of the Prague School of linguistics and stayed on, for fear of

Stalin, in academic jobs in Czechoslovakia until 1939. Then, fleeing from the Nazis, he moved first to Scandinavia and from there, in 1941, to the USA (Terras 1985:208), where he died in 1982. Thus, through his personal history, he was able to bring together the approaches to literature and language of Russia, Western and Central Europe, and the USA over a period of sixty years.

In Prague he worked with Mukarovsky, whose views on literary language were, if anything, even more extreme than his: 'The distortion of the norm of the standard is ... of the very essence of poetry' (Mukarovsky 1932 (Quoted in Burton 1980:5)). The two men shared, in other words, a view of literariness as a deviant use of language. Together with other linguists of the Prague School, they developed the notion of linguistic foregrounding, though the roots of the idea go back to earlier formalist work (see O'Toole and Shukman 1977:34; van Peer 1986:5–26). With this increased emphasis on language as opposed to textual form, the formalist interest in longer stretches of discourse began to be forgotten: a tendency reflected in the increasing substitution of the novel, drama, and epic by lyric poetry as the object of study.

Poetic function and poetic form

Jakobson was to continue developing these ideas throughout his life. In 1958, at a conference in Indiana, he summed up his views (and the conference) with a particularly lucid and elegant paper (Jakobson 1960), which is undoubtedly the single most influential and often cited contribution of linguistics to literary analysis this century (Carter and Simpson 1989:1; Fabb et al. 1987:1) and which has dominated Anglo-American stylistics ever since. Its clarity and lack of equivocation also makes it a useful target for those critics who wish to reject a scientific formal linguistic approach to literature altogether.

Jakobson's proposals and their place in the history of functionalist theories of language have already been discussed for their relevance to discourse analysis. The theory serves as a means of characterizing either individual utterances or even particular types of discourse. This application to discourse typology confirms the claim that Jakobson's proposal ignores discourse structure, for he seeks to define a discourse type by its formal linguistic features, showing how in certain discourses and utterances one function dominates the others (see also Jakobson [1935] 1978). In literature, the dominant function is the poetic. Meaning is carried not by the relations of signs to the world, but rather by the relation of signs to each other, either inside or outside the text—by, in other words, the specific linguistic choices, their deviations from the norm, and the patterns which they create. In the words of the most famous sentence of this paper, italicized by Jakobson himself: '*The poetic function projects the principle of equivalence from the axis of selection into the axis of combination*' (Jakobson 1960:358).

In many ways, the objections which may be made to this thesis of Jakobson's concerning the language of literature are similar to those which may be made to the structuralist thesis about text structures. I have already touched upon the weaknesses of the implication that literariness can be found at one level in isolation. In Jakobson's argument, the concentration on language and the exclusion of other levels is vulnerable at many points. Jakobson writes of 'reference' and 'a principle of equivalence'. Yet it is not clear what this 'reference' and 'equivalence' are to. It cannot be, in the case of language with a poetic function, equivalence to some other linguistic form, since the uniqueness and unparaphrasable nature of literary linguistic choices is exactly Jakobson's point. Presumably, though the explicit statement of this inference is carefully avoided, the 'equivalence' is to some conceptual representation in the mind of its users. But this is not clear, and understandably so, since to introduce individual readers, and therefore the notion of individual variability, would undermine Jakobson's point that literariness is to be found in language itself without any reference to the world or the people in it. Related to this is the difficult problem of norms and deviations. Definition of a deviation depends on the definition of a norm. What is normal will vary with individuals and in history. There is thus a degree of arbitrariness in the choice of the yardstick of normal language, just as there is in structuralist choices of standard patterns extant in some texts on which others are variations. 'Normality' is relative to a system as a whole and is thus vulnerable to changes within that system; a literary text will in fact—to be deconstructionist about the issue—even shift the norm by virtue of its own existence, for it too is a part of the totality of language. Norms and deviations will exist not only through comparison with the language as a whole, but also through comparison with the expectations and patterns set up by the text itself (Halliday [1964] 1967; Burton 1980:7; Leech and Short 1981: 55–6; Wales 1989:118). The characterization of literariness as a particular use of the code is, moreover, dependent upon showing that such uses do not occur in 'non-literary discourse'. Yet it is not difficult to demonstrate that non-literary discourse is also full of patterning and deviation. Werth (1976) demonstrated as much for a *Sunday Times* article on pest control. (The counter-claim that such instances are merely examples of 'literariness' within non-literary texts is blatantly and hopelessly circular.) It is also true, as Culler has observed (1975b:55–74), that the patterns and deviations discovered by Jakobson are not absolutes, engendered by a total and objective linguistic description, but functions of the linguistic elements he chooses to look for in the first place.

Stylistics and 'representation'

Yet all these objections notwithstanding, it is indisputable that the Jakobsonian approach has spawned a vast number of perceptive and valuable studies of individual works of literature, not only in the many analyses by Jakobson himself but also in the sizeable literature of stylistics which developed during the sixties, seventies, and eighties (see especially Fowler 1966; Fowler 1975; Leech 1969; Widdowson 1975; Ching, Haley, and Lunsford 1980; Leech and Short 1981; Carter 1982a).[20] In the stylistics of this period:

> there is never any real doubt expressed about the fact that in order to write about style in a linguistically justifiable way, we must be able to relate the language used in a text, or by an author, to the conventions of the language as a whole. All practical stylistics papers carry this assumption.
>
> (Burton 1980: 5)

In this respect, stylistics was based upon Jakobsonian premises. The main differences from Jakobsonian analysis are, perhaps, a reluctance to state overtly that literariness can be defined as a feature of the code on the one hand, and a readiness to connect formal linguistic features to interpretations on the other. This latter practice may be summed up by the term 'representation' (Widdowson 1984: 150–60; 1992: 16–31). A simple example would be the claim that a breakdown of normal syntax reflects a breakdown of order in the fictional world or the mind of a character, as it might be said to do, for example, in the novels of William Burroughs. Another example would be to say that the morphemic and tonal alternation of 'see' and 'saw' in the words from Dylan Thomas's *Under Milk Wood* 'see-sawing like the sea' (1954: 7) 'represents' the alternating motion of both a see-saw and the sea, aurally because 'see/sea' is higher than 'saw', and, in meaning, because when there are waves, things appear and disappear: you see them, you saw them . . .

Yet whereas Jakobson was in the habit of listing, with a claim to inclusiveness, the formal patterns and deviations in a work without

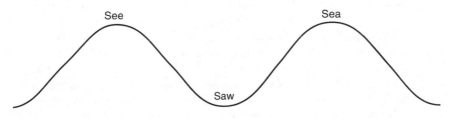

Figure 5.3: 'See-sawing like the sea'

comment, a practitioner of stylistics is more likely to select a few linguistic features and demonstrate their connection to a particular interpretation. This exposes stylistics to the charge that its apparently scientific nature is a sham, that there is no rigorous basis to the selection of features. (For a discussion of this challenge, see Carter 1982b.) It can be said that the interpretation does not derive from the linguistic analysis, but rather that the linguistic analysis is used, *post hoc*, to support an intuitive interpretation (Fish 1980:68–97; 246–68), and that stylistics selects only those texts which bear out its own assumptions. Many of these problems have been more recently acknowledged in stylistics, which, in the seventies and eighties, began to move away from the linguistic emphasis of a Jakobsonian approach and to assimilate a wider view of literature as discourse which must embrace both context and its users (Widdowson 1975; Leech and Short 1981:257–87; Carter 1982b; Carter 1989; Carter and Simpson 1989:1–20; Short 1989c; Short and van Peer 1989; Widdowson 1992). This, it seems, is a wise direction, for the Jakobsonian approach is so rich that it is far better to build upon it, despite its shortcomings, than to reject it out of hand.

Conclusions

For all their limitations, their over-emphases and under-emphases, the contribution of formalism, structuralism, and stylistics to discourse analysis and literary theory remains immense. The single most persistent element in these theories, developed in different ways by structuralism and stylistics, is the formalist notion of 'defamiliarization'.

My aim in the following chapters will be to build upon this notion, and to show how formalist and structuralist ideas may combine with linguistic description on the one hand, and description of world schemata on the other. In doing so, I hope to suggest ways in which defamiliarization may take place, not at one level in isolation, but in their interaction. I shall term such interaction 'discourse deviation'.

Notes

1 Making explicit use of schema theory, de Beaugrande proposes an approach to literature which combines the individual psychology of readers with formal linguistic and textual description. He argues against the abandoning of the quest for a definition of literariness which has resulted from a general disillusion with the Jakobsonian approach, and proposes two principles which he regards as characteristic of all literature. The first principle is that of 'alternativity'. Literature, he argues, allows us to enter alternative worlds in which alternative schemata, including alternative language and text schemata,

are used in processing. These schemata, though similar to those used in the real world, are quite distinct from them. The second principle is that of 'super-coherence'. According to this principle, the details of a literary work all fit together and are components of the schemata which interpret them in a way which is quite unlike the real world. Everything in a literary work is significant. (The paradigm case, he suggests, is the use of detail in the Sherlock Holmes stories.) It may be, he suggests, that the literary text thus compensates for the illogicality, lack of connection, and disorder of the real world. This view echoes Tomashevsky's view that certain motifs (pages 136–7) (and Barthes' view that certain functions) must all contribute to the overall theme (pages 150–2). As Chekov put it: 'there is no point in having a loaded gun on stage unless it is going to go off'.

2 The final section heading 'Cognitive literary scholarship' in Lodge (1988) is, in this respect, misleading.

3 What de Beaugrande (1987:58) describes as the principle of 'alternativity'.

4 He later moved away from these views more voluntarily (Shklovsky 1966:298). Shklovsky was also still publishing and expressing certain aspects of formalist theory, however, in 1940: see the quotation on page 131.

5 Ironically, by these definitions, 'socialist realism' is a misnomer. Rather than distracting from its own devices, it manipulated highly formal conventions, though lacking the impeding of form to promote interest. (In this sense it is itself highly formalist, and arguably owes more to the traditions of Russian orthodox iconography than to either socialism or realism (Achildiev 1989).)

6 For a later Freudian version of this theory see Bloom 1973.

7 Todorov (1966b), incidentally, together with Erlich [1955] 1980, was instrumental in introducing Russian formalist ideas to the West.

8 Grammatically, *The Inheritors* is in the third person. Nevertheless it is very much from Lok's point of view (Halliday 1973:103–38; Black 1993). *What Maisie Knew* is also in the third person, but limited to what Maisie perceives.

9 The examples from Shakespeare are my own, not Tomashevsky's.

10 An interesting parallel could be drawn between these three categories of motivation and Halliday's three functions of language: the ideational, interpersonal, and textual.

11 There is a good deal of controversy over whether Bakhtin was a Marxist or simply paid lip service to Marxist ideas to avoid persecution. If the latter, he was not in any case successful, as he was arrested and exiled for religious activities in 1929. Forgacs (1982:160) assumes that he was a Marxist, as does Bennet (1979: 75–82) and Hymes (1989). Clark and Holquist (1984:38) on the

other hand and Terras (1985:34–6) more convincingly suggest that, though he may have shared some of the anti-capitalist aspirations of the October revolution, he was never a Marxist, and, deeply though warily, anti-Stalinist. Generally, Bakhtin's position remains an enigma. There is a simple explanation of the scholarly controversy. Marxists and non-Marxists, united in their esteem for Bakhtin, both wish to prove that he shared their point of view. For further discussion, see Cook 1994a.

12 See Chaucer (ed. Robinson) [1957] 1966 *Canterbury Tales*: line 1760.

13 This reductionist view of the mind is rejected by AI but accepted by many of its opponents. Searle ([1980] 1987) and Edelman (1992), for example, accept the argument that intelligence is indissolubly wedded to the biology of the human brain.

14 In his autobiography, Buñuel ridicules such attempts to interpret his films (Buñuel [1982] 1983:174, 222). Nevertheless, he and his friends themselves made structuralist analyses of films, constructing grammars predicting likely outcomes (Buñuel [1982] 1983:132).

15 This also applies to mental models theories (Johnson-Laird 1983).

16 Barthes also refers to Tomashevsky's theory of theme and motif ([1966] 1977:89), and there is some connection, though not necessaily a one-to-one equivalence, between his use of the term 'action' and Tomashevsky's 'motif'.

17 Propp's [1928] 1968 use of the term 'function' is closer to Barthes' 'action'. Barthes divides functions into two kinds, 'cardinal functions' which, like Tomashevsky's 'bound motifs', are essential, and 'catalysers', which are not. These are analogous to the obligatory and optional elements of the sentence in grammar. The logic of the level of detail to be included is, therefore, that catalysers must be included, although it may not be immediately evident that they are catalysers. To give an example of my own: in Steven Soderbergh's film *Sex, Lies and Videotape*, one of the characters loses an ear-ring while in bed with her sister's husband. When her sister later finds the ear-ring she takes it as evidence of the adultery. The loss is thus a catalyser, though this is not immediately evident.

18 I regard the parallel development of Jakobson's literary theory and structuralism as essentially distinct, a bifurcation of the formalist legacy; I do this despite the fact that Jakobson's theories are sometimes classed as 'structuralist' (de George and de George 1972) and he himself sometimes worked with more 'mainstream' structuralist analysts (Jakobson and Lévi-Strauss [1962] 1972).

19 For an argument in favour of conceptual representation systems and against Wittgenstein see, for example, Fodor 1976.

20 Throughout this period, there is a growing attention to discoursal as well as linguistic features. Thus, for example, though Leech and Short (1981:1) has, in its own words, 'the same aim' as Leech 1969, it takes more account of discourse and language context. The work which initiated the change of emphasis is Widdowson (1975).

6 Incorporating the reader: Two analyses combining stylistics and schema theory

Introduction

It will be useful at this point to combine the kind of schema theory analysis developed in Chapters 1 and 3 with a more formalist analysis concentrating particularly upon language. In the analyses which follow, I shall first apply the Jakobsonian methodology to two texts: the first an advertisement, the second a poem. For the moment, my analyses ignore the issue of establishing linguistic norms and deviations, and assume this to be unproblematic. I then contrast these stylistic analyses with descriptions in terms of interpretative schemata. By so doing, I hope to illustrate some of the strengths and weaknesses of the two approaches and also ways in which they interact.

Text Three: 'Elizabeth Taylor's Passion' (advertisement)

The nine-word text in the advertisement (Figure 6.1) contains an extraordinarily concentrated exploitation of every linguistic level, in a way which not only reinforces and represents the message, but, in the best traditions of stylistics, is inseparable from, and identical to it. It is a gift to formal stylistic analysis, and, if such matters were simply quantifiable—a ratio of stylistic points to words—would be a great lyric poem.

Graphology

On a graphic level, the varying lengths of the four lines allow the text to reproduce iconically the hexagonal shape of the perfume bottle which is pictured below it. In this way, the advertisement makes use of a graphological device which is occasionally—though sporadically—used in poetry (van Peer 1993). (Each stanza of George Herbert's 'Easter Wings' for example represents the shape of an angel's wings; Lewis Carroll's 'Mouse's Tale' in *Alice in Wonderland* is written in the shape of a mouse's tail; Apollinaire has 'Calligrammes' whose letters picture their subject: a mirror, a train, a night sky, falling rain.)

Figure 6.1: Advertisement for Elizabeth Taylor's Passion

Phonology

In a Jakobsonian view, the patterning of stressed and unstressed syllables to create rhythm, and of phonemes to create rhyme, alliteration, consonance, assonance, and the other sound effects of verse, is at once both a deviation from the code and an imposition of order upon it. It is a deviation—the argument goes—because in other more 'normal' uses of the code, where the focus is on meaning rather than form, such sound effects occur at random. It is an imposition of order because it enables the language to be analysed by a set of prosodic rules which, like the rules of phonology, grammar, and semantics, can both predict and restrict possibilities.

Leaving these arguments temporarily aside, and assuming that phonic regularity is unusual, literary, and a feature of text, the stress patterns of the advertisement are as follows:[1]

⌣ / ⌣ ⌣ / ⌣ ⌣ / ⌣ ⌣ / ⌣

Be touched by | the fragrance | that touches | the woman

The rhythm, in other words, is absolutely regular. It consists of four amphibrachs: a metrical unit comprising a single stressed syllable between two unstressed syllables. And as an amphibrach has the quality of being the same backwards and forwards, it follows that a succession of an equal number of amphibrachs can be divided into two halves, of which the second half is a reversal, an exact mirror image, of the first. The name

⌣ / ⌣ ⌣ / ⌣

Eliza | beth Taylor

moreover, is also amphibrachic, and the rhythm of the advertisement thus mimics the name of the product, in much the same way as its shape reproduces the shape of the bottle.

Lexis

The advertisement exploits lexical ambiguity, both at the relatively fixed semantic level of denotation, and at the discoursal level of meaning in context. Thus, at the semantic level, 'touches' means both 'to bring or be brought into physical contact with' and also 'to arouse positive emotion'. 'Woman' means both 'adult, female, human being' and also 'femininity' (as it does in a sentence like 'It brings out the woman in you'). Both of these lexical items, when taken in the context of the pictorial part of the advertisement, and in the context of its function of persuading a reader to buy a product, take on further meaning. The noun phrase 'the woman', with its definite article assuming a specific identifiable referent, can now mean either 'the woman in the picture' (i.e. Elizabeth Taylor) or 'the woman reading the advertisement' (i.e. you, the reader), and in fact invites the reader to identify with Elizabeth Taylor, presumably on the assumption that readers will wish to take on certain of her qualities. Here the advertisement makes use of a common discoursal ambiguity in advertising whereby the second person pronoun is used to refer to both the addressee, the reader, and also to a character in the advertisement. (Something similar occurs in songs, for example: 'Well it ain't no use to sit and wonder why babe/ If you don't know by now' (Bob Dylan).) A further complication is introduced by the fact that the reader may be a potential buyer of the product for somebody else, rather than for personal use. Indeed, luxury items such as perfumes are often bought as presents—hence their intensive advertising in the weeks before Christmas. As perfume is often a token of sexual attraction, and as advertisements seem to assume an exclusively heterosexual world, the targeted reader may also be a man, buying it for a woman (Cook 1992: 103). Thus 'the woman' comes to mean 'your actual or desired female partner' and 'touches' appeals to the reader by suggesting a means—albeit vicarious—of emotionally or physically touching the desired person. In this case 'the woman' may perhaps even take on an extra dimension of meaning: 'the female part', 'the vagina'. Interestingly, these latter discoursal ambiguities are only present when the text is read as an advertisement. They are not formal features of text, in the Jakobsonian sense.

Grammar

Grammatically, as well as phonically, the text is both deviant and patterned. Using the nul sign '$\emptyset$' to mark the ellipsis of the pronoun 'you', its grammatical structure may be analysed as:

$_{MCl}$[$\emptyset$ (Be touched) (by (the fragrance $_{RCl}$[(that) (touches) (the woman)]))]

The deviance is in the use of the passive imperative, an exceedingly rare form. ('Be seated' is an exception, but 'be kissed', 'be killed', 'be seen', 'be amused', would be similarly odd.) The patterning is in the clause structure, for the relative clause which postmodifies the noun 'fragrance' exactly reverses the main clause of which 'fragrance' is a part. Indeed, if we write in the ellipted 'you' as 'you, the woman' and replace the relative pronoun 'that' by the noun it stands for ('the fragrance'), then the relative clause is a back transformation of the passive main clause to its active form:

[Woman, be touched by the fragrance] is a transform of
[The woman is touched by the fragrance] is a transform of
[The fragrance touches the woman]

This is odd, because the usual function of a relative clause, as of any modifier, is to add information which will help identify the referent of the head word. Here the relative clause simply repeats the meaning of the main clause. This creates a grammatical mirror image. The embedded relative clause reflects the main clause, as illustrated in Figure 6.2.

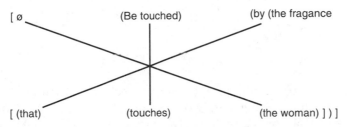

[ø   (Be touched)   (by (the fragance

[(that)   (touches)   (the woman)])]

Figure 6.2: Grammatical parallelism in Text Three

The break between the two clauses coincides with the half-way point in the rhythm which is also reversed after the half-way point. The grammar is mimed by the sound which mimes the grammar—(to use the same device myself). The woman is touched by the perfume which touches the woman.

Representation

The language of this advertisement, then, reveals regularities, similarities, ambiguities, and polysemies of the kind revealed by classic Jakobsonian analyses. The point is, however, that it is not difficult, in the traditions of stylistics, to go further than mere formal analysis and suggest ways in which these exploitations of the code reinforce, amplify, and add to the meaning in ways which would be lost if paraphrased. Taking this even further, the specific linguistic choices of the advertisement may be seen as creating a unique meaning which cannot be separated from its form. The reader is invited to become like Elizabeth Taylor through the use of a bottle of perfume. Perfume as a substance which, when used for seduction, enables the wearer, after the initial adornment, to attract by doing nothing more, is concerned with an unusual relationship of passivity and activity. (Note also that the active clause is subordinate to the passive clause.) It is also, as something used before the mirror in the privacy of the bathroom or bedroom, concerned with narcissism, reflection, and contemplation of the self. It is also, being bodiless and verbally indefinable, akin to an abstract concept, while being simultaneously, as something sexually attractive and perceptible at the most intimate distances, inherently sensual and physical, concerned both with romantic and with sexual love. In this perfume advertisement, as in many others, the perfume is seen, not as attractive in itself, but as something which releases a dormant attractiveness in the wearer. All of these features may be related to the linguistic features described above: the imitation of the bottle's shape by the graphic form and of the filmstar's name by the prosodic unit, the reversible rhythm and grammatical structure, the ambiguous lexis denoting both the physical and abstract, the confusion of referents, the embedding of the active within the passive, the redundancy of meaning.

Schemata

So far, following Jakobson, I have analysed the formal sub-sentential features of the advertisement. No mention has been made of the plans or the goals of the author, the character (Elizabeth Taylor), or the reader. Yet, for the advertisement to function as a coherent communicative act rather than to be merely a superfluous and meaningless (if grammatical) bit of text, certain themes and plans must be recognized by the reader, if only subconsciously. At this level there is even less certainty than there can be concerning norms of language and significant deviations. Allowing for the usual fuzziness in distinguishing themes, plans, and scripts, I interpret relevant schemata to be:

Π   A   SELL PRODUCT
Π   A   ATTRACT ATTENTION
Π   A   SUGGEST PERFUME FULFILS Π R

Π   C   (LIZ TAYLOR) BE ATTRACTIVE
Π   C   (LIZ TAYLOR) BE SUCCESSFUL
Π   C   (LIZ TAYLOR) WEAR PASSION PERFUME (already executed)

Π   R   (FEMALE) BE ATTRACTIVE
Π   R   (FEMALE) BE FEMININE
Π   R   (FEMALE) OBTAIN SEXUAL SATISFACTION
Π   R   (FEMALE) IMITATE ATTRACTIVE WOMEN (LIKE LIZ TAYLOR)
$S R   (FEMALE) WEARING PERFUME

Π   R   (MALE) OBTAIN SEXUAL SATISFACTION
Π   R   (MALE) TOUCH WOMAN
Π   R   (MALE) BUY PERFUME
Π   R   (MALE) GIVE PERFUME

No explicit mention of these plans and themes is made in the text, and in asserting them I can appeal only to my own intuition and cultural knowledge, though this is likely to be shared by other readers. This is in the advertiser's favour, for should he or she wish to deny the interpretative use of such themes and plans, it is very hard to prove their existence. (This avenue of retreat is often to deny sexual suggestiveness in advertisements, by attributing it to one reader's mind.) Yet it may be safe to assume that readers with a similar cultural background will have the same intuitions about how the advertisement works. In fact, it is the advertiser's assumption that receivers share and recognize these themes and are susceptible to the suggestion that they may be fulfilled by buying the perfume, which enables them to go unsaid. They are—in every sense—schematic, stereotypical, and predictable.

Conclusions

I hope to have shown that, in this text, the formalist notion of defamiliarization operates only at the linguistic level, not at the schematic and discoursal level. In so far as this text is classified as an advertisement and not as a work of literature, that classification appears to view the schematic level as more important. This judgement, however, will vary with the schemata of the reader.

A way of avoiding this conclusion would be to say that the defining feature of advertisements in terms of the six Jakobsonian functions[2] is that the conative function (see pages 37–40) is the dominant one. In contradiction of this, I would argue that the conative function also involves reader interpretation and is thus also schematic. It is also vulnerable to changes outside the text. If the product ceases to be available for purchase, the conative function will be invalidated, though the advertisement may endure (Cook 1988).

Text Four: 'First World War Poets' by Edward Bond

You went to the front like sheep   1
And bleated at the pity of it
In academies that smell of abattoirs
Your poems are still studied

You turned the earth to mud   5
Yet complain you drowned in it
Your generals were dug in at the rear
Degenerates drunk on brandy and prayer
You saw the front—and only bleated
The pity!   10

You survived
Did you burn your general's houses

Loot the new millionaires?
No, you found new excuses
You'd lost an arm or your legs   15
You sat by the empty fire
And hummed music hall songs

Why did your generals send you away to die?
They saw a Great War coming
Between masters and workers   20
In their own land
So they herded you over the cliffs to be rid of you
How they hated you while you lived!
How they wept for you once you were dead!

What did you fight for?   25
A new world?
No—an old world already in ruins!
Your children?
Millions of your children died
Because you fought for your enemies   30
And not against them!

We will not forget!
We will not forgive!

To many readers who value and admire both the lives and the poetry
of the First World War poets, this poem is likely, and no doubt
calculated, to cause offence and outrage, and this reaction in turn will
lead to a strong rejection of any claim that it is literary. Indeed, a
colleague whom I consulted over this analysis felt moved, on every
occasion we discussed it, to voice his deeply-felt disgust with it, and
deny its status as a poem. Yet these feelings (with which, to some
extent, I am in sympathy) may aid my purpose here. It is precisely as a
text whose literary status is in doubt, that this poem, like the perfume
advertisement, is of particular interest. If the appellation 'literary'
functions largely to indicate approval, then the reader's agreement or
disagreement with the views expressed are likely to be crucial. If, on the
other hand, as the formalists claimed, 'literary' is a term for discourse
which defamiliarizes through the manipulation of form, then the case
may remain open. Certainly, by violently contradicting views which are
deeply ingrained and treasured by many readers, it sets out to disturb.
But then so does mere abuse which focuses on what is most valued by
the abused. It is the manner rather than the fact of the challenge which
is my concern.

Yet the form of this poem seems also markedly 'unliterary'. Arguably,
it is, both linguistically and schematically, the polar opposite of the

perfume advertisement analysed above. Linguistically conformist and unoriginal, it is innovative and disruptive at both the text-structural and conceptual levels. (Again, these judgements are those of one reader—the present writer—but assumed to hold for some other readers, on the assumption that certain schemata are shared.) My argument is that this text is literary without being linguistically deviant or patterned, while the previous text is not literary, despite a significant concentration of both patterning and deviation. As such, my argument can be instantly demolished by the claim that this is 'not literary' or 'not a poem'. Against this I can say only that it is presented as a poem by writer and publisher (in the 'poems' section of a book entitled *Theatre Poems and Songs*) and that this classification is accepted by bookshops and literature courses. It is also graphologically set out as a poem in that line breaks are an intrinsic part of the text and do not depend on the width of the page, and lines are grouped into stanzas. There is also an absence of conventional punctuation, fairly common in twentieth-century poetry. Thus, though there may well be readers who reject its pretensions to be poetry, I shall proceed as though (and indeed I believe that) it is.

To say, as I do of this text, that a stretch of language shows no significant deviation or patterning, is open to challenge from two directions. It assumes, first of all, consensus about linguistic norms, where no absolute consensus exists. Secondly, it is a negative claim, and thus hard to demonstrate, being vulnerable to refutation. Nevertheless, it seems reasonable. As with the advertisement for Elizabeth Taylor's Passion, I shall, following Jakobson, assume the issue of linguistic norms to be relatively unproblematic.

Graphology and phonology

On the graphological level, the only features of note are those already mentioned above: the conventional lineation and stanza divisions of poetry, and the absence of conventional punctuation. On the phonic level, there is little regularity. Line by line, the syllable count is as follows: 7, 9, 11, 7; 6, 7, 9, 10, 9, 3; 3, 8, 6, 7, 7, 7, 6; 11, 7, 7, 4, 14, 8, 9; 5, 3, 10, 3, 6, 9, 5; 5, 5. Although there is a tendency towards six- and seven-syllable lines, there are many other lengths too. Similarly, though there are lines which fall into metrical patterns reminiscent of more conventional poetry

   ˘   /   ˘   /   ˘   /
You turned the earth to mud
   ˘ ˘   /   ˘   /   ˘ ˘
Yet complain you drowned in it

the effect is immediately broken:

   ˘   / ˘   ˘   ˘   / / ˘ ˘ /
Your generals were dug in at the rear
˘ / ˘ ˘ / ˘ / ˘ ˘ /
Degenerates drunk on brandy and prayer

There is no rhyme except the (possibly accidental) half rhyme in lines 7 and 8 between 'rear' and 'prayer', perhaps in lines 12 and 14 between 'houses' and 'excuses', and the internal echo between 'generals' and 'degenerates' in lines 7 and 8.

The overall effect is thus of language whose phonic regularity is no greater than that of discourse types (for example bureaucratic prose) where attention is traditionally supposed to be on meaning rather than sound, and less than that of other discourse types excluded from the literary canon such as advertisements, prayers, football chants, etc. Arguably, however, there is just enough patterning—in syllables, prosody, and rhyme—for expectations to be set up and immediately dashed: a feature which is reinforced by the contrast between the traditionally 'poetic' graphology and the lack of 'poetic' phonology. That, at least, is how it seems to me.

Grammar

The grammar of the poem, like its phonology, seems pointedly 'unpoetic'. Occasional glimpses of patterning or 'poetic' syntax serve only to highlight their absence elsewhere. For example there is a degree of parallelism between sentences beginning with the subject 'you'. There is also parallelism in the two lines:

How they hated you while you lived!
How they wept over you once you were dead.

which both follow the pattern:

$_{\text{MC1}}[\ _{\text{AvP}}(\text{How}) \ _{\text{NP}}^{\text{S}}(\text{they}) \ ^{\text{P}}(\text{PAST}) \ _{\text{NP}}^{\text{Od}}(\text{you}) \ _{\text{ACl}}[\ _{\text{cj}}(\text{TEMPORAL}) \ _{\text{NP}}^{\text{S}}(\text{you}) \ ^{\text{P}}(\text{PAST})]]$

This adjective phrase 'dead', though it has no syntactic parallel with the preceding line, is semantically linked to 'lived'. Such parallelism is, however, often found in political rhetoric, a discourse type with which this polemical diatribe, by virtue of its subject matter, has much in common. There is also fronting of a prepositional-phrase adjunct in lines three and four—a construction much favoured in poetry. Interestingly, this comes, like the syllabic and prosodic patterning referred to above, near the beginning of the poem, and thus establishes a hint of convention, making its later absence more marked.

Given the length of the poem (186 words), however, syntactic patterning and deviation are not intense, especially when compared with that in the advertisement (nine words).

Lexis and metaphor

The lexis is 'ordinary' rather than 'poetic'. Almost the only lexical cohesion of note is the lexical chain created by the sustained metaphor of sheep: 'like sheep', 'bleated', 'abattoirs', 'bleated', 'herded'. But this comparison is a cliché: a fact which, paradoxically, makes it deviant in poetry, where, traditionally, clichés are avoided. In poetry, comparisons like the following (from Craig Raine's poem 'The Behaviour of Dogs'), are in fact far more 'normal':

Their feet are four-leafed clovers
that leave a jigsaw in the dust.

They grin like Yale keys that tease
us with joke shop Niagara tongues

The only other metaphor in Bond's poem is another standard one—that of drowning in mud—about which I have more to say below.

Intertextuality

Poor in prosodic, grammatical, lexical, and metaphorical innovation, the poem is rich in intertextual meanings. These, like schemata, must be described with a specified reader or group of readers in mind. At this point it is necessary to become personal, especially as this is a poem written by, and perhaps primarily for, members of the post-war generation in Britain. I am such a reader myself, and I assume that there are several allusions which will be shared by others like me. The intertextual allusions which I have noticed are listed in Table 6.1 (overleaf). For other readers there may well be more or less, and the effect of the poem may be quite different.

Schemata

Here again, hypotheses must relate to particular readers. Let us specify, then, British readers who received a Christian education during the twenty-five years following the Second World War. For these readers, a good deal of time and emotional intensity was devoted to:

—study of the First World War poets (especially Wilfred Owen)
—study of the New Testament (in the Authorized or Revised Standard version)

Evoked reference	'Trigger' in poem
'My subject is war and the pity of war.' Wilfred Owen ([1920] 1931:40)	'bleated at the pity of it' 'only bleated/ The pity!' (lines 2, 9–10)
'He was brought as a lamb to the slaughter.' (Isaiah 53:7)	'like sheep . . . abattoirs' (lines 1,3)
'Guttering choking drowning' (Wilfred Owen: *Dulce et Decorum Est*'	'You turned the earth to mud/ Yet complain you drowned in it' (lines 5–6)
'The whole herd rushed down the steep bank into the lake and died in the water.' (Matthew 8:28–32)	'they herded you over the cliffs to be rid of you' (line 22)
'We will remember them.' (Laurence Binyon: 'For the Fallen')	'We will not forget!' (line 32)
'Then Jesus said, Father forgive them for they know not what they do.' (Luke 23:34)	'We will not forgive' (line 33)
'Father forgive.' 'Lest we forget.' (On war memorials)	

Table 6.1: Intertextuality in Text Four

—an annual Remembrance Service
—study of nineteenth- and early twentieth-century poetry.

We can therefore hypothesize that, for such readers, the intertextual references listed above will evoke the following schemata. In fact, it was the intention of the educators of that time to inculcate such schemata. For each schema, I give only a selection of default elements.

Θ R/C/A MAKE LIFE BETTER

$S R FIRST WORLD WAR

In execution of (misguided) plans: Π BRITAIN DEFEND EMPIRE; Π BRITAIN HELP FUTURE GENERATIONS; Π BRITAIN BUILD 'NEW WORLD'.
Events: Slaughter of young men; maiming of young men.
Results: Sympathy for veterans/invalids; war poetry (see $S WAR POETRY); Second World War; Π AVOID REPETITION.

$S R WAR POETRY

Track 1: 'patriotic' poets: Rupert Brooke, Laurence Binyon, and others.
Track 2: 'anti-war' poets: Wilfred Owen, Siegfried Sassoon, and others.
ARE sensitive, brave, good, wasted.

Events: writing poetry about $S A FIRST WORLD WAR.
Results: Sympathy for soldiers, 'Anti-war' feelings.

Π R STUDY 'ANTI-WAR' POETRY
Result: helps prevent war.

Π R REMEMBER WAR DEAD
Result: helps prevent war.

Π R FORGIVE ENEMIES
Result: brings reward, makes life better.

Π R MAKE SACRIFICES
Result: better society.

$S R POETRY (A TEXT/ LANGUAGE SCHEMA)
HAS rhythm, rhyme, and other sound effects, elevated language, figurative language, original language.

The poem challenges every element in the scripts and plans (as I have described them), its poets and their poetry, and the efficacy of remembrance. It also represents (in the sense defined above) a contradiction of $S R POETRY. In formalist terms it defamiliarizes received ideas of war, war poetry, and poetry in general. Thus, possibly, it suggests a connection between the conventions of poetry, the conventional philosophy of proponents of war, and conventional anti-war views. It acts out, in its own poetic form (or lack of it), the revolution which it advocates in the political sphere. Yet, paradoxically, it also very obviously, and presumably self-consciously, does what it criticizes — 'bleats' and does not act. In this sense it is iconic and self-reflexive.

The literariness of this poem can not then be described in simple Jakobsonian terms as a deviation from linguistic norms, or as a patterning of elements which would otherwise occur at random. In fact in purely textual terms it is singularly lacking in linguistic interest. Only with reference to schemata (including text and language schemata), can an argument be made for its literariness at all. Interestingly, one of the schemata it breaks is precisely that which demands that literary language be innovative.

Incorporating the reader

The analyses on pages 161–7 and 167–73 point clearly to the limitations of Jakobson's attempt to identify and characterize 'literariness' at the linguistic level in isolation. The density of formal patterning and deviation in the advertisement will not raise it, in most people's estimation, into the literary canon. The poem, by contrast, lacks formal patterning and deviation, yet may still be regarded as literary. Whether it is so regarded will depend upon the reader, and it is precisely the kind of poem which, because of its viewpoint and technique, will arouse very different judgements. Such judgements will vary with the political outlook, world and text schemata of the reader, and the degree to which the attempted disruption of them is valued. On the other hand, both the advertisement and the poem are vulnerable to reclassification as audiences change. It is not difficult, in the contemporary world, to imagine a readership which might reclassify both.

   This reader-dependency of 'literariness' was overlooked by Jakobson, despite the fact that the terms in which he chose to express his theory imply very strongly the presence of the reader. If language has a poetic 'function' then it must *do* something *to somebody*—the reader—and if that function reflects a 'set towards the message', then it must be a 'set' *by somebody*—again the reader. Unlike the Jakobsonian approach, much recent literary theory has shown acute awareness of reader variations, and their effect on interpretation. Dimensions of inter-individual difference (such as class, gender, culture, age, and education) have been brought to the fore, as have intra-individual differences (such as mood, the context and purpose of reading, and age). While rejecting formalist, structuralist, and New Critical approaches to reader variation (see Wimsatt [1949] 1954), this reader-centred movement can point to the centrality of the reader in much older approaches. The Aristotelian view of tragedy, for example, is couched in terms of effect upon the reader, while Wordsworth's view of poetry as 'heightened sensation' or Coleridge's dictum of the 'suspension of disbelief' both appeal to the relation of reader and text, rather than to features of text in isolation. In the 1920s and 1930s, I. A. Richards stressed 'response' to poetry, though only the response, as he termed it, 'of the right kind of reader' (Richards 1926:10). This last remark betrays a confident belief in the reading of the academic establishment as the correct reading, privileging one group of readers over others, bestowing on it a right to 'correct' the 'wrong' readings of others (Richards 1929). It is a view still present, half a century later, in Culler's notion of 'literary competence', an ability (analogous to Chomsky's linguistic competence) which can, and in Culler's view should, be transmitted institutionally (Culler 1975b:113–31; 1988:3–57). These approaches accept and justify the critical *status quo*. Other approaches to the reader, however, influenced by the deconstructionist attack upon all centres and 'transcendental signifiers', have emphasized the equality of all readings, or tried to shift the centre from one social group to another: from the middle to the working class, or from a patriarchal to a feminist readership.

   The diversity of reader-centred approaches is thus vast, both synchronically and diachronically, and it is not my intention to attempt to survey them. From among the many reader-centred approaches, I shall isolate two contradictory tendencies relevant to my own discussion. The first tendency is one which seeks to incorporate reader variation as an element in the construction of discourse, but regards the reader's response as delimited by the nature of the text in question. The second, influenced by deconstruction, is one which rejects the existence of autonomous text, reversing the apparent direction of communication from author through text to reader, and regarding text and even author as the creation of the reader. This second view rejects—often ingeniously, sometimes playfully—the approaches of discourse analysis, formalism, structuralism, and linguistics. These two opposing approaches to the role of the reader are well summed up by the debate between Wolfgang Iser and Stanley Fish. The former approach likens the perception of text to the perception of stars in the sky: 'Two people gazing at the night sky may both be looking at the same collection of stars, but one will see the image of the plough, and the other will make out a dipper. The "stars" in a literary text are fixed; the lines that join them are variable' (Iser 1974: 282). The latter approach is summarized by Fish's rejoinder to this analogy in which he claims that the reader supplies 'everything: the stars in a literary text are not fixed; they are just as variable as the lines that join them' (Fish 1981:7). This leads Fish (1980:21–58) to attack both linguistics and formal stylistics, suggesting a new 'affective stylistics'[3] which will replace the traditional dichotomies such as text/reader and subject/object with a monistic view in which there is no text separate from the reader (Fish 1972). Even 'linguistic fact' such as parallelism is, in Fish's view, interpretation. (We shall return to this in more detail when discussing an example of Fish's rejection of stylistics on pages 214–16.)

Iser, and other 'reception theorists', on the other hand, though they emphasize both the reader and the process of reading over the text and the product of reading, are prepared to accept text as a component in the reading process. In this they trace their roots back to the work of the Polish literary theorist Roman Ingarden, and particularly to his book *The Literary Work of Art* published in 1931. As Ingarden's work and its continuation in reception theory has certain elements in common with the approach I am advocating, I shall give a brief outline of it here as it is expressed in this most influential work. I shall regard reception theory—despite the many other influences upon it—as, fundamentally, a continuation of his work.

Roman Ingarden's *The Literary Work of Art*

Ingarden was a pupil of the phenomenologist Husserl. In this he shares a common influence with the Gestalt tradition in psychology, in which his contemporary Bartlett developed the first ideas of schema theory. In fact Ingarden even uses the word 'schema', though in a rather different sense to Bartlett.[4] (Both Bartlett and Ingarden had perhaps inherited the term indirectly from Kant.)

In Ingarden's view: 'What is essential and valuable in the literary work of art is considered to be what develops in the reader under the influence of the reading' (op.cit.: 18–19) and 'what develops in the reader' is the product of four strata. The first of these is the stratum of 'word sounds' and 'phonetic formations' and the higher orders built upon them. The second stratum is that of 'meaning units'. The third that of 'schematized aspects of the text' and the fourth that of 'represented objectivities'. The first two of these strata essentially encompass, though in less detail, the area marked out by modern linguistics, and acknowledge the objectivity of the text (though Ingarden worked outside the Saussurean tradition, and was also dismissive of the formalists (Grabwicz 1973: xv)). With an argument which could be used against Fish today, Ingarden simply observes that if there were no shared intermediate level between substance and reader, then every copy of a book would be a different text (op. cit.: 12). Thus: 'One may not [. . .] foist upon the literary work various objects which are altogether foreign to it [. . .] the view that the literary work is nothing but a manifold of experiences felt by the reader during the reading is [. . .] false and its consequence absurd' (op.cit.: 15).

In explaining the third stratum, that of 'schematized aspects', Ingarden employs Gestalt and phenomenological theories of perception, observing that in perceiving something, we never see it in totality, but only 'aspects' of it, which we combine to make a 'concretization' of the experience (op.cit.: 255–64). To make this concretization we make use of existing 'represented objectivities', previous experiences of the same or similar experiences. It is the same, in his view, with reading. The discourse presents meaning units provided by the first two strata, in such numbers and combinations that they enable the reader to make 'individual concretizations' (op.cit.: 265). Thus if, for example, the action of a novel takes place in Rome, the reader will provide details from a 'represented objectivity' of the real Rome (op.cit.: 30).[5] Successful 'concretization' thus depends on the representation of previous experience and, in this sense, Ingarden's theory resembles schema theory.[6] Similar ideas can be seen in later developments of 'reception theory', most especially in the notion of 'the horizon of expectations':[7] 'an intersubjective system or structure of expectations, a 'system of references' or a mind-set that a hypothetical individual might bring to any text' (Holub 1984: 59).

What is inspiring in Ingarden's work, however, is its attempt, for all its many omissions and obscurities, to present a balanced and holistic view of the literary work, which neither excludes the individual reader nor denies the text. His arguments against both extremes are as valid today as they were fifty years ago. Like schema theory, with which they have a good deal in common, these arguments have undergone a long period of eclipse before resurfacing again in recent decades. There is not space here to explore contemporary versions of these theories in full, but I recognize here the similarity of the endeavour, and the following words of Ingarden's sum up very well the kind of approach to which I adhere in the next two chapters: 'only a detailed analysis of both the individual strata and the kind of connection arising from them can disclose the peculiar structure of the literary work' (op.cit.:33).

Notes

1 This is how I perceive them. Contrary to Fish (1980:309), who argues that even features such as alliteration are put into a poem by the reader, I believe that other English-speaking readers would perceive these stress patterns in the same way.
2 See Figure 2.2.
3 Making a positive use of the term used so disparagingly by Wimsatt ([1949] 1954) when he coined the phrase 'affective fallacy'.
4 'Here we see once again that a literary work is a schematic formation. In order to see this, however, it is necessary to apprehend the work in its schematized nature and not confuse it with the individual concretization that arises in individual readings' (op.cit.:265).
5 It is this process, which in Ingarden's view leads to a 'characteristically pulsating mode of experiencing' literature (op.cit.:269), 'as one reads, objects appear vividly only from time to time in momentarily actualised aspects' (op.cit.:268).
6 The similarities between Ingarden's views and those of schema theorists like Bartlett should be clear from the above. The terminology, however, is confusing. 'Schemata' in my sense correspond most closely to Ingarden's 'represented objectivities', while in my terms Ingarden's 'schematized aspects' are best described as discourse features triggering schemata in the reader.
7 'The horizon of expectations' also derives from Gadamer (see pages 51–3, and Holub (1984:58–63)).

PART TWO

7 A theory of discourse deviation: schema refreshment and cognitive change

Introduction: the argument so far

Part One has surveyed ideas from three fields—discourse analysis, schema theory, and literary theory—and has attempted to describe both the contribution they may make to a characterization of literary discourse, and their shortcomings. Chapter 2, on discourse analysis, examined approaches to discourse in general, while also noting some of the features of literary discourse not easily accounted for. Chapter 3 described in detail one version of schema theory, and Chapter 4, through the detailed analysis of two texts, suggested that a difference between discourse types may reside in the types of schemata they evoke and the relationships between them.

Both the discourse-analysis and the AI approaches, however, have a tendency to regard schemata as static representations brought to bear upon text, and neglect ways in which certain texts may rebound upon the schemata used to interpret them, leaving those schemata radically altered. It is here that the Russian formalist notion of defamiliarization can make a crucial contribution to a theory of the relation between literary text and reader's mind and, with this in view, Chapter 5 examined this characterization of literary discourse, and some of its descendants, in detail.

The three main levels at which this defamiliarization may take place are those of language, text, and sense perception. Bringing different terminologies together, these levels can be referred to as those of *language schemata*, *text schemata*, and *world schemata* (though the last of these may be derived from discourse as well as perception). The Russian formalists concentrated most of their attention on how discourse as a whole may disrupt expectations, but the post-formalist 'scientific' approach to literary discourse divided into two, with each direction concentrating upon one level of the literary work in isolation. The structuralist approach, treating discourses as products rather than processes, concentrated upon conformities and deviations from postulated text structures, without reference to reader variation or linguistic realization. The Jakobsonian and stylistics approach, on the other hand, concentrated upon linguistic form below the sentence, attempting to characterize literariness as patterning and deviation at this level only, again without reference to reader variation. We have, then, three emphases: on the world (whether observed directly or through discourse), on text structure, and on language.

The two analyses in Chapter 6 attempted to demonstrate the weaknesses of the Jakobsonian approach in isolation, and the greater power of a linguistic description working in concert with a description related to certain reader-specific schemata. The formal approach, in other words, should not be abandoned, but supplemented by some description of the reader. Sadly, however, existing approaches which do take more account of the reader are often marked either by a rejection or an ignorance of linguistics, discourse analysis, and other formal descriptions of text (including, by implication, AI text theory).

Against this background, this chapter attempts to bring together insights from the various approaches described so far, and to propose a theory of literariness as a dynamic interaction between linguistic and text-structural form on the one hand, and schematic representations of the world on the other, whose overall result is to bring about a change in the schemata of the reader. I shall call this dynamic interaction 'discourse deviation'. The aim is to use schema theory as a way of taking account of reader variation and non-linguistic knowledge, though without abandoning the insights and descriptive apparatus provided by discourse analysis, formalism, structuralism, and Jakobsonian stylistics. In particular, I wish to suggest that in certain types of discourse, change in high-level schemata takes place through linguistic and text-structural deviation, but that (as is the case in many advertisements) such deviation is no guarantee of such change. This approach, however, of its nature, can never assign the quality of 'literariness', once and for all, to a given text, but only to a given discourse: to a text, in other words, in interaction with a particular reader.

The need for schema change

In Chapter 4, I tried to demonstrate that schemata are an essential element in the establishment of coherence. We need schemata in order to understand discourse. Yet as well as helping understanding, schemata may also hinder and prevent understanding if they are too inflexible. It seems reasonable to say that human beings need to adapt to new situations, to experiment with new possibilities, and that rigid, unchanging schemata would not always be helpful.

So far, the description of schema theory has emphasized the role of schemata in creating coherence during the processing of texts. The influence described has been one-way. Schemata have been represented as relatively fixed structures acting upon texts to create discourse. There is, however, another side to this process. Texts may change schemata.

The interaction may not be one-way, but reciprocal and dynamic. While any interaction with new experience or text may be of this kind, and may effect changes in schemata while simultaneously using them in processing, there may also be experiences and discourses whose primary function[1] is to alter schemata, making the mind better equipped for processing in future. A particular relation between schemata on the one hand, and language and text structure on the other, may effect exactly this kind of change. Many works which are regarded as literary may stimulate this kind of relation. Furthermore, it seems reasonable to suppose that discourse which functions in this way should not be intimately concerned with other functions of language such as efficient co-operation in manipulation of the physical world, or the establishment and maintenance of social relationships. When these functions are dominant, it may be better to keep to established patterns rather than experiment with new ones. (Repairing the brakes on a car or greeting an old friend are not times to try out new procedures.) Thus a type of discourse removed from immediate practical and social functions is best suited to changing schemata.

Prelude to the theory: earlier accounts of schema change

Before proceeding with my own theory, I shall discuss the approach to schema change in the works of the two major schema theorists, Bartlett and Schank, while also noting two important weaknesses in their approach. These weaknesses are: the failure to take account of the effect on schemata of different linguistic and text-structural arrangements of the 'same' conceptual 'content'; the failure to comment on the existence of discourse types whose primary function may be to effect changes in schemata.[2]

'Turning round upon' schemata: Bartlett (1932)

Awareness of a need to describe a dynamic and reciprocal interaction between schemata and new experience, so that both process each other, is present in Bartlett's seminal work *Remembering* (1932). Though in general concerned to show the role of schemata in the processing of new experience, whether textual or sensory, Bartlett at several points voices an engaging awareness of his theory's need to account for influence in the opposite direction (the effect of experience on schemata), and of its inadequacy in this respect.[3]

Drawing together the findings of his research into a 'theory of remembering' (1932: 197–215), he voices constant concern about the rigid temporal sequencing of events in schemata as he describes them. (His theory contains no Schankian hierarchy which will enable an intelligence to connect one schema to another through a schema at a higher node, thus jumping over schemata at the same or intermediate levels (see Figure 7.1).) His comments on this type of rigidity apply to a non-hierarchical schema theory in general, not only to the issue of temporal sequencing. These comments are so much to my present purpose, and so emblematic of the concerns I wish to pursue in this chapter, that they are worth quoting here at length:

> In remembering, we appear to be dominated by particular past events which are more or less dated, or placed, in relation to other associated particular events. (. . .) If only the organism could hit upon a way of turning round upon its own schemata and making them objects of its reactions. . .
> (Bartlett 1932:202)

> An organism has somehow to acquire the capacity to turn round upon its own schemata and to construct them afresh. This is a crucial step in organic development. It is where and why consciousness comes in; it is what gives consciousness its most prominent function. I wish I knew exactly how it was done.
> (ibid.:206)

> To break away from [the immediately preceding reaction or experience] the 'schema' must become, not merely something that works the organism, but something with which the organism can work. (. . .) its constituents may perhaps begin to be reshuffled on a basis of purely physical or physiological determinants. This method is not radical enough. So the organism discovers how to turn round upon its own schemata, or, in other words, it becomes conscious.
> (ibid.:208)

And Bartlett concludes this section with a question:

> How are our active organized settings, our schemata, developed?
> (ibid.:212)

The theory of dynamic memory: Schank (1982a)

To some extent, an answer to this question of Bartlett's is suggested by Schank in further developments of the theory of schemata types described in Chapter 3. These ideas are stated most fully in the book *Dynamic Memory* (Schank 1982a).[4] Where *SPGU* centred very much upon text processing, *Dynamic Memory* deals more with experience in general. Conclusions are presumed to apply in a similar way both to direct experience and to experience gained via text. This is a major weakness of schema theory.

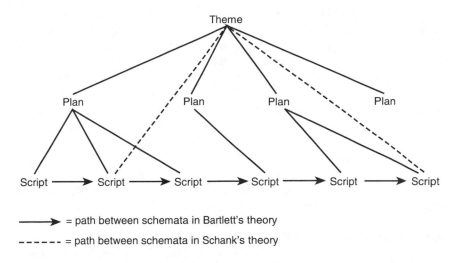

Figure 7.1: Serial connection in Bartlett's theory of memory: non-serial connection in a Schankian hierarchy

SPGU, as we have seen, is an explanation of how various types of schema may be applied in text processing. *Dynamic Memory* deals with the reverse of this process and describes how schemata may be constructed and changed. Schank's starting point is the observation that the phenomenon of being reminded of one experience by another, though frequent and important in people's lives, is inadequately and rarely dealt with in the psychological literature (ibid.: 19). He suggests that an investigation of the connections which evidently exist between apparently disparate experiences may help in the understanding of memory and schematic knowledge (ibid.: 19–36).

Schank gives many examples from his own life of odd instances of reminding. These illustrate how connections are made between quite disparate scripts or plans by reference to a common goal or theme (see Figure 7.1). Schank's approach is, like Ingarden's, heavily phenomenological, in that he is prepared to admit introspection into his own mental life as evidence. Such an approach may gain a certain degree of validity if the theorist's introspections ring true with other people. For myself, I can say that my own experience of reminding *does* resemble Schank's; but *you*, the reader, must judge for yourself whether your own experience of 'being reminded of something' is similar. Rather than repeat one of Schank's many examples I shall give a similar one of my own.

Some time ago I was working at the University of Leeds, living there during the week in term-time, and returning to my home in Edinburgh every weekend. As the drive is two hundred miles, I was always anxious to leave work as quickly as possible. One Friday evening, while hurriedly dealing with some last-minute business in the office of my department, I noticed a letter addressed to one of the students lying on the counter of the office, in a place where the student would be unlikely to find it. Three hours later, while driving in dark and rain on an empty stretch of a major road in Scotland, I saw a plank in the road in front of me, which, not having time to avoid, I drove over. The plank reminded me of the letter! Why? The 'low level' explanation that they were both rectangular objects lying on a surface is not convincing. The world is full of such objects and I had already encountered many of them in the intervening period—a briefcase on the back seat of a car, a sandwich on a plate—without being reminded of the letter. An explanation of the reminding is provided more convincingly (through a combination of introspection and Schank's theory) at a 'higher level'. This is that both objects evoked in me a common theme and plan. The theme is to act in a socially responsible manner. This theme would instigate a suspension of more self-centred plans—to leave work quickly, to reach my destination—and the substitution of more altruistic plans. In the first case this would have involved putting the letter in the right place, and in the second, stopping the car, going back and removing the plank. (As it happens, I did neither.)

In *Dynamic Memory*, Schank suggests that such strange remindings provide us with a glimpse of connections through higher levels of schemata. In a later book, *Explanation Patterns* (Schank 1986), he suggests that the task of explaining unusual events—whether to others or to oneself—may provide us with similar glimpses. Reminding and explanation reveal the kind of connections which provide the basis for changing and reconnecting schemata. Like Bartlett, Schank is aware that schemata cannot be too rigid. They must change and re-form.

With this in mind, he introduces two fundamentally new ideas to schema theory. The first is that *re-membered* experiences are *dis-membered* in the mind, and the parts stored separately (my pun here is significant!). Dismembered parts are stored in a new category of schema: Memory Organization Packets (MOPs). They generalize memories as much as possible into broad categories. Each MOP contains a number of 'scenes' (defined as 'physical settings that serve as the basis for reconstruction' (ibid.: 15)) connected to goals. Scripts are then reconstructed by bringing together several MOPs. Usually three types of MOP are needed to construct a script: one concerned with personal needs, one concerned with social interaction, and one concerned with physical entities. MOPs are thus not themselves text-processing schemata, but a means of constructing text-processing schemata. Schank suggests, for example, that the schema used for a visit to the doctor is composed of three MOPs: one containing scenes about Health Protection (personal), one containing scenes about a Professional Office Visit (physical), and one containing scenes about Making a Contract (social) (1982a:98). Each of these contains ordering rules for its own scenes. Brought together, these three MOPs yield a sequence of scenes which, when read horizontally, are very much like a script as described in *SPGU* (see Figure 7.2).

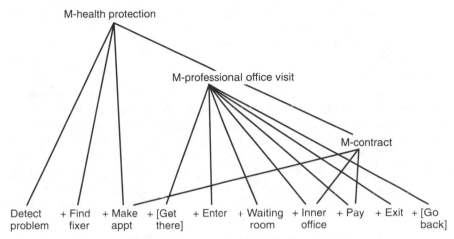

M-health protection

M-professional office visit

M-contract

| Detect problem | + Find fixer | + Make appt | + [Get there] | + Enter | + Waiting room | + Inner office | + Pay | + Exit | + [Go back] |

Figure 7.2: Construction of script through MOPs (Schank 1982a:89)

There are several advantages to this description. It is at once more economical and more fluid than a view of schemata as fixed ready-made representations such as scripts. It explains why it is that people may remember a part of a script without generating the whole (for example, that something happened in a waiting room, but not *which* waiting room) and also why some experiences remind us of others (they are organized in the same MOPs). It also remedies a number of the problems created by the large and rigid nature of scripts, enabling the construction of new ones and more leeway in the ordering of events.[5] Changes do not have so many repercussions on other elements of the script (which are stored elsewhere). Smaller schematic units, called 'scenes', allow for greater fluidity. A scene in this new formulation is a single location or process associated with a goal (MOPs are collections of scenes which share the same goal). Buying a ticket is, for example, a scene associated with the goal (or plan) TRAVEL; boarding a bus is another such scene. Both would belong to the same MOP. Two similar experiences are 'mushed' together into the same scene. We may remember, for example, that something happened while we were boarding a bus, but not—if we have done this many times—on which specific occasion.[6] Significant departures from the expectations generated by a scene—for example 'the time I boarded a bus but it broke down'—are retained together with the scene. These are 'failures' of the predictions generated by the scene.

When the same failure occurs twice, a new scene is generated. In this example, this new scene would be a 'bus breakdown scene'. Elements which this new scene has in common may then link up (nobody pretends to explain quite how) with the same element in another scene or MOP. In the bus breakdown, this might be a MOP containing scenes of frustration or scenes of mechanical failure. Similar links are manifested by the mental phenomenon of being reminded.

In Schank's view, schemata and memory are one and the same thing. The general picture of memory—as the title *Dynamic Memory* suggests—is one of schemata in constant flux: schemata which are used in processing but also changed by processing (a view compatible with both connectionist and neural Darwinist views of mind (Martindale 1991; Edelman 1992:141)). Each new experience creates new scene combinations through the bringing together of MOPs, but this very process creates new scenes which are then filed away under new MOPs. One scene may, of course, belong to several MOPs—a fact which explains many odd instances of reminding, like the plank-and-letter one described above. The elements of schemata are constantly being broken down and re-formed into new schemata. Introspection into instances of reminding affords us glimpses of the kind of process this is. Connections are achieved very much by reference to goals and plans, though these, as Schank emphasizes, are often mysterious and the subject of speculation rather than certainty. This is because the goals and plans and specific experiences of individuals vary widely. There can therefore be no final description of the processing of a given experience or of its effect on the schemata used in that processing. There can only be descriptions valid for particular individuals, and even then there is an inevitable uncertainty.

In the context of Schank's theory of reminding, it is interesting to note that the analyses here have suggested that connections between schemata in literary discourse are at higher levels, whereas in many non-literary types of discourse with language patterning (such as advertisements) connections are established through one 'prop' (such as the product) at the lowest level. If the theory of Dynamic Memory is correct, connections at higher levels provide the greatest potential for schema change.

A weakness in schema theory

Both Bartlett and Schank recognize the need for human beings to change and reorganize schemata. Schank provides a substantial account of how this may be done. Yet neither theorist pays much attention to the role of language and text structure in this process. Both have a tendency to treat direct sense experience of the world and experience of a (real or fictional) world through language as the same. For Schank in particular, the building blocks of schemata are conceptual dependency representations, and the linguistic or text-structural origin of those representations is abandoned once it has been 'translated' into the new language. Thus, though there are times when he recognizes the role of a lexical choice in creating a link (Schank 1982a:25, 111) or the role of schema theory in disambiguating anaphoric reference (Schank and Abelson 1977:38–41) or even the role of text structure (in discussing why *West Side Story* reminds people of *Romeo and Juliet* (Schank 1982a:33)), Schank does not develop the role of language or text structure in any detail. This tendency remains in *Explanation Patterns* (1986), where 'sentences' are treated as equivalent to 'facts'. Significantly, though he several times refers to jokes as manifesting strange connections between schemata (Schank 1982a:25, 32–7; 1986:16, 20), none of the jokes which he cites in evidence rely heavily upon wordplay or linguistic innovation. Similarly, on a text-structural level, all the stories used by both Bartlett and Schank have, in formalist terms, unmarked *syuzhet*. Their ordering of events, in other words, is that of their *fabula* (see pages 134–5).[7]

In the remainder of this chapter, and in the next, I shall attempt to remedy this shortcoming in schema theory by developing and applying a theory of how deviation at the linguistic and text-structural level may be linked to changes in schemata, creating an overall effect of discourse deviation. I shall also suggest that the primary function of some discourses may be to effect such changes.

A theory of literary discourse: Schema refreshment and cognitive change

In the Schankian view, the ability to break down existing schemata, reassemble new ones, and draw new connections, is synonymous with intelligence and adaptability. Yet in the picture he draws of this constant and dynamic interaction, the process of renewal is viewed as a consequence and not a motivation of experience. The experiences he describes are still primarily sought out for social and material ends. Any change they may effect in schemata exists as a by-product. He does not consider the possibility of there being experiences whose primary—and perhaps unique—function for the individual is to effect changes in schematic organization. This oversight is connected with Schank's failure to draw a distinction between linguistic and direct sensory experience. Direct interaction with the world or with other people does not always allow the maximum and most creative degree of play. Its consequences are too important and affect the individual too closely. For these reasons, change is best effected through a kind of linguistic experience which, though it may describe interaction with other people or the environment, is not itself part of that interaction.

Experience of language which is written,[8] rather than spoken and performed, enables the individual to withdraw from social interaction, and this too may ensure greater freedom and experimentation. Though there are institutionalized events which allow people to come together to experience such playful uses of language communally—comedy shows, plays, performances of songs[9]—the act of reading to oneself, by its very nature, is private.[10] The mass literacy which has come to Europe in the last two hundred years (Hobsbawm 1975:191–2) has thus changed the nature of discourse processing, diminishing the stature of the communal experience and raising that of private experience. Comedy and song have largely been demoted to the status of sub-culture; poetry is increasingly treated as written rather than spoken text; the novel—once a junior branch—has been canonized (see page 133); the popularity of drama has waned. Television and film can, in this respect, be regarded as either communal or private. Many people watch television alone, often as a substitute for company, and film (in the cinema, not on videotape), though it involves the gathering of crowds, is—because of its non-reciprocal nature, and because it is experienced in the dark—essentially private: more like reading a book than going to a play. Taking all of this into account, in what follows I deal mainly with written discourse, read silently. With this qualification, let us return to the issue of the difference between linguistic and sensory experience.

Experience may be divided into three types: that which is perceived directly without the mediation of language (though it may also include language); that which comes to us entirely through language, but we believe represents an independent reality; and that which exists only through language, with no accessible corresponding reality in the world, though it creates an illusion of one. Much literary discourse is of the last type. This is not only true of fiction. Even literary discourse derived from and representing independent 'facts' is unlikely to have the same immediate impact upon the reader as a discourse reporting a situation which directly affects the reader, or in which the reader can intervene. The boundaries here are fuzzy. Some discourses apparently derived from an independent reality (a memorandum, for example, or a summons to court), may directly involve their reader, while others (for example, newspaper reports), though also representing reality, may be so far beyond the reader's control or experience, that they are to all intents and purposes of the same status as the illusory world of a literary discourse. We must also bear in mind the post-modernist notion of the retrospective effect of discourse in creating 'facts' from which they apparently derive, the reversal of cause and effect (discussed on pages 126–7).

Despite this fuzziness and complexity, and the issue of the differences between communal and private experiences of discourse, it seems reasonable to identify a group of texts of no immediate practical or social consequence. I propose that the illusory experience offered by such texts provides the individual with the opportunity to reorganize schemata without the fear of unpleasant practical or social consequence.

In this definition, it is important to stress the word 'immediate'. The reorganization of schemata may have eventual social and practical consequences. *Crime and Punishment* may change our attitude to various phenomena in the world: to the murder of old women for money, to religion, to prostitution, or to poverty. It may also change our attitude to language and discourse: to detective novels, narrative viewpoint, or the structure of the clause.[11] But its effect on future action is delayed. One can read a literary work in order to solve an immediate problem, of course, but arguably that would not be to read it as a literary work.

I shall treat changes in schemata as having three aspects (see Figure 7.3). Existing schemata may be destroyed. New ones may be constructed. New connections may be established between existing schemata. I shall refer to these three processes as 'schema refreshment' (I shall also use the term 'schema disruption' to describe a general effect on existing schemata. Disruption is a pre-requisite of refreshment.)

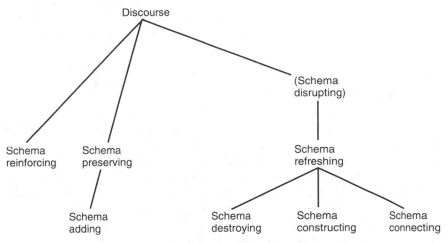

Figure 7.3: Discourse effects on schemata

My claim is that the primary function of certain discourses is to effect a change in the schemata of their readers. Sensations of pleasure, escape, profundity, and elevation are conceivably offshoots of this function. So too is the high social esteem afforded to discourse with no other apparent social or practical function. Conversely, it seems that discourses attempting this function but failing (for a given individual) are not simply ignored, but often violently attacked by those individuals and dismissed as boring or even harmful. (Consider the opprobrium and vitriol attracted by a 'bad joke' or 'unsuccessful novel'. The Edward Bond poem analysed on pages 167–73 for example, attracts very strong disapproval from some people.) The degree of schematic change, and thus the assignment of esteem, will depend upon the schemata which the reader employs in interpretation, and on his or her own receptiveness and ability or wish to change. There are discourses rejected because they seek to cause too sudden and too drastic a change: hence the frequently negative initial reception of revolutionary or avant-garde art which is later elevated to a very high status. There are, of course, times when people have good cause to resist change suggested by a particular discourse. Though change in general may be desirable, there is nothing inherently commendable in accepting a particular change. For these reasons, my claim that certain discourses are 'schema refreshing' can never specify the quality in particular texts. The quality of schema refreshment is reader-dependent. Nevertheless, a given text may possess this quality for a large number of people. We may contrast schema-refreshing discourse with discourse which is 'schema preserving', leaving existing schemata as they were, and discourse which is 'schema reinfor-cing', leaving existing schemata stronger than before. (In connectionist terms, increasing the 'strength' of a schema may mean increasing the weightings in neural connections,[12] and the result of this will be that the schema is activated more readily, and departures from it accepted less easily.) Sometimes, discourse may simply add to existing schemata, while preserving their basic structure intact. This is the case with the addition of Gore-Tex fabric as a new prop in script-like schemata representing Scotland or holidays on pages 109–18.

The category of schema-refreshing discourse, whose primary function is to effect change in schemata, will include many of those discourses described as 'literary'. This is not to say, however, that all literature is schema refreshing or that all schema-refreshing discourse is literature. The borders of the two types are not absolutely coterminous. (Nor, for that matter, are they precise.) Certainly, there are many discourses which are not generally accepted into the canon of literature, but whose primary value is the disruption of schemata. These may be divided into two types. Those which disrupt schemata through conventional (even 'ready-made') text and language structures, and those whose disruption of world schemata is matched by deviant text and language structures.[13]

The former category will include, among other instances, scientific and journalistic prose which disrupts rigid and strongly-held schemata. Consider, for example, the following passage from a serious work of popular science, Stephen Hawking's *A Brief History of Time*:

At first, I believed that disorder would decrease when the universe recollapsed. This was because I thought that the universe had to return to a smooth and ordered state when it became small again. This would mean that the contracting phase would be like the time-reverse of the expanding phase. People in the contracting phase would live their lives backward: they would die before they were born and get younger as the universe contracted.
(Hawking 1988:150)

Here we seem to have extreme schema disruption: a serious and learned suggestion that time can go backwards. Yet it is apparently expressed in the most unremarkable, lucid, and 'transparent' prose, in a book with a very conventional text structure. (It is, in fact, the interaction of the serious genre with its conceptual content which makes this book schema disrupting. In science fiction, such ideas are already banal.) It is worth noting, however, that the apparent separation between disruptive content and disruptive form is not as simple as it seems. Firstly, the expression of new scientific ideas often leads to innovative uses of language. Examples are phrases like 'cosmic soup', used to describe the early stage of the universe, 'cosmic censorship' to describe the inaccessibility of information in a black hole, and the attribution of 'charm' to particles with particular properties. In fact, the passage quoted above contains examples of such innovations in the neologisms 'recollapsed' and 'the time-reverse'. Secondly, the 'weird' findings of modern science are often verbalizations in natural language of findings originally expressed in formal languages.

The category of non-literary schema-disrupting discourse includes many jokes, comedy routines, graffiti, and advertisements. The exclusion of these discourse types from the literary canon may be attributed to a number of causes (Cook 1990b). Firstly, though they share many features with literary discourse, they often have a dominant function considered alien to literature, for example to establish group identity or to give voice to taboos. Secondly, they are often concerned with communal rather than individual creative identity, and the former, in a literate culture, is often regarded as inferior. Thirdly, they are often disruptive of language and text schemata, while preserving or reinforcing world schemata. This last feature is particularly true of advertisements. The analyses on pages 109–18 and 161–7 have highlighted sub-sentential patterning and deviation, but there is also, on occasion, deviation from expected text structure. If, for example, the expected text structure of a television commercial reflects the 'rule' that it begins, runs continuously for approximately twenty-five seconds, and ends, then a number of advertisements are text-structurally deviant. In 1989–1992, for example,

British television carried an advertisement for Gold Blend coffee, telling a story in instalments. Completion of the story was delayed. (In formalist terms this canonizes the junior branch of advertisement, making it closer to the senior branch, in television terms, of soap opera.) A building society ran two advertisements in parallel with each other—one 'gloomy' version, one 'cheerful' version—on two commercial channels simultaneously, advising viewers to switch channels according to preference. In the USA, a firm ran a series of parody advertisements for spurious products, interrupting each one with a cartoon rabbit advertising the firm's product. These examples will be referred to in the next section.

Conversely, there are arguably discourses within the literary canon which are far from 'schema refreshing'. It might be said, for example, that the novels of Jane Austen evoke, maintain, and indeed reinforce quite rigid schemata about acceptable and desirable behaviour. On the other hand, it might validly be claimed that this view is retrospective; we have only to compare Jane Austen's depiction of the behaviour of the rural middle and upper classes in, say, *Emma* (published in 1816) with Fielding's depiction of the same classes in, say, *Tom Jones* six decades earlier (1749) to appreciate how 'schema-breaking' the world of her novels may have been in its own time. Literary discourses which were once schema-refreshing become schema-reinforcing.

This applies as much to text schemata and language schemata as it does to world schemata. In fact, as innovation in language use often accompanies innovation in content, the acceptance of new attitudes and subject-matter often entails acceptance of new approaches to language. A good example is Wordsworth and Coleridge's *Lyrical Ballads*, which aimed to disrupt norms of both poetic language and poetic subject-matter, yet rapidly became the stereotype of poetry. Similarly, in our own century, departure from conventional punctuation in poetry, which once often accompanied iconoclastic attitudes and unconventional subject-matter, has now become banal.

This tendency of new form and content to become not only accepted but conventional, leads to a lack of fit between the literary canon and the category of 'schema-refreshing discourse'. This is hardly surprising, as the canon tends to be defined, not for specific readers, but for—and by—a dominant social group speaking in institutions at a particular time in history. The concept of schema-refreshing discourse, on the other hand, must be related to as many variations as there are between epochs, individuals, and social groups. (That is why what I have just said about Jane Austen is highly personal and disputable, and can never have the status of a fact.) Educational institutions, however, have a tendency to be a step behind. They canonize what was once (and exclude what is currently) schema-refreshing. Yet, despite the emasculating effects on literature of institutions, time, and fame, the literary canon does provide many examples of schema-refreshing discourse, and I shall treat it as the major source of such discourse.

This feature of literature—that it is often primarily schema-refreshing—accounts for the inability of many approaches to discourse analysis to cope well with the coherence of literary discourse. Accounts of coherence at the linguistic or text-structural level are only partial. Pragmatics, adopted in discourse analysis to remedy this inadequacy, works best with the discourse of 'the bulge': civil exchanges between acquaintances whose relations are neither too intimate nor too disparate in power (Wolfson 1988; also, see page 42). There is thus a tendency to interpret the primary functions of all discourse as either co-operative (manipulating the environment together with others) or polite (creating and maintaining social relations), or, to use Hallidayan terms, as ideational or interpersonal (see pages 37–40). The function of schema refreshment comes under neither of these headings. Added to these two, it effects a third major function of discourse (as already suggested on page 44).

To some extent it is true that any discourse alters schemata. A discourse which did not would be both totally superfluous and utterly boring, realizing the most catastrophic misjudgement of the interlocutor.[14] There are two apparent qualifications to this general truth. Firstly, there is the paradox that statement of the obvious arouses a particular kind of interest. Encountered in the surreal dialogues of the Theatre of the Absurd, for example, it stimulates a search for the goals behind such extreme failure of communication. The second qualification concerns the deliberate re-processing of a discourse. People re-read a favourite book or poem, or watch a film that they have seen many times before. It might be argued that in these cases there can be no further change of schemata, as whatever changes the discourse may encourage have already taken place. It is more likely, however, that each repetition yields a new interpretation, especially as an individual reader changes between readings. Alternatively, subsequent readings may yield the same changes as the first reading, but serve to reinforce them. If the reader likes the changes, this may be seen as desirable. (In connectionist terms, this last effect is equivalent to increasing the 'weightings' of connections; in neural Darwinist terms, it is an instance of the mind evolving towards new structures.)

Yet, although most discourse effects *some* change in schemata, there are differences of degree. Looking back over the texts analysed in earlier chapters, we may see, for example, that the biographical sketch of Balzac provides (for its projected reader) a good deal of new information about its subject. It adds to the script-like 'Balzac schema' which we may presume any educated English-speaking adult to have available. It may also add (through 'double inclusion', see page 118) to schemata concerning child-rearing, post-revolutionary France and so on. Similarly, the advertisements for Elizabeth Taylor's Passion, and for Gore-Tex, may provide new information about Elizabeth Taylor and Scotland, or about what to wear when we wish to be attractive, comfortable, or stylish.[15] Yet they effect no radical change in schemata. These discourses are instances of schema addition rather than refreshment. They affect the level of script-like schemata, but not of plans or themes. The advertisements confirm the unremarkable facts that most men and women wish to be attractive and comfortable. Similarly, the Balzac biography may confirm a schematic expectation that great writers triumph over suffering and difficult circumstances. In contrast, the description of Raskolnikov, even in the opening paragraphs of *Crime and Punishment*, demands reorganization of assumptions about human behaviour and motivation. It begins to build new schemata which are incomplete, mainly because the themes and plans behind them are unknown. The Edward Bond poem stands or falls by its challenge to deeply ingrained high-level assumptions about poetry, poets, and the war dead. (Many would say it falls, but it is worth noting that it may do so in two ways: either because it fails to evoke acceptance of the changes it advocates, or because its attempt to demolish and rebuild schemata is not perceived — in which case it is simply considered to be bad poetry, or insensitive.)

All the examples are perhaps extremes. The Balzac passage is a plain presentation of biographical facts, the advertisements embody rigid unquestioned values. *Crime and Punishment*, by contrast is, for many people, one of the most rewardingly disturbing discourses of all. The Bond poem attempts to overturn sacred assumptions. Such examples have been chosen for their extremity. In general, we might expect the distinction between schema-refreshing discourse, and discourses which are schema-preserving or reinforcing to be more 'fuzzy', and best represented by a cline. In terms of prototype theory, *Crime and Punishment* is prototypical of schema-refreshing discourse, as are the three literary texts analysed in the next chapter.

In all that has been said so far, both in the analysis of approaches to discourse analysis, and in the summary of literary theory, three major levels have been acknowledged in discourse (whether literary or non-literary). These, in the broadest terms, are the levels of language, text structure, and world knowledge. We may relate these to the approaches described in Table 7.1. (In this table cohesion, being both sub- and super-sentential, belongs to both levels 2 and 3.) The equation of the role of knowledge (in discourse analysis) with that of the reader (in literary theory) may seem strange, but is valid on the grounds that — in a sense — the sum of a person's schemata is that person, and, conversely, schemata are as variable as readers.

Schema theory	Discourse analysis	Literary theory
1 (world) schemata	knowledge	the reader
2 text schemata	functional structure (defined pragmatically)	structure (defined intertextually)
	formal links (cohesion)	Linguistic form
3 language schemata	grammar	

Table 7.1: Correlation of levels in schema theory, discourse analysis, and literary theory

There is an understandable, but regrettable, tendency in various approaches to focus on one of these levels to the detriment of the others. This is most evident in literary theories where the legacy of formalism has fragmented into an exclusive emphasis on language (Jakobson), on text structure (structuralism), and on the reader (in those reader-response theories which deny an autonomous text). Literary theorists of these schools have tried vainly to identify literariness in terms of deviation and conformity at one and only one of these levels. In discourse analysis this atomizing approach is less in evidence. The inability of purely formal and textual approaches to cope with coherence has been recognized. Discourse analysis could indeed be defined as the attempt to bring together knowledge, text structure, and language. Yet it is also true that in discourse analysis the schematic organization of knowledge has often been regarded as fixed. Schemata are brought to bear upon the interpretation of discourse rather than affected by it. For this reason, pragmatic and text-structural approaches to discourse, though they work well for discourse primarily motivated by the politeness and co-operative principles, are weak in dealing with literary discourse. AI text theory, on the other hand, falls into the opposite trap from structuralism and Jakobsonian stylistics. While it pays attention to knowledge, it has a tendency to ignore the complexities created by differences in linguistic and text-structural form.

A theory of literary discourse: discourse deviation

If it is the primary function of a particular category of discourse to effect the refreshment of schemata, it seems likely that that refreshment will take place, not at one of the three levels discussed above, but in the relation between them. The 'world' of a literary work, whether or not it originates in, or relates to some external world, is an illusion brought into being through the language and text structure. It is reasonable, therefore, to suppose that the schemata the literary work evokes through these two levels may also be refreshed through these two levels. Literary theoretical approaches concentrating on deviation and patterning at the linguistic and text-structural levels, and the Schankian approach concentrating on the schematic level, all fail to show how patterning and deviation at one level affect patterning and deviation at another. Just as discourse and its quality of coherence can be described only as the interplay of levels and not at any level in isolation, so can the elusive quality of 'literariness'. Where there is deviation at one or both of the linguistic and text-structural levels, and this deviation interacts with a reader's existing schemata to cause schema refreshment, there exists the phenomenon which I term 'discourse deviation'.

This definition is complicated by the fact that schemata, in the broadest sense, include not only schemata of the world but also schemata representing text structures and the language itself ('text schemata' and 'language schemata' respectively). The highest level, in other words, contains the other two. It is thus feasible that schema refreshment, effected through language and text structure, may on occasion be refreshment of schemata of language and text structure. In other words, we may come away from a discourse with our mental representation of the language altered (as the first readers of 'Jabberwocky' came away with the word 'burble') or with some new notion of text structure (as the first readers of *The Mysteries of Udolpho* came away with the genre of the Gothic novel, or the first readers of Freud with the genre of the psychoanalytic case study (Foucault [1969] 1979:206)). These new linguistic and text-structural schemata will, in turn, have effects upon representations of the world. A further complication is that the deviations at the linguistic and text-structural levels effecting schema refreshment may not be deviations at that level only, but rather in their choices at that level in relation to one of the others. Thus Alexander Pope's mock-epic *The Rape of the Lock*, which describes trivial events in a grand style, is an instance of discourse deviation not for its structure and linguistic form in isolation, nor in schematic representation of the events it describes in isolation, but in the mismatch between the two. Deviation, moreover, whether defined at one level or as an interaction between levels, is never absolute, but always relative to the expectations of a specified reader. Literature students, for example, who commonly have no direct experience of the epic form which mock-epic parodies, do not initially find *The Rape of the Lock* either disturbing or amusing. The same is true for Jane Austen's parodic novel *Northanger Abbey* (another favourite on literature courses) when readers have no experience of the Gothic novel.

The texts analysed so far all reveal the futility of analysis at one level only. The sub-sentential patterns and deviations of the perfume advertisement neither cause, nor derive from, any schema refreshment. In the Bond poem, it is the lack of sub-sentential patterning and deviation, interacting with a degree of stereotypical poetic text structure and combined with an attempt at schema refreshment, which constitute discourse deviations.

The task of a theory of discourse deviation must therefore be to show how schema refreshment is effected through language and text structure, to relate linguistic and text-structural features to particular changes in schemata. There are reasons why a complete description of these relations is impossible. The quantity of relations would clearly be vast: a multiplication of whatever complexities might be described at one level in isolation. Limitations, moreover, are not only quantitative but qualitative. Firstly, the description must involve a description of the relevant pre-existing schemata of a specified reader. As such, the description remains speculative and open-ended (the number of potential readers, or of schemata employed by any particular reader, being virtually infinite and inaccessible). Secondly, it is in the nature of the literary beast to be unpredictable. Predictions are schematic. Schemata are predictive. Yet the effect the theory seeks to describe is schema disruption. What could be predicted would not be disruptive.

Nevertheless, we may speculate both about the effects in general of the interaction of linguistic and text-structural deviation with schemata, and also about particular interactions in given literary texts. In the remainder of this chapter, I shall undertake the first of these tasks. The next chapter is devoted to the analysis in terms of discourse deviation of three well-known and frequently analysed literary texts ('The Tyger' by William Blake, *The Turn of the Screw* by Henry James, and 'The Windhover' by Gerard Manley Hopkins.

The theory continued: Interactions between world, text, and language

Let us start in a simplified way and discuss the possible interactions of deviation and normality at the three major levels. If we represent these levels with the letters S for (world) schemata evoked by the discourse (a notion which is elaborated below), T for text structure, and L for language, and follow each with + for norm or − for deviation (where 'norm' means 'conformity to schematic expectation' and 'deviation' means 'difference from schematic expectation'), we have the possible combinations listed below.

The most complex deviations, at more than one level, in examples 6

	Exemplified by	Location
Schema reinforcement/ preservation		
1 S+ T+ L+	Balzac biography	page 49
2 S+ T+ L−	Elizabeth Taylor's Passion	Chapter 6
3 S+ T− L+	*Kim*; Gold Blend advertisement	page 143; page 194
4 S+ T− L−	(no example)	
Schema refreshment		
5 S− T+ L+	'First World War Poets'	Chapter 6
6 S− T+ L−	'The Tyger'	Chapter 8
7 S− T− L+	*The Turn of the Screw*	Chapter 8
8 S− T− L−	'The Windhover'	Chapter 8

Table 7.2: World, text, and language schemata

to 8, are yet to be analysed. In 1 to 5, a number of points need to be made in glossary of each of the combinations and examples.

1 The biographical sketch adds new defaults to schemata, but there is no fundamental rearrangement. Stereotypes of writers are reinforced.

2 The combination of 'poetic' language and lineation with the schemata evoked by an advertisement may once have been itself schema-refreshing. (There is a paradox here: that the means of schema refreshment, deviant language, when combined with an absence of schema refreshment, was—in the early days of advertising—itself odd and therefore schema-refreshing. In a given context, in other words, the absence of schema refreshment is itself schema refreshing. This may be one of the reasons that advertisements on occasion evoke such hostility. They set up an expectation of schema refreshment by adopting its means, but leave this promise unfulfilled.

3 The departure of *Kim* from a posited text structure of 'initiation' novels has been discussed. Seeing this novel as the departure and some of the others as the norm, depends, of course on the perception of the reader. But this only emphasizes the relativity of 'norm' and 'deviation'. For a given reader who does see the others as the standard, *Kim* will be marked. The Gold Blend and similar text-structurally deviant advertisements are discussed on pages 193–5. Now that people are perhaps immured to word-play in advertisements, such text-structural devices are an effective option (see Cook 1992:218).[16]

4 The difficulty of providing an example suggests a causal connection between the combination of linguistic and text-structural deviation and change to world schemata.

5 This example is complex. The contrast of 'ordinary language' with a conventional poetic layout and iconoclastic sentiments is potentially deviant, but only in the combination of these features. The poem presents the opposite paradox to 2. It is the absence of text-structural and linguistic deviation which, combined with the expectations set up by poetic form, 'represents' the schema-refreshment advocated by the poem. Another example which might be relevant here is the extract from *A Brief History of Time* discussed on page 193. This scientific example is, as already noted, not as straightforward as it seems. Paradigm-breaking scientific prose may employ more linguistic innovation than popularly believed. These qualifications, and the general difficulty of finding an example to fit this category, suggests (like the absence of an example in 4) that there is a connection between formal deviation and changes to schemata.

(Texts 6, 7, and 8 are dealt with in detail in Chapter 8.)

This relatively simple model may be made more complex in a number of ways. If we accept the existence of the three schemata types: world schemata, text schemata and language schemata (represented respectively by: $S(W)$, $S(T)$, $S(L)$) we can assume that all of these are present in the mind of any reader. A reader's feeling that the text structure or linguistic choices of a given discourse are normal or deviant derives from a comparison of its text structure (T) and its language (L) with the reader's pre-existing text schemata $S(T)$ and language schemata $S(L)$. The interaction of these interactions creates the illusion of a 'world' in the discourse (W), which can then be compared with the world schemata of the reader, yielding a judgement as to the normality or deviance of that illusory world.

Judgements about the normality or deviation at any of the three levels in the discourse are not, then, as simple as Table 7.2 suggests. They arise from the comparison of the schemata at each level in the reader with the three levels of the text. The 'world' of the discourse, however, can only come into being through the interaction of its language and text structure with the language schemata, text schemata, and world schemata in the reader. Let us represent this stage by stage (though without any implication that these stages are chronologically the stages of interpretation).

Each reader possesses schemata at each level ($S(W)$, $S(T)$, $S(L)$). A given discourse has language and text structures (L, T). None of these

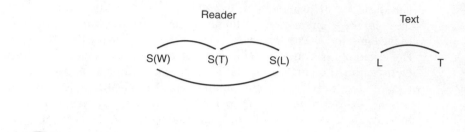

Reader   Text

S(W)   S(T)   S(L)   L   T

——⌣ = interaction

Figure 7.4: Schemata, text, and language (1)

levels are discrete; they interact with each other as shown in Figure 7.4.[17]

The comparison of the language of the discourse with the language schemata of the reader, and of the text structure with the text schemata of the reader, yield judgements concerning the deviance or normality of the language and text structure, as shown in Figure 7.5.

These judgements, however, and the extensions of them described below, are, of course, not final for a whole discourse. They will change with each stage in the process of reading, and will be different at different 'places' in the product of reading. Also, they may describe any feature of the language or text structure and any possible combinations. They will also change on re-reading and within and between readers. Deviation and normality, moreover, are not absolute conditions, and clearly there can be degrees of either. Bearing all this in mind, the possible permutations of the descriptions provided here are clearly immense.

The interaction of world schemata S(W) with the interaction of S(T), S(L), L and T produces an (illusory) world (W) (which may change or

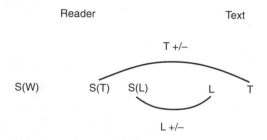

Reader   Text

T +/−

S(W)   S(T)   S(L)   L   T

L +/−

Figure 7.5: Schemata, text, and language (2)

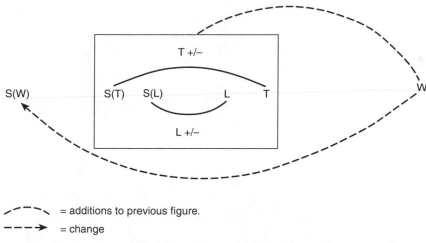

```
        = additions to previous figure.
- - - ►  = change
```

Figure 7.6: Schemata, text, and language (3)

add to existing schemata or yield new ones) as shown in Figure 7.6. (Each figure adds to the previous one.)

This world in the discourse is compared with the reader's world schemata S(W), allowing a judgement of the deviance or normality of the world of the discourse, as shown in Figure 7.7.

So far, however, the interaction is one way. Schemata are applied to text, creating discourse. An experience of deviation, however, will rebound upon the schemata which were used to establish it in the first place. A deviant text structure, for example, will alter a reader's text schemata, as shown in Figure 7.8.

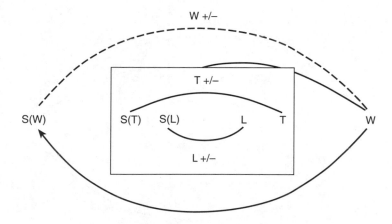

Figure 7.7: Schemata, text, and language (4)

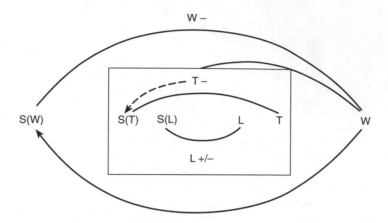

Figure 7.8: Schemata, text, and language (5)

Deviant language may change language schemata, and a deviant world may change world schemata, as shown in Figure 7.9.

There will also, I believe, be instances in which a deviant text structure or use of language will directly affect the world schemata of the reader, as shown in Figure 7.10. This is discussed further in the next chapter.

In fact, as the 'world' of a discourse comes into being only through language and text structure, it may be that in discourse (as opposed to direct experience) it is *only* by altering text and language schemata that we can alter world schemata. That is to say, the overall interaction of all elements will yield an effect of deviation from expectation, and

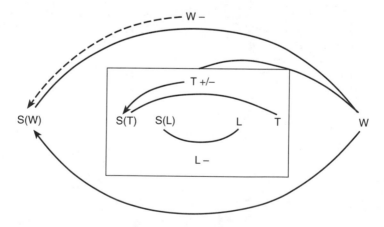

Figure 7.9: Schemata, text, and language (6)

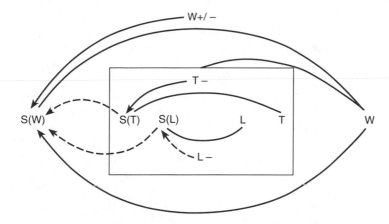

Figure 7.10: Schemata, text, and language (7)

consequent schema change. It is this phenomenon which is discourse deviation, and it is hoped to illustrate it in the next chapter. The analyses of advertisements in earlier chapters, on the other hand, illustrate that textual and language deviation is no guarantee of discourse deviation. The process of interaction, in other words, does not go beyond that shown in Figure 7.7. The potential for discourse deviation can only begin after that point. The process I am describing is dynamic. When schemata change, the interaction begins again with the newly-formed schemata. This may explain why people enjoy re-reading texts which initiate this process for them.

As these relations apply at any stage in a reading, they would be more truly represented in three dimensions (Figure 7.11), as combinations of elements will be different at different times in the reading.

The suggestion that changes in text and language schemata can affect world schemata, or that world schemata can change text and language

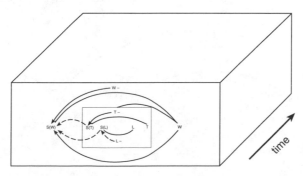

Figure 7.11: Interactions in time

schemata, implies a degree of belief in linguistic relativity, in that it sees S(W)s as being potentially affected by language and text, and vice versa.

It is through the interaction of existing schemata and text (which creates discourse) that the reader infers the world schemata of the discourse. These are usually attributed to the author or narrator (see Figure 7.12).

Introduction of further distinctions within the levels of world, text structure, and language would cause the possible combinations and interactions to proliferate. We might, for example, distinguish S(W)s which are script-like schemata, plans, and themes. In Chapter 8, I shall attempt to illustrate some possible interactions through the analysis of three literary discourses.

Defamiliarization revisited

The idea of 'schema refreshment' through discourse deviation is essentially the Russian formalist concept of defamiliarization restated in the light of AI text theory and discourse analysis. From AI, it borrows the idea of schemata, and from discourse analysis the idea that discourse is a reader-variable process of relating knowledge, text structure, and language, rather than any of these in isolation. Formalism, discourse analysis, and AI all have contributions to make to each other.

Although the formalists had taken the idea of a defamiliarization of reality and direct sense perception as their starting point (see pages 138–9), they soon moved away from this approach to deal with defamiliarization only at the level of text structure and linguistic form. If the idea of the defamiliarization of non-linguistic perception persisted in formalist theory at all, it did so only as a metaphor of the defamiliarization of text structure and language. To all intents and purposes, description of this aspect of defamiliarization was abandoned as a matter of principle. Having narrowed the field by inflicting this exclusion upon themselves,

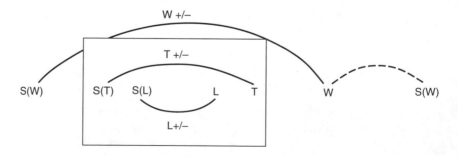

Figure 7.12: Schemata, text, and language (8)

the formalists were further limited, as Bakhtin points out, by the lack of a rigorous theory of language (Bakhtin [Volosinov] [1929] 1973:78; Bakhtin [Medvedev] [1928] 1978).[18] In addition, they sought to exclude both author and reader, the sender and receiver of the literary message, whose presences—as we have seen in Chapter 2—are so essential for any satisfactory explanation of coherence. For these reasons, the formalists tended—or intended—to concentrate upon text structure (see pages 133–9). Yet much of their work, ironically, far from being about the impersonal objective form of autonomous texts, does describe the interaction of text structure and reader, pointing the way towards resulting changes in a reader's representations of the world. (Here the world and representations of the world are treated as the same.) Thus, an inconsistency between formalist theory and practice produced some of their best work and ideas.

It is, in fact, difficult to see how the concept of defamiliarization can exclude the reader, and refer to a quality of text rather than to a quality of discourse. Ironically, this central weakness in the theory is suggested by the word itself. (These points are as true of the Russian word *ostranyenie* as they are of its English translation.) Though a neologism, the word 'defamiliarization' may be regarded as a nominalization of a verb. This verb would be transitive and always predicate an object, with an optional adjunct 'for x'. The text defamiliarizes *something for someone*. The 'something' is the world (though in a sense which includes texts and language) and the 'someone' must be the reader. The use of the nominal, however, enables the formalists to avoid both implications. Defamiliarization is, in fact, reader-dependent: a relationship between a reader and an object of perception (even if that object of perception is another text, or the language itself). This is why many of the formalist devices can only be identified for specific readers. Canonization of the junior branch, for example, assumes a point in history; what is junior for one generation of readers is not so for the next. *Skaz* relies on the notion of a narrator different in identity or attitude from the reader. Impeded form would be better described as 'impeding form', for it impedes the perception of the reader, which in turn depends upon the reader's experiences. Familiarity with a particular language or genre will surely result in easier processing. Bared form is bared to, and dependent upon perception by, the reader.

We are brought back to the Bakhtinian adage:

Meaning does not reside in the word or in the soul of the speaker or in the soul of the listener. Meaning is the effect of interaction between speaker and listener produced via the material of a particular sound complex. It is like an electric spark that occurs only when two different terminals are hooked together. Those who ignore theme (which is

accessible only to active, responsive understanding) and who, in
attempting to define the meaning of a word, approach its lower,
stable, self-identical limit, want, in effect, to turn on a light bulb after
having switched off the current.
(Bakhtin [Volosinov] [1929] 1973:102–3)

In his own practice, Bakhtin went on to examine the effect on readers
of text-structural and linguistic devices and their role in discourse.
He never separated his analyses from historical periods and particular
readers, a particular state of the world. In this sense he was not a
'formalist', and disavowed the term. Yet perhaps some future development of formalism might have incorporated and benefited from this
insight into the user-dependency of language, had not historical events
intervened.[19]

The irony of the situation, then, is that while the formalists had
rejected the relationship of literature to the world as naïve, and had
also avoided the issue of the reader-dependency of literary effect, they
nevertheless left behind them an impressive body of analyses and a
theoretical framework describing exactly this interaction of world and
reader through unfamiliar form. Concepts like *skaz*, *syuzhet*, canonization,
and bared form are already a stage beyond text-structural deviation, as
they begin to relate textual features to readers. It is but a short step
further to describe (as I attempt to demonstrate in the next chapter)
how this interaction changes readers' schematic representations of the
world (including schematic representations of texts and language). In a
similar way, Jakobson's work on literary language provides an unrivalled
descriptive framework, but fails to take the next step, and describe the
effect on readers, allowing for all the possible variations which that step
involves. The formalists' and Jakobson's insistence on 'defamiliarization'
as an aspect of form alone restricted them. They describe the means of
defamiliarization but not its result. Nevertheless, their descriptions of
these means remain as potent as ever.

The claim here is that schema theory provides a way of attempting
at least a partial description of readers. The idea that certain discourses
have a primary function of refreshing schemata reaffirms, in new and
potentially more precise terms, the formalist concept of defamiliarization.
It rescues the concept from some of its own internal contradictions and
remedies its narrow focus. No-one, however, should belittle the genius
of the original concept of defamiliarization. It is more like the culmination
of research into discourse, schemata, and literary language, than an idea
advanced before all the major work in these fields in this century had
been undertaken. It is perhaps another case of cause and effect reversed.

It is the genius of the idea that it came first, like a conclusion based on evidence which had yet to be gathered.

Notes

1 'Function' is again used primarily in the sense of 'effect on the receiver' rather than 'intention of the sender' (see also pages 36–7).

2 Edwards and Middleton (1987) point out that Bartlett frequently uses conversation as evidence, but fails to pay direct attention to conversation as a discourse type. The same could be said of Schank's use of jokes.

3 Though writing before Popper, he is, in his frank admission of this weakness, a model of Popperian rigour.

4 Though their origin is in an earlier paper (Schank 1980). During the 1980s, Schank developed and applied his ideas to a number of other areas too: to teaching reading (Schank 1982b); to translation (Lytenin and Schank 1982); to news analysis (Schank and Burstein 1985). His book *Explanation Patterns* (Schank 1986) deals with the ways in which the task of explaining unusual events can both develop intelligence, and demonstrate it.

5 MOPs are, in Schank's view, very much like the goals and plans of *SPGU*. In fact he seems to suggest that goals and plans are so similar as to be conflated into this one new category. The greatest change, then, is in the conception of scripts. Although the possibility of large ready-made scripts is still accepted, the idea is far more that the majority are assembled as needed. Corresponding to the demotion of large, rigid scripts, is a far greater emphasis on goals and plans.

6 This is my own example. Transportation in Schank's examples is invariably by rented car or aeroplane.

7 Bartlett's and Schank's choices of texts are perhaps significant. Bartlett uses myths and jokes; Schank favours jokes and anecdotes. These discourse types, like advertisements, serve to reinforce schemata rather than disrupt them. In *Explanation Patterns* (1986:124–34) Schank deals at length with proverbs, which perform a similar function.

8 Or at least heard in private.

9 Recording can make listening to songs, shows, and plays a private experience too.

10 In the modern world, we take reading to ourselves for granted. In antiquity it was not so. St Augustine is reported to be the first person to have read silently to himself. For further comment on the effects of literacy on experience of discourse, see Buchan (1972); Steiner (1972); Ong 1982; Halliday (1985:xxiii–xxv); Ellis and

Beattie (1986:231, 248–9); Olson and Torrance 1991; Halverson 1991.

11 Dostoevsky frequently appears to change view in mid-clause, often through the insertion of a parenthesis. This is an effect which can survive translation, as in the following:

> The aged General Ivan Drozdov, a former friend and fellow-officer of the late General Stavrogin, a most worthy man (in his own way of course), a man we all know to be extremely stubborn and irritable . . .
> (*The Devils* trans. Magarshak 1953:38)

12 See Chapter 3. This comment assumes that connectionism is a psychological as well as a computational theory.

13 For discussion of ready-made units in language, see Bolinger (1974), Pawley and Syder (1983), Cowie (1990), Nattinger and DeCarrico 1992.

14 For discussion of an AI view of what make discourse interesting, and the role of a reader's attention focus in processing, see Schank et al. (1982), Grosz (1986).

15 This information is in fact misleading. It is unlikely that Elizabeth Taylor wears such a cheap perfume, and the picture in the Gore-Tex advertisement is not a picture of Rannoch Moor (see Chapter 4, note 10).

16 This change is reflected in a move from linguistic to discoursal concerns in analyses of advertising. Compare, for example, Leech (1966) with Vestergaard and Schroder (1985).

17 As in linguistic analysis, description of them must 'shunt' (Halliday 1976:59).

18 Similar criticisms of the formalists, for attempting to limit their concerns to the textual level, were made by Ingarden (Grabwicz 1973:lxv–lxvii). Bakhtin also criticized Saussurean linguistics for isolating language from its users and encouraging a dualist view. In this, he pre-dates similar views in modern discourse analysis by forty years.

19 Unlike the formalists, who were forced mostly into minor editorial and philological work (Terras 1985:60, 407, 480), Bakhtin, with considerable mental agility and acumen, managed to keep on producing theoretical writings throughout the Stalin period. He even successfully defended a doctorate implying criticism of hegemonic and monolithic ideology (Clark and Holquist 1984:263, 295–320). This work, entitled 'Rabelais and the History of Realism', on carnival culture of the Middle Ages, was later expanded and published as a book, *Rabelais and His World* [1965] 1968. While expressing orthodox Marxist-Leninist views in its eulogy of folk culture and

condemnation of the Roman Catholic Church, its championing of humour and parody against a monolithic and humourless authority could be interpreted allegorically as a criticism of Stalinism. It is impossible to tell how the relationship between Bakhtinian and formalist criticism might have matured and developed in different circumstances. The friendship which developed between Bakhtin and Shklovsky in their old age in the 1970s may be some indication of the potential for reconciliation and mutual benefit between the two trains of thought (see Shklovsky 1966:298; Clark and Holquist 1984:340–3).

8 Application of the theory: three literary texts

Introduction

The previous chapter has advanced a theory involving schema refreshment, cognitive change, and discourse deviation. The description has, however, been made in the most general terms. This generality is inevitable, both for reasons of quantity—the possible interconnections of formal features and schemata being virtually infinite, and for reasons of quality—the essential feature of discourse deviation being its defamiliarizing unpredictability.

The theory, however, cannot remain so hypothetical. In this chapter, I shall apply it to three texts, hypothesizing about the relations between formal features and schemata, and suggesting that the overall effect of these relations is discourse deviation and their outcome is schema refreshment. These analyses are intended to show examples of the kinds of interconnection which may exist. They make no attempt to be exhaustive descriptions, either of discourse deviation or of the texts themselves.

The three texts chosen are all notorious as battlegrounds of interpretative disagreement. They have each been analysed many times over, according to the tenets of very different critical approaches. For present purposes, this disagreement is an advantage. First of all, it suggests the richness of the texts themselves; their ability to affect, in different ways, a wide variety of readers. Secondly, it provides an opportunity to contrast the theory proposed here with others I have described before. The texts chosen are:

- 'The Tyger' by William Blake
- *The Turn of the Screw* by Henry James
- 'The Windhover' by Gerard Manley Hopkins.

In each of the analyses, it is important to emphasize the reader-dependency of interpretative schemata, of new schemata or schematic connections generated by the reading, and of judgements of linguistic and text-structural deviation. They hold true for one reader (me, the writer) and assume successful intuitive conscious access to schemata. Differences among readers will produce new readings. Nevertheless, it seems likely that the readings here will hold true for other readers whose experience of language and the world is sufficiently similar.

Text Five: 'The Tyger'

The Tyger

Tyger! Tyger! burning bright
In the forests of the night,
What immortal hand or eye
Could frame thy fearful symmetry?

In what distant deeps or skies   5
Burnt the fire of thine eyes?
On what wings dare he aspire?
What the hand dare seize the fire?

And what shoulder, & what art
Could twist the sinews of thy heart?   10
And when thy heart began to beat,
What dread hand? & what dread feet?

What the hammer? what the chain?
In what furnace was thy brain?
What the anvil? what dread grasp   15
Dare its deadly terrors clasp?

When the stars threw down their spears,
And water'd heaven with their tears,
Did he smile his work to see?
Did he who made the Lamb make thee?   20

Tyger! Tyger! burning bright
In the forests of the night,
What immortal hand or eye,
Dare frame thy fearful symmetry?

Earlier controversy

In an eloquent plea for the reader-dependency of interpretation and the inability of any one interpretation to be absolute, Stanley Fish (1980: 339) has mockingly listed some of the rival interpretations which this poem has generated. Thus Raine (1954), adducing obscure cabbalistic writings in evidence, concluded that the tiger is 'Evil' and the answer to the final question a decisive 'No'. Hirsch, in contrast, saw the tiger as 'holiness' because: ' "Forests" ' suggests tall straight forms, a world that for all its terror has the orderliness of the tiger's stripes and Blake's perfectly balanced verses' (Hirsch 1964:247, quoted by Fish 1980:339). Taking up this refrain, other critics have regarded the tiger as both good and evil; others still as being beyond good and evil. Hobsbaum (1964) regarded the tiger as a mystery; Doxey (1970),[1] citing biographical evidence that Blake was apprenticed to an engraver who made engravings for astronomers, thought the tiger must be a stellar constellation. Stevenson (1969), in a New Critical vein,[2] decides that the tiger is the poem itself, and the answer to the last question, 'What immortal hand or eye, / Dare frame thy fearful symmetry?', therefore 'the poet', Blake. Sardonically, Fish points to the foolish finality of all these readings, observing simply that they cannot all be true. Amusingly, he picks out the presence of some dogmatic phrase such as 'there is no doubt' in each reading, at exactly the point where the critic is being most speculative and presenting the critic's own view as a final truth, elevated above all others (Fish 1980:340). Thus (my italics):

> The answer to the question is *beyond all possible doubt*. (Hirsch)

> *There can be no doubt that The Tyger* . . . is a poem which celebrates the holiness of tigerness. (Raine)

> *It is quite evident that* the critics are not trying to understand the poem at all. (Hobsbaum)

Ironically, and possibly self-consciously, Fish also uses such a phrase in pointing this out:

> Whenever a critic prefaces an assertion with a phrase such as 'without doubt' or 'there can be no doubt', *you can be sure* you are within hailing distance of the interpretative principles which produce the facts he presents as obvious.
> (ibid.) (my italics)

Jokingly, he observes that the subject of the poem might as well be interpreted as 'indigestion' caused by eating tiger meat instead of lamb (ibid.:348). Each reading, in his view, is true only for one reader or a group of readers who share values and interpretative strategies: an 'interpretative community'. In a sense, all the interpretations above are those of one such community. They all share a belief in the possibility of a single interpretation supported by evidence.

Fish's attack on the readings listed above is, from the point of view being advanced here, more easily accepted than the attack he makes in another essay (Fish 1980:246–67) on the stylistic analysis of the poem by Epstein (1975). This is because Epstein makes use of the supposedly rigorous and scientific approach to the language of the poem as text which I have so far taken for granted in my approach to both discourse analysis and literary theory: in contrast to Epstein's method, the other readings listed above seem arbitrary and intuitive. Fish, however, dismisses this linguistic approach for being quite as arbitrary as any other: the reading of yet another interpretative community, presented, quite wrongly, as fact.

Epstein catalogues a number of deviant linguistic features, which, in his view, create the ambiguity of the poem and its power to generate so many rival interpretations (ibid.: 63–9). Thus, he points to the uncertain grammatical analysis of a number of phrases in the poem. In the first stanza, 'burning bright', for example, may be read in three ways. 'Bright' may be an adverb modifying the participial adjective 'burning' which postmodifies the noun 'tyger'. This reading is equivalent to an analysis of the noun phrase as

(tyger, tyger [(who) (is burning) (brightly)])

Alternatively, by analogy with such phrases as 'boiling hot' and 'hopping mad', the word 'bright' may be read as an adjective postmodifying the noun 'tyger'. The adjective is itself modified by the participle 'burning'. In this reading the meaning is equivalent to

((burning bright) tyger)

or

(Tyger, tyger [(who) (is) (burning bright)])

A third, subtly different reading, is made by analogy with such clauses as 'the candle was burning blue' and 'the moon was shining bright'. Here the candle/moon is burning and becoming bright as a result. The verb phrases are, in Epstein's words, 'quasi-predicative':

(the tyger) (is burning) (bright)

A similar ambiguity exists in the phrase:

(in (the forests (of (the night))))

Here 'in' may mean either 'within/ as an integral part of' (as in 'there is hydrogen in water') or 'contained in but not part of' (as in 'there are fish in the water'). 'Forests of the night' may be read to mean that the tiger is burning in the night which possesses forests. Alternatively, by analogy with phrases such as 'ye of little faith', 'the knight of the woeful countenance', or 'the lady of the lake', it may be read to mean that the tiger is burning in the forests which have the quality of the night. The first reading might mean something like 'in the thick tangled night', the second reading something like 'in the dark forests'. A combination of the threefold interpretation of 'burning bright' with the double interpretation of the 'forests of the night' yields six possible readings. These are all formal ambiguities of text rather than discourse but, as there is no disambiguating context for the poem, their effect remains.

Having made these linguistic points, Epstein continues to make a discoursal one (ibid.: 69–74). He explains the power and disturbing quality of the poem's questions by relating them to an analysis and typology of English questions, showing how the form of questions is dependent on the shared knowledge of questioner and answerer. Distinguishing 'yes/no' questions, which ask for an assertion of the truth of the whole proposition, from 'wh' questions, in which an interrogative word replaces the unknown element of the clause, he goes on to point out three levels of the latter category, distinguished by what he describes as the 'ignorance factor'. By way of exemplification he asks us to imagine the following dialogue:

Q1 What do I press?   primary question
A1 The button.
Q2 What button?   secondary question
A2 The red button.
Q3 What red button?   tertiary question
A3 The red button marked 'start'.
(Epstein 1975: 72)

This sequence is a co-operative 'homing in' on the required information, the increasing specificity of the noun phrase gradually pinpointing the required answer. (In this respect, it is reminiscent of the given/new structure of discourse described on pages 50–1.) The questions of 'The Tyger' are, as Epstein observes, of a secondary and tertiary kind. They disconcert because they assume the primary sequence and a degree of shared knowledge which the reader does not have.

On what wings dare he aspire?
What the hand dare seize the fire?

More interesting than the immediate answers to these questions would be knowledge of the primary questions and answers from which they derive. More interesting still would be to know who is talking to whom.

Applying the theory

Fish's attack on Epstein reflects an unfortunate parting of the ways between formal description of a literary text and a pluralist acknowledgement of reader variation. But, as I am trying to show, the two need not be mutually exclusive. Relatively stable formal features interacting with varying knowledge and preconceptions will yield as many valid interpretations as Fish could desire. In this section, I shall attempt to describe a possible interaction of the poem with a reader's schemata, and the way in which changes in these schemata may be effected through the poem's formal features. In this I shall, unlike Fish, accept the linguistic and pragmatic analysis of Epstein as valid for all speakers. But, unlike Epstein, I shall attempt to show some ways in which these features create interpretations. To do this, we need first to speculate about the schemata evoked by the poem.

What follows, then, is not an interpretation in the literary critical sense, but a description of how such interpretations may be produced. Interpretations derive from the interaction of schematic predictions — about language and text structure as well as the world — with the specific linguistic structures and text structure of this poem. Different interpretations derive from differences in world schemata (or possibly from slight differences in text and language schemata[3]). The power of the poem lies in its openness to different interpretations arising from different initial schematic assumptions. If, for example, we assume that many people, perhaps the majority, regard the poem as being in some way about cosmic creation and destruction and the forces of good and evil, then the poem will not exclude people with widely different schemata of these forces and events, reflecting differences in religious beliefs and knowledge. This does not in any way imply anything about Blake's schemata. He might, for example, have had a very literal idea of creation, believing that God made animals in the sky. But if so, neither this, nor any other specific religious assumption, is so precisely present in the poem that it would exclude a reader with different schemata about creation. In contrast, we might compare the poem with, for example, the Creed in the Anglican *Book of Common Prayer*, which contains such lines as:

> I believe in God the Father Almighty Maker of heaven and earth and in Jesus Christ his only Son our Lord. ... I believe in ... The holy Catholick Church; The Communion of Saints.

This statement is too explicit to be accommodated into Moslem, Jewish, or atheist schemata, or even into the schemata of other Christian denominations. This is not true of 'The Tyger'.[4]

A reader's interpreting schemata

Let us postulate the following, scriptlike schemata ($S), and list under each $S name the words and phrases from the poem referring to defaults, and the relationship they have to the main concept. Words listed under each $S are all 'headers in the text' in the sense used on page 82. For reasons given on pages 121–2, I shall no longer list default elements under the headings used for scripts. The important feature of a scriptlike schema is only that it contains quite specific defaults. In the contents of the scriptlike schemata described below, there is a dominance of qualities and attributes (IS) and actions (event). It is often shared attributes and actions which create a metaphoric link from one schema to another. Furnaces, stars, and eyes are all bright. Spears and starlight both move fast and straight.

1 $S TIGER
   Props:
   —Locations 'forests'.
   —HAS 'heart', 'sinews', 'brain', 'eyes'
   $S EYES: ARE 'bright'
   IS: 'deadly', 'fearful'
   Results: "deadly terrors".

2 $S FORESTS
   Prop: HAS 'tyger'
   IS dark.

3 $S NIGHT
   IS dark
   IS like 'deeps'
   Props:
   —HAS 'skies'
   —HAS 'stars'
   $S STARLIGHT: MOVES
   IS 'bright'

4 $S BLACKSMITH
   Props:
   —HAS/ MOVES 'hand', 'eye', 'shoulders', 'sinews'
   —Instruments: 'hammer', 'chain', 'furnace', 'anvil' 'fire'
   $S FIRE: IS 'bright'
   Events: 'grasp', 'beat', 'clasp'
   Result: 'work'

5 $S ARTIST
   Props: HAS/ MOVES 'hand', 'eye'
   Results: 'symmetry', 'art', 'work'.

6 $S GOD
   IS 'immortal', 'dread', 'fearful'
   Results: 'deadly terrors'
   Track: $S PAGAN GODS
   ARE 'stars'
   Instance: Thor/ Zeus
   IS blacksmith (see $S BLACKSMITH)
   Prop: Instrument: bolts

Event: throws
Sub track: $S Greek gods.

7 $S SPEAR-THROWER
Instrument: 'spears'
Event: throws.

8 $S TEARS.

Plans and themes

The above schemata fall into two groups. Those for tigers, forests, and night may each contain the other two (a case of double inclusion, see page 118). This group, however, has no immediate connection to the remainder; the schemata for blacksmith, artist, God, spear-thrower, tears. We may suppose that, for many readers, these lower-level schemata associate with each other in various ways through a common plan or theme of a character, or of the reader. Thus schemata of a blacksmith, an artist, and God all share the common theme of creation (and perhaps the use of fire); the tiger and certain manifestations of God share the theme of destruction. Tiger, forests, the night, God, and spear-throwers can all be frightening and may invoke in the reader a theme of self-preservation, executed through a plan of escape.

Schema connections

Each of the lower-level schemata will include elements which find no mention in the poem (blacksmiths work on horses for example). The contents evoked in the poem, however, yield a number of cross-references. Thus both the tiger and the blacksmith have sinews. The tiger's eyes are like fire, which a blacksmith uses, and, being points of light, they are also like stars. Forests are dark like the night, which contains stars, which in turn are associated with the gods. One of the gods (Zeus or Thor) was a blacksmith who threw thunderbolts. Starlight, which is part of the night, is like the throwing of spears. And so on . . . The fact that some of these connections may be peculiar to me, does not invalidate the principle of this kind of connection.

The overall effect of the poem, then, is to bring together these schemata either by choosing elements which they already have in common, or by establishing new links between them. The result is the creation of a new and unique composite schema, drawing together elements of the original ones. (It is tempting to use the poem's own imagery of the forge—but this is perhaps too near to interpretation.)

This interweaving is not only, however, achieved through the choice of items shared by the different schemata, nor through their linear mixing, nor through the evocation of shared higher-level schemata (plans and goals) of either characters or readers. It is also effected through the use of ambiguous 'deviant' linguistic structures of the kind observed by Epstein, writing, we may observe, in the stylistics tradition which derives from the formal approach to literary language of Roman Jakobson (see pages 152–5). Thus, for example, the opening lines:

Tyger! Tyger! burning bright
in the forests of the night,

bring together into a single noun-phrase words which evoke three schemata, and which can later be linked to a god and to the blacksmith. They also, through the formal ambiguities described by Epstein, allow various hierarchical connections between those schemata. Thus, if we read 'in' as 'within' (i.e., an integral part of) we may regard the tiger as part of $S FOREST or $S NIGHT; if we read it as 'in, but not part of' ('among') we may treat it as a separate schema. The two readings of 'forests of the night' will allow night to be a part of $S FORESTS, or forests to be a part of $S NIGHT. The same holds true of the second stanza. Here 'the fire of thine eyes' allows fire to be part of eyes, or eyes to be part of fire, and it is this second option which seems to be taken up in the final line, where the image of a fire that may be seized triggers $S BLACKSMITH. Whether or not these comments hold true for a significant number of readers, we might suppose that the kind of Jakobsonian detail catalogued by Epstein effects some degree of schema refreshment along these or similar lines.

Nor is this linking effected only through grammatical ambiguity or lexis shared by different schemata. Sound effects such as rhyme, alliteration, assonance, and consonance will create links between words which reinforce or contradict their semantic connections. Thus 'bright' connects with 'night', 'frame' with 'fearful', 'skies' with 'eyes', and so on.

The adjectival presence of God

One strange feature of the poem, which might with reason be used against this analysis, is that there is no lexical item referring directly to three of the major schemata I have proposed: $S BLACKSMITH, $S ARTIST, $S GOD. The same is true of the sub-schemata which depend on them: $S PAGAN GODS, $S SPEAR-THROWER. These are evoked, not by a lexical item referring directly to them, but by reference to elements of the schema. For example, 'hammer', 'furnace', and 'anvil' evoke $S BLACKSMITH. In the case of $S GOD, the evocation is even less direct, effected through adjectives which commonly collocate with God: 'immortal', 'dread', 'fearful', and effects which God produces—

'deadly terrors'. The dependent schemata are evoked through association with other schemata: Thor/Zeus was a blacksmith, using an anvil, associated with the stars from which he threw spears/bolts.

This merely implied presence need not, however, weaken my claim for the validity of these schemata. (It was, in any case, never an absolute claim but was only supposed true for certain readers.) The absence of a word referring to these schemata as a whole might be taken as leaving their contents floating free for recombination. In addition, their presence through implication makes them both more powerful and more mysterious. Again, we may make use of Epstein's stylistics analysis, though this time drawing upon its pragmatic rather than its linguistic aspects. Just as the use of secondary and tertiary questions makes the primary questions from which they derive—and the identity of questioner and questioned—more remote, so too does this evocation of parts of schemata without reference to their unifying concept. It is this vagueness which gives the poem the power to yield many interpretations, and which underlines the uncertainty and reader-dependency of the schemata I have tentatively advanced.

Text structure and text schemata

For speakers of a given language, textual schemata are perhaps more reader-variable than either (world) schemata or language schemata. They depend very much upon experience of other texts, and this is more likely to vary between individuals than experience of the world or of the language. A given text, for example, may appear highly unoriginal to a particular individual but highly original to another, if the former has experience of other texts with the same structure, while the latter has no such experience.

'The Tyger' is no exception to these general principles. It is one of a series of poems, the *Songs of Innocence and of Experience*, and also a poem which is (like many advertisements) presented together with a picture. To a reader who knows the series of poems, or the picture, its meaning will be effected by interaction. Arguably, this effect on meaning is part of its text structure, for the poem itself is part of a larger whole, and takes on meaning through its relation to other parts of that whole.

The poem may also take on meaning through its relation to other known and relevant text structures. It is presented as a 'song', and its structure may be compared to that of a song. Its first and last stanzas, through their repetitions, are like refrains, and they frame the intermediate stanzas in way which is often found in ballads (Buchan 1972: chapters 6–8). The questions are also 'ballad like'. Another possible parallel is with the unanswered questions of the Book of Job in the Bible (Epstein 1975: 63). The text-structural level, however, cannot be examined in

Figure 8.1: 'The Tyger' from Songs of Experience

isolation from the language level, for the questioning is conveyed by the interrogative clause structure. The refrain is not exactly a refrain: 'Could' has become 'Dare'. Significantly, this difference between first and last stanzas was made by Blake at a late stage in the drafting of the poem (Abrams [1962] 1986:2489–90). If it *is* significant, and if the ballad or song is a relevant text structure, then it is worth noting that such attention to precise linguistic choice would not be available to the balladeer in a pre-literate culture. In such a tradition, despite modern assumptions about verbatim memory, the words were most likely never repeated exactly (Ellis and Beatty 1986:248–51). There is a tension between Blake's use of features of song and ballad form and his precise attention to linguistic detail, evidenced by a comparison of the final and earlier drafts. The ballad form was a genre whose social status diminished with the coming of literacy. As a pre-literate genre at a period on the verge of an explosion of literacy, it was also doomed to change and die (Buchan 1972). Blake exploits the form, changes it, and elevates it.[5] It is a classic case of the formalist device, 'canonization of the junior branch'. It is genre defamiliarization.

For certain readers, then, a text schema which may be evoked is that of a ballad or song. By varying the refrain and leaving questions unanswered, the poem deviates from the expectations created by this schema. This schema is thus refreshed. The deviation at text-structural level in turn suggests or points to deviation at the level of (world) schemata. It may even be that if some new (world) schemata have come into being through the first five stanzas in ways which I have been at pains to describe above, then the virtual repetition of the first stanza may highlight how the schemata it evoked the first time round have radically changed by the time it recurs.

Paradoxically, the above comments, while they may have been true of readings by Blake's contemporaries, or of literature specialists today, are not likely to hold true for the majority of readers. Blake's poetry—and this poem in particular—is so widely anthologized and known that it has itself become a model, a stereotype and a source of a text-structural schema. By contrast, the ballads and the Book of Job are less well-known. The poem's ability to defamiliarize through evoking and departing from text-structural expectations is thus weakened, if not destroyed. This only serves to illustrate a degree of reader dependency in discourse deviation. To some extent, it is at the mercy of reader variation.

Text Six: *The Turn of the Screw*

Superficially, Henry James' novella *The Turn of the Screw* and William Blake's 'The Tyger' are very different kinds of text. The former is an extended piece of narrative prose, whose grammar, though elaborate, could be described as 'non-deviant', while the latter is a short lyric poem, in rhymed and rhythmic verse, containing linguistic deviations (as observed by Epstein). In Bakhtinian terms, the former has the many narrative voices of the novel, the latter the single narrative voice of the short lyric poem. Despite these differences, they are both classed as literary, both are widely read and studied, and both have attracted a great deal of critical attention, resulting in bitter dispute and widely differing interpretations. These differences of form, and similarities of response, may give rise to interesting points of comparison and contrast. In terms of the present theory, they are both instances of discourse deviation, though the schemata they 'refresh' and the formal means they use to effect this are rather different (though not perhaps so different as might at first appear).

Skaz and schemata

It is a truism that any author who opts for an exclusively first-person narrative accepts the inevitable limitation of the single point of view. Within the terms of the fiction, no events can be related which are not known, either first or second hand, to the narrator. Yet the first-person narrative also involves an unstated contract with the reader: that the story-teller will, in Gricean terms, be co-operative: clear, true, relevant, and as brief as necessary (see pages 40–1). Departure from this contract is perceived as 'deviant' and defamiliarizing. The obscurity of narratives such as those in, for example, Samuel Beckett's trilogy, is viewed as remarkable. The same deviation is perceived when narrators' assumptions and knowledge lead them to state the obvious at great and defamiliarizing length. This is the point made in Shklovsky's formalist analysis of Tolstoy's story *Kholstomer* (Shklovsky [1917] 1965), where the narrator is a horse who explains as new the nature of human institutions and behaviour already coated with 'the glass armour of the familiar' for any human reader (Shklovsky [1940] 1974:68). (Other examples of such unusual narrators and their defamiliarizing effect have already been cited on pages 135–6 above.) Above all, perhaps, within the fictional world, the narrator is assumed to be truthful. Though a fictional world is of its nature in one sense untrue, nevertheless it is possible for a narrator to tell untruths within that world, to withhold a fact, mislead, or give contradictory reports (Short 1989). That is why Agatha Christie's *The Murder of Roger Ackroyd* (a detective story whose first-person narrator does not confide in the reader that he is the murderer) has such a defamiliarizing effect: it makes us examine again our schematic assumptions about the reliability of narrators. We assume that the narrator has told us not only the truth, but the whole truth. (Again I am here generalizing from my own response in the belief that it is shared by others.)

In general, this reliability of narrators is overruled only where the demands of the co-operative principle are outweighed by those of the politeness principle (cf page 43), in particular when narrators feel it incumbent upon them to be modest and withhold information concerning, for example, their own attractiveness or honesty. In this case, however, the reader may resort to the view of other characters expressed within the narrative. A good example of this is Nick Carraway, the narrator of *The Great Gatsby*, who, though extremely self-deprecating, has his reliability established by the confidence he evokes in the two main characters, Jay Gatsby and Daisy Buchanan, and his attractiveness attested by the attentions of a third character, Jordan Baker. This is a kind of parallax, the fixing of an object by observation from two points of view at once: a relativist scientific notion significantly mused upon at length by Bloom in Joyce's *Ulysses*.[6] Where the narrating voice is to be doubted, we resort to that of a character. In a first-person narrative, this is of course an illusion, because the evidence for the apparently withheld truth is in fact presented by the voice which appears to withhold it. It is, however, a convention which works. Information is also withheld to create suspense, though, in this case, the deprivation is only temporary. A more difficult kind of unreliable narrative is that of the person who, while being our only source of truth, is yet untrustworthy. There are many examples of such narrators in literature, some of whom have already been mentioned. The first narrator in *The Sound and the Fury*, for example, is mentally deficient; another narrative in the same novel is a racist. *Faithful Ruslan*, a novel by Georgi Vladimov, is told by an aggressive and violent guard dog. From a certain sexist point of view—very common among readers—the narrator of the main part of *The Turn of the Screw*, being a young and unmarried woman, is in this category of unreliable narrators! Yet the reader who does not totally question her reliability (and therefore her representation of other characters), may rely to some extent upon parallax: the viewpoints of other characters.

The Turn of the Screw is a concentric narrative of the kind described on pages 143–6. As such, for many readers, it conforms to a known text schema and sets up certain expectations. The degree of embedding—the number of narratives within narratives—is, however, unusual. The book is written by Henry James, but adopts a first-person narrative 'I' (though he begins, significantly, by talking about 'us': a group of people assembled together on Christmas Eve). Within this narrative is a further narrator 'Douglas', who gives an account of how he came by the journal of a young woman. This journal is then presented in its entirety, and forms by far the greater part of the novella—114 pages of 121 in the

Penguin edition. Within the first-person narrative of the journal, are the narratives of other characters. Miles, the little boy, gives an account of his school; Mrs Grose, the housekeeper, relates various facts and opinions of her own. (This structure is presented diagrammatically in Figure 8.2.) The novella finishes with the end of the journal. There is no return to the narrative of 'Douglas' nor the 'I' of the opening pages. In this respect it is the same kind of incomplete concentric narrative as *Notes from the Dead House* (see pages 143–6).

The journal itself is the young woman's account of how she was employed by a 'person . . . in Harley Street' (page 11)[7] to act as governess for his two children, Miles and Flora. The governess recounts how she became aware of the presence in the house of the ghosts of two servants, Quint and Miss Jessel, how the children were also aware of their presence, and indeed were possessed by them. The governess tells of her struggle with the ghosts for possession of the children, and of her efforts to convince the housekeeper, Mrs Grose, of the ghosts' existence. The story ends with the death by heart failure of the boy, Miles, in his governess's arms as she struggles to persuade him not to look at the ghost of Quint.

In addition to being, quite literally, a number of voices inside other voices, each layer of the narrative differs in discourse type and medium from the layer above and below. It is a journal inside a ghost story inside a novel. As such, it is writing presented through speech presented through writing. Moreover, and significantly in terms of the preconcep-

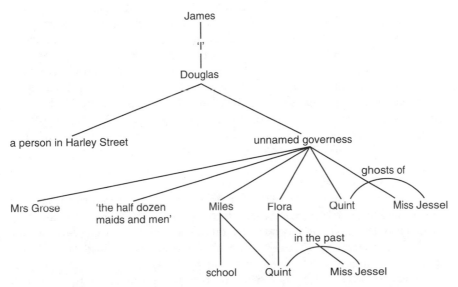

Figure 8.2: Narrators and characters in The Turn of the Screw

Discourse type	Mode	Voice	Pronoun used
novel	writing	author/narrator	'we'/'I'
ghost story	speech	man	'I'
journal	writing	woman	'I'
speech (of characters)	speech	characters	'we'

Table 8.1: Layers of narrative in The Turn of the Screw

tions of many readers, it is the voice of an emotional and hasty young woman inside that of a reticent and serious middle-aged man.

The 'hearsay principle'

The Turn of the Screw, like 'The Tyger', has attracted a good deal of critical controversy. Rival interpretations centre mostly, with a quite startling naïvety, on the question of whether the ghosts exist! Edmund Wilson ([1934] 1960), for example, with dogmatic certainty, expounded an argument citing various pieces of evidence from her narrative, that the governess is suffering from a neurosis inspired by the suppression of her sexual feelings towards her employer, that the ghosts are a figment of her imagination, and the death of the children her doing. Forty years later, Sheppard (1974) is at passionate pains to refute the argument detail by detail, insisting that the ghosts are real and the children evil. The fifteen studies in Willen's (1960) anthology of critical essays on the story, and the twenty-one in Scura's (1979) anthology, almost all debate the issue in the same terms. Quite apart from the primitive assumption of the reality of the fictional world, such readings ignore the embedded narrative structure, and the consequent uncertainty created by the interplay of levels: an interplay which makes the interpretation doubtful even if we treat this fictional word as real. Just as the linguistic structure of 'The Tyger' prevents a decisive interpretation, so does the text structure of *The Turn of the Screw* (Culler 1975b: 137). Such a view is perhaps reflected—though the author's view carries no more authority than any other—in James's own frequently-quoted description of the work as an 'irresponsible little fiction . . . a piece of ingenuity pure and simple' (Sheppard 1974: 5).

The futility of attempts to give a definitive judgement on the truth of the embedded narrative is a result of what I shall call the 'hearsay principle'. This can be explained by analogy with the approach to the truth of narratives in court. It is a well-known legal principle that, while a witness is bound to tell the truth on pain of prosecution for perjury, that same witness's evidence about somebody else's evidence is unreliable, even if the witness believes it to be true. It is 'hearsay evidence', and inadmissible. The witness may be honestly reporting the account he or she heard, but that account may itself have been untrue. If this is so at one remove, for every further remove the uncertainty increases. In *The Turn of the Screw*, we have a narrative inside a narrative inside a narrative inside a narrative: evidence about evidence about evidence about evidence. At so far a remove, even if we treat the account as one of fact instead of fiction, it is quite impossible to be sure of anything. The reliability of any one narrator in the chain may be undermined by the unreliability of any other. For the story to be true, it must be true at every level. Ironically, many readers may feel that in this insubstantial quicksand of voices, the most reliable voice is that of the character Mrs Grose the housekeeper, a 'stout simple plain clean wholesome woman' (page 15): a down-to-earth, matter-of-factual, common-sensical person whose views are to be trusted far more than those of the self-indulgent, more impressionable governess, influenced by her own romantic readings and preconceptions.[8] (In the terms of schema theory, such readers might say that the governess's schemata lead her to expect ghosts in an old house by default.) Reliance on Mrs Grose's testimony, however, quite inverts the removes of the narrative. For her voice exists only within and through the voice of the governess. Everything she says is hearsay at the furthest remove. The most reliable voice, and the one we can hold most accountable, must be the closest to us. Our judgement should rely most heavily on the outer narrative, the 'I' with which the novel opens, speaking confidently for 'us', or—if he is unavailable—perhaps 'Douglas'. (Interestingly, in *Wuthering Heights*, a similarly stereotypically reliable housekeeper is to be found in one of the outer levels.) Yet the end of *The Turn of the Screw* offers no return voyage back through the circles of this narrative solar system. The tale finishes abruptly with the death of Miles. We are offered neither the opinion of the narrator, nor Douglas, nor even of Mrs Grose.

The Turn of the Screw as discourse deviation

For the reasons outlined above, I believe there can be no solution to the problem of the veracity or sanity of the governess's narration. As in 'The Tyger' it is the form of the text which, in interaction with reader schemata, will create differing interpretations. And, as in 'The Tyger', it is a form which may interact with widely different schemata, causing their disruption and refreshment. The defamiliarizing effect of *The Turn of the Screw* is far more a question of the interplay of (world) schemata with text schemata and the *skaz* of the various narrators, than is the case in 'The Tyger' where deviation relies far more on lexical combinations and grammatically ambiguous sub-sentential structures. *The Turn of the*

Screw leads to the disruption of schemata about the very act of story-telling itself.

Let us hypothesize that in reading *The Turn of the Screw* a number of relevant processing schemata will be activated, from the very inception of the framing narrative. (It may well be that schemata activated in the opening of a discourse have a tendency to persist throughout.) The book begins:

> The story had held us, round the fire, sufficiently breathless, but except the obvious remark that it was gruesome, as, on Christmas eve in an old house, a strange tale should essentially be, I remember no comment uttered till somebody happened to say that it was the only case he had met in which such a visitation had fallen on a child. The case, I may mention, was that of an apparition in just such an old house as had gathered us for the occasion—an appearance, of a dreadful kind, to a little boy sleeping in the room with his mother and waking her up in the terror of it; waking her not to dissipate his dread and soothe him to sleep again, but to encounter also, herself, before she had succeeded in doing so, the same sight that had shaken him. It was this observation that drew from Douglas—not immediately, but later in the evening—a reply that had the interesting consequence to which I call attention. Someone else told a story not particularly effective, which I saw he was not following. This I took for a sign that he had himself something to produce and that we should only have to wait. We waited in fact till two nights later; but that same evening, before we scattered, he brought out what was on his mind. (*The Turn of the Screw* [1898] 1969:7)

Let us suppose that this opening activates, among others, schemata concerning Ghost stories, Ghosts, Narrations, and Men. The following pages relate how Douglas goes on to produce the journal of the young woman, which he then reads to the assembled company. (Bear in mind that the fact that Douglas's 'tale' is written may—though not necessarily—make it seem more reliable as a true account of the governess's words than a mere verbal report. Note also that the initial use of 'we' in the outer narrative suggests plurality and consensus, contrasting with the singular and correspondingly isolated 'I' of the journal. The fact that there are two children, leads to a further contrast of 'I' and 'we'.) The journal begins:

> I remember the whole beginning as a succession of flights and drops, a little see-saw of the right throbs and the wrong. After rising, in town, to meet his appeal, I had at all events a couple of very bad days—found myself doubtful again, felt indeed sure I had made a mistake. In this state of mind I spent the long hours of bumping,

swinging coach that carried me to the stopping-place at which I was to be met by a vehicle from the house. This convenience, I was told, had been ordered, and I found, towards the end of the June afternoon, a commodious fly in waiting for me. Driving at that hour, on a lovely day, through the country to which the summer sweetness seemed to offer me a friendly welcome, my fortitude mounted afresh and, as we turned into the avenue, encountered a reprieve that was probably but a proof of the point to which I had sunk. I suppose I had expected, or had dreaded, something so melancholy that what greeted me was a good surprise.
(*The Turn of the Screw* [1898] 1969: 14)

Let us suppose that this opening activates schemata concerning Journals, Governesses/Young Women, and Summer. Arrival by a young woman at a country house may also evoke text schemata derived from the conventions of the Gothic novel.[9] The schemata evoked, and their contents, will of course vary considerably between individuals. But supposing that those listed here are possible, indeed likely, we may observe that they fall into three main categories: schemata about the world, schemata about narrators, and schemata about discourse types. (Schemata about discourse types are here included under the heading 'Text schemata';[10] schemata about narrators are treated as world schemata.) There are also schematic connections between the categories: ghost stories are told on Christmas Eve for example. Relevant schemata are:

(World) schemata:

$S GHOSTS	(relevant plans: Π R/C SEEK EVIDENCE)
$S CHRISTMAS EVE	(relevant plan: Π A/C ENTERTAIN)
$S SUMMER	
$S MEN	(relevant plans: Π C JUDGE, Π C ADVISE)
$S GOVERNESS	(relevant plans: Π C PROTECT CHILDREN, Π C PERFORM DUTY)

Text schemata:

$S GHOST STORIES	(realizing plans: Π ENTERTAIN, Π FRIGHTEN)
$S NARRATION	(realizing plans: Π INFORM/ Π ENTERTAIN)
$S JOURNALS	(realizing plans: Π REMIND/ Π RECORD FACT)

Within this framework, the potential for interplay, contradiction and variation is quite immense. The contents of a (world) schema $S GHOSTS, for example, varies widely. For some people, who do not believe in ghosts, $S GHOSTS can only exist as part of $S GHOST STORIES. Gender stereotypes cause similar divergence. For some people $S YOUNG WOMAN will contain such default attributes as 'unreliable', 'romantic', 'credulous', and $S MAN will contain their opposites. Other people will not share these preconceptions. Each schema about narrators and discourse types will contain a default attribution of reliability. The combination of schemata in *The Turn of the Screw*, however, leads to contradiction: writing is more reliable than speech—but journals are more reliable than ghost stories—but middle-aged men are often considered more reliable than young women.

Knowledge of what types of evidence are reliable is of crucial importance to an individual. To call assumptions into question is to undermine the basis of all knowledge. Given the particular combinations of these elements in *The Turn of the Screw*, it is quite simply impossible to maintain all the relevant schemata intact. One or another must be wrong. If the journal is more reliable than the ghost story, then the young woman is more reliable than the man. Let us look at the contradictions which exist between the pointers to reliability in Douglas's narrative and the governess's narrative as set out in Table 8.2.

	Governess		Douglas	
Discourse type:	journal	R+	ghost story	R−
Narrator:	young woman	R−	middle aged man	R+
Medium:	writing	R+	speech	R−
Text schema:	inner narrative	R−	outer narrative	R+
Goal:	truth	R+	entertainment	R−
World:	ghosts exist	OR	ghosts don't exist	

R+   = a schema default of reliability
R−   = a schema default of unreliability

Table 8.2: Reliability associated with schemata

One relatively simple effect of this is to disrupt schemata which attribute unreliability to young women or non-existence to ghosts. Readers have to choose between world and textual schemata. (Edmund Wilson, revealing more about himself and his time than the story, chose to treat the telling of a ghost story as fact and a journal as untrue, but to preserve a schema in which young women are unreliable.) The doubt resulting from the irreconcilable demands of different schemata might perhaps be referred finally to the author-ity of the author (the pun is significant) or the parallax views of characters, especially Mrs Grose. It is the story's refusal to conform to the text schema for concentric narrative, setting up an expectation that doubt will be resolved through a return to the outer narrative, which makes schema disruption inevitable

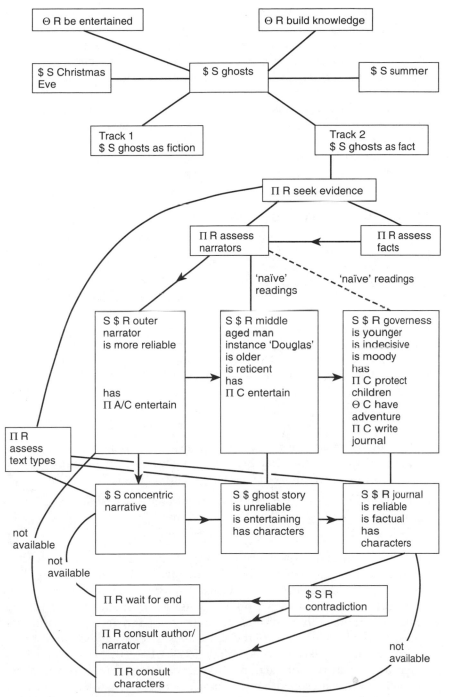

Figure 8.3: Interaction of a reader's schemata in The Turn of the Screw

and irresolvable. Figure 8.3 (above) attempts to describe the relationships between schemata and the inevitable circularity of a reader's attempts to solve the question of whether the ghosts exist.

In *The Turn of the Screw*, world schemata and text schemata are in a dynamic interaction. Each disrupts the other. The only way to solve the problem is to change one set of schemata for another. Without this refreshment of existing schemata, the problem must remain unsolved: and that too would violate a schema, for it is surely a default of a puzzle, that it must have a solution! As discourse is the totality of text and communicative situation, this kind of instability can more justly be described as discourse deviation than formal deviation.

Text Seven: 'The Windhover'

The Windhover:
To Christ our Lord

I CAUGHT this morning morning's minion, king-   1
  dom of daylight's dauphin, dapple-dawn-drawn Falcon, in
    his riding
  Of the rolling level underneath him steady air, and striding
High there, how he rung upon the rein of a wimpling wing
In his ecstasy! then off, off forth on swing,   5
  As a skate's heel sweeps smooth on a bow-bend: the hurl and
    gliding
  Rebuffed the big wind. My heart in hiding
Stirred for a bird,—the achieve of, the mastery of the thing!

Brute beauty and valour and act, oh, air, pride, plume, here
  Buckle! AND the fire that breaks from thee then, a billion   10
Times told lovelier, more dangerous, O my chevalier!

  No wonder of it: shéer plód makes plough down sillion
Shine, and blue-bleak embers, ah my dear,
  Fall, gall themselves, and gash gold-vermilion.   14

Like 'The Tyger' and *The Turn of the Screw*, this poem has attracted considerable critical attention and controversy. Dunne (1976) lists seventy-three studies devoted exclusively to this poem, and it figures prominently in general works on Hopkins. Most studies, however, are chiefly concerned with meaning, interpretation, and the relationship of the poem to Hopkins' other works, or to his ideas, rather than upon linguistic detail (an exception is Milroy 1977:210–13). My own analysis concentrates upon the interaction of the grammar and lexis of the poem with a reader's interpretative schemata, and a consequent effect of schema change.

A reader's schemata for 'The Windhover'

Let us suppose that this poem triggers script-like schemata representing: Christ, morning, a knight, a falcon, a skater, fire, and ploughing. These seem to be the most prominent schemata in my own reading of the poem and, as before, I make the assumption that such schemata are likely to be similar to those of readers with a similar cultural background. Below, I suggest some default elements in these schemata, quoting words from the poem corresponding to these elements. The assignment of features to these six schemata is justified in the discussion which follows. As in 'The Tyger', there are a large number of connections between schemata through props, attributes, and results they have in common. These connections are indicated by cross references 'see $S X'.

$S CHRIST
Header in text: 'To Christ our Lord'
IS eldest son, like 'dauphin' (see $S KNIGHT)
IS like 'dawn' (see $S MORNING)
IS a champion like 'chevalier' (see $S KNIGHT)
Events:
—rose in the 'morning' (see $S MORNING)
—talks of a 'kingdom'
—sheds 'gall' and blood from 'gash'
Results: 'kingdom', 'ecstasy', 'mastery' (see $S KNIGHT), 'beauty' (see $S CHRIST).

$S MORNING
Header in text: 'this morning/ morning's'
IS 'dapple'
Events: 'dawn'
Results: 'daylight'.

$S KNIGHT
Instance:
—dauphin (eldest son like Christ: see $S CHRIST)
—'chevalier'
IS a 'minion'
Props:
—location: 'kingdom'
—'drawn' sword, 'plume', 'falcon' (see $S FALCON)
Events: 'riding', 'striding', 'rung upon the rein'
HAS: 'mastery', 'valour', 'pride'
Results: 'gash'

$S FALCON
Header in text: 'Windhover', 'Falcon'

Props:
—location: 'air'
—'wing'
IS 'high', 'a bird', 'a thing', 'brute',[11] 'blue-bleak', 'gold-vermilion'[12]
HAS 'plume'
Events: 'gliding', 'rebuffs the big wind'
Results: 'mastery', 'beauty' see ($S CHRIST, $S KNIGHT, $S SKATER)

$S SKATER
Events: 'sweeps smooth on a bow bend'

$S FIRE
Results: 'embers'
ARE 'blue-bleak'
Events: glow 'gold-vermilion' (see $S FALCON) like 'gash' (see $S KNIGHT, $S CHRIST)

$S PLOUGHING
Props: 'plough', 'sillion'[13]
Events: 'sheer plod'
Results: 'plough down sillion shine'

These schemata may well, before the reading of the poem, be relatively unconnected. Interpretation will be a relationship between them established in the reader. One interpretation, for example, (influenced by knowledge of Hopkins's religious beliefs) is that the ecstasy caused in the narrator by the beauty of the bird gives way to a control over that beauty, a submission to the will of Christ, echoing the control of the bird over its element, air (metaphorically expressed as the control of a knightly rider over a horse), and an acknowledgement of a higher authority (again expressed metaphorically through the knight, though this time referring to his subservient position in the kingdom, as 'minion' and 'dauphin'). This is the reading which I shall describe here, not in the belief that it is an only reading, but in illustration of possible interactions between linguistic features and schematic representations. The poem foregrounds elements which the schemata I have detailed have in common, thus drawing the different schemata together. Christ, like the knight and the falcon and potentially the narrator, has mastery. Like the knight and potentially the narrator, he submits to a higher authority.

I hope to show that, significantly, these script-like schemata also relate through higher-level schemata: life themes of appreciating beauty and serving Christ. New connections effect in the narrator (in this interpretation) a change of the plans which execute these themes, changing them from plans of passive contemplation to plans of work and control. The narrator is no longer content to be mastered by natural beauty, but must master it as a sign of obedience to a higher authority.

These changes are expressed through lower-level associations between schemata suggested by lexical and grammatical deviation, and ambiguity. The focus here must be on how these different schemata are brought together, and how the change of plan is reflected in the process of the poem. As it develops, the poem appears to change the high level schemata which give it coherence.

I shall consider relevant high-level schemata to be:

Themes: Θ SERVE CHRIST; Θ BE MASTERED BY BEAUTY; Θ MASTER BEAUTY
Plans: Π REJECT BEAUTY; Π WORK HARD; Π ATTAIN CONTROL

Phonological and graphological features

'The Windhover', unlike 'The Tyger', is highly idiosyncratic at every linguistic level: 'counter, original, spare, strange' (to borrow a description from another Hopkins poem).[14] The rhythm, line lengths, and line breaks are unorthodox and, though there is a rhyme scheme, the grammatical unit at the end of which the rhyme occurs is constantly changing.[15] There is also marked use of graphological devices, notably capitalization of whole words, hyphenation, and stress marks. These, it might be argued, are only present when the poem is experienced visually. On the other hand, they are clues to stress and emphasis.

As already stated, my major concern will be with the connections between the grammatical features of the poem and changes in the schemata of a reader. Nevertheless, with a poem of such marked phonological and graphological structure, and with such a marked relation between this structure and the grammar, it would clearly be foolish to leave this aspect of the poem out of account.

The rhythm of the poem is represented below. Stressed syllables are capitalized. In Figure 8.4 the overall rhythm is represented line by line by '+s' (stressed syllables) and '−s' (unstressed syllables). Table 8.3 lists some overall patterns.[16]

I CAUGHT this MORning MORning's MINion, KING-
dom of DAYlight's DAUphin, DApple-DAWN-DRAWN FALcon, in
his RIding
Of the ROlling LEvel underNEATH him STEAdy AIR, and STRIding
HIGH there, how he RUNG upon the REIN of a WIMpling WING
In his ECstasy! then OFF, OFF FORTH on SWING,
As a SKATE'S HEEL sweeps SMOOTH on a BOW-bend: the HURL
and GLIding
ReBUFFed the BIG WIND. My HEART in HIding
STIRRed for a BIRD,—the achIEVE of, the MAStery of the THING!

BRUTE BEAUty and VAlour and ACT, oh, AIR, PRIDE, PLUME, HERE

BUckle! and the FIRE that BREAKS from thee THEN, a BIllion TIMES told LOvelier, more DANgerous, O my CHEVaLIer!

No WONder of it: SHEER PLOD makes PLOUGH down SIllion SHINE, and BLUE-bleak EMbers, AH my DEAR,

FALL, GALL themSELves, and GASH GOLD-verMILion.

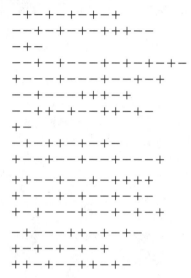

```
−+−+−+−+−+
−−+−+−+−+++−−
−+−
−−+−+−−−+−+−+−+−
+−−−+−−−+−−+−+
−−+−−−+++−+
−−++−+−−++−+−
+−
−+−++−+−+−
+−−+−−+−−+−−−+
++−−+−−+−++++
+−−−+−+−−−+−+−
+−+−−−+−−+−+−+

−+−−−++−+−+−
+−+−+−+−+
++−+−−++−+−
```

Figure 8.4: Stress patterns in 'The Windhover'

'The Windhover' as discourse deviation

It is not intended, nor is it possible, to give an exhaustive account of all the linguistic features of this poem which may result in the disruption and refreshment of the schemata I have hypothesized, or of any others. It is so rich and so complex that such an attempt could take up another book, while still not doing full justice to the poem's potential to mean. Of necessity I shall select a small number of linguistic features and speculate on their effect upon reading. I shall concentrate most of my attention upon the opening lines. One possible grammatical analysis of these lines is as follows:

[$^S_{NP}$ (I) $^P_{VP}$(CAUGHT) $^A_{NP}$(this morning) < $^{Od}_{NP}$(morning's minion) $^{Od}_{NP}$(king-dom of daylight's dauphin) $^{Od}_{NP}$($_{RCl}$[dapple-dawn-drawn] Falcon $_{PP}$(in (his riding (Of (the rolling level underneath him steady air))))) and $^{Od}_{NCl}$ [[^{P}(striding) ^{A}(High) ^{A}(there)] ^{A}(how) ^{S}(he) ^{P}(rung) $^A_{PP}$(upon (the rein (of (a wimpling wing)))) $^A_{PP}$(In (his ecstasy))]>]

Line	Syllables	Stresses	Elision disrupting	Rhyme	Graphological features
1	10	5	word	A	capitalized word/ word-break
2	16	7	phrase	B	word-break/ hyphens capital
3	16	6	clause	B	
4	14	5	clause	A	
5	11	5	clause	A	
6	15	7	clause	B	
7	10	5	clause	B	
8	9 or 10	5	NONE	A	
9	14	8	clause	C	
10	13	5	phrase	D	capitalized word
11	13 or 14	5	NONE	C	
12	12 or 13	5	clause	D	stress marks
13	9	5	clause	C	
14	10	6	NONE	D	

Table 8.3: Graphological and phonological features of 'The Windhover'

It needs to be emphasized that this analysis is one of many possibilities. I have, for example, treated 'how' as an adverb initiating the clause 'how he rung upon the rein of a wimpling wing in his ecstasy'. Yet 'how' could also be treated as an exclamation, making this clause an interpolated exclamation. I have treated 'striding high there' as embedded within this clause. But it could also be incorporated into the prepositional phrase 'in his riding/Of the rolling level underneath him steady air' as a co-ordinate of 'his riding . . .'. (Support for this reading is perhaps given by the semantic and phonological connections between 'riding' and 'striding', and 'underneath' and 'high'.) There are also many alternative analyses of 'dapple-dawn-drawn' and 'the rolling level underneath him steady air'. Both of these phrases are discussed in detail below.

In the analysis set out above, the predicator 'CAUGHT' has four objects: three noun phrases of growing complexity which are in apposition to each other, and one noun clause co-ordinated with these three appositional noun phrases.

[^{S}(I) ^{P}(CAUGHT) ^{A}(this morning)]

| | direct object 1: | (morning's minion) |
| appositional | direct object 2: | (kingdom of daylight's dauphin) |

appositional	direct object 3:	(dapple-dawn-drawn Falcon in his riding Of the rolling level underneath him steady air) and
co-ordinated	direct object 4:	[[striding High there] how he rung upon the rein of a wimpling wing In his ecstasy]]

The final noun clause, describing the bird's action, is treated grammatically in the same way as the noun phrases which precede it, as though it were another appositional noun phrase. What the bird is doing—a process—is treated in the same way as the bird itself. In this sense, this fourth clausal object could be treated as another unit in apposition.

A further multiplication (indeed explosion) of valid analyses arises from doubt over the end of the first sentence. In the above analysis, I have treated the exclamation mark after 'ecstasy' as the end of this sentence, although there is a case for incorporating all the lines before the first full stop. This latter analysis, however, raises a host of new problems. Is 'then off' to be interpreted as a new beginning, or in co-ordination with 'rung' through an ellipted 'went': i.e., 'I CAUGHT . . . the falcon . . . and I CAUGHT . . . how he rung upon the rein . . . and I CAUGHT how he then went off'? But if we read it in this way, how are we to cope with the potentially autonomous SPOd clause, 'the hurl and gliding rebuffed the big wind'? Such syntactic complexities and switches of direction do not yield easily to a grammar designed for more sedate and conventional structures. They are, by the norms of such grammars, deviant. A loose stylistics reading might well claim that they iconically represent both the sudden changes of the bird's flight pattern, the wind, the excitement of the beholder, and—eventually—his change of heart.

Let us concentrate our attention on one or two features. The first line exploits lexical ambiguity, syntactic mobility, sound patterning, and a highly unorthodox line-break in mid-word, to bring together all of the major schemata I have suggested, and to presage the change of heart from unbridled excitement to self-disciplined control which is—in this reading—the poem's central concern. 'I' immediately introduces the narrator as a centre of attention. 'CAUGHT' exploits the many meanings of the verb: 'to catch sight of', 'to understand', 'to gain control of', but also 'to be infected by'. It is, thus, an action in which the 'I' may be either the agent or the patient, active or passive. The unusual post-verbal positioning of the adjunct 'this morning' allows it to be associated alliteratively with the direct-object noun-phrase that follows it. It would, in final position, otherwise be delayed by the string of appositional objects.[17] The highly idiosyncratic line-break in the middle of the word 'king/dom' allows it to be—for a split second in the process of reading—the word 'king' (for this last point, see Widdowson 1987:245). The first two appositional noun phrases both delay the noun 'Falcon', which is the literal—as opposed to metaphorical—direct object and, while doing so, bring all of the major schemata together. The falcon is the servant of the morning, and is a prince and eldest son (like Christ), heir to the kingdom of daylight: and all this has been 'CAUGHT' (captured?) by the 'I', or has 'CAUGHT' (infected) him. The effect is a fusion of these disparate schemata, a foregrounding of the elements they have in common, giving each the potential to disrupt and change the other.

The growing complexity of the noun-phrases leading up to the word 'Falcon', with ever longer and longer premodification, followed by a sudden switch to lengthy postmodification after it, foregrounds this word syntactically. The grammatical structure may be illustrated as shown in Table 8.4.

Modifier type	Premodifiers	Head	Postmodifiers
Determiner	(this	morning)	
Noun + 's	((morning) 's	minion)	
Noun phrase + 's	(kingdom (of daylight))'s	dauphin)	
Clause	([dapple-dawn-drawn]		
		Falcon	
Complex Prepositional Phrase			(in his riding (of (the rolling level underneath him steady air))))*

Table 8.4: Noun-phrase structure in the opening of 'The Windhover'

'Falcon' stands out, balanced between eighteen syllables of heavily premodified appositive noun phrases leading up to it, and seventeen syllables of complex postmodification. If we are to believe the psycholinguistics claim that left-branching in English noun phrases is harder to process than right-branching (Milroy 1977:213), this change will lead to greater ease of processing, and therefore to a release of tension. The syntactic foregrounding of 'Falcon' is echoed, moreover, in its rhythmic foregrounding:

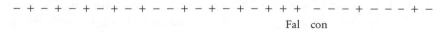

− + − + − + − + − + − − + − + − + − + + + − − − + − − − + −

Fal   con

and its orthographic foregrounding through the capitalization of its initial letter. There is also a change of rhythm, with a greater mean number of unstressed syllables between beats after the climactic syllable

'Fal'. It is hard to imagine how more emphasis could fall upon a single word.

The last and most complex of the premodifiers in this introductory succession of noun phrases is 'dapple-dawn-drawn'. This may be analysed as either:

(dapple- [dawn-drawn] Falcon)
or
([(dapple-dawn) -drawn] Falcon)

Where a single hyphen would have disambiguated, the repeated hyphen supports either reading. The fronting of a relative clause to function as a premodifier is, in most grammatical descriptions, deviant;[18] but it allows the creation of a number of effects for a reader who is open to them, all of which unify the schemata we have suggested. The two analyses above explain how 'dapple' may modify either 'Falcon' or 'dawn'. 'Drawn', like 'CAUGHT', has many meanings, in which the agency of the action is different, and the bird more or less active or passive. It may mean 'attracted to' (drawn towards), 'pulled by' (drawn out by), 'unsheathed' (drawn), 'sketched' (drawn against)—this last meaning applies if the bird is visualized in silhouette against the morning light. Had the phrase employed the more normal postmodifying relative clause construction, it would have been difficult to create all these multiple readings together, as the distinguishing prepositional and adverbial particles of the phrasal verbs disappear only when the clause is fronted. Combining this lexical and grammatical ambiguity, we find, when we rewrite the premodifying relative clause in a postmodifying position, that it may mean (at least) all or any of the following:

(The   falcon [which was drawn towards the dapple dawn])
(The dapple falcon [which was drawn towards the   dawn})
(The   falcon [which was drawn out by the dapple dawn])
(The dapple falcon [which was drawn out by the   dawn])
(The   falcon [which was drawn   by the dapple dawn])
(The dapple falcon [which was drawn   by the   dawn])
(The   falcon [which was drawn against the dapple dawn])
(The dapple falcon [which was drawn against the   dawn])

This grammatical structure enables the words 'dapple-dawn-drawn' to bring together three of the major interpretative schemata: $S MORNING, $S KNIGHT, and $S FALCON. This unity is reinforced by the sound parallelisms (the alliterative /d/ and the assonantal /ɔ:/) which are also made possible by this construction.[19]

Taken together, these grammatical features of the opening lines create a unique connection of the suggested schemata. My claim is that they also facilitate changes in the highest levels of schemata. Firstly, the potential for multiple interpretations creates a general atmosphere of openness, fluidity, and change. More specifically, particular ambiguities represent particular changes in themes and plans. The passive and active meanings of 'CAUGHT' and 'drawn' represent different and contradictory attitudes to natural beauty. Is it something to master, or be mastered by? The inclusion of a clause describing a process (as though in apposition to a series of noun-phrases describing an entity) reflects the fluidity and changeable nature of the poem's perception. This is a poem about change and interconnection, but these motifs are present, not only at the most abstracted conceptual level, but at the level of linguistic detail. It is as though linguistic choice directly penetrates and changes the highest abstractions—themes and plans—without any recourse to the intermediate stages of representation described in schema theory (see Chapter 4). The qualities I am describing are thus functions of particular linguistic choice, NOT (to borrow one of Hopkins's typographical devices) of an abstracted representation in 'another language' (a formal non-linguistic representation system like Conceptual Dependency). In this respect, the poem's blurring of the distinction between events and entities is significant, for this distinction is the basis of all such non-linguistic systems of representation. The combination of linguistic choices with a reader's schemata and a resultant change in those schemata is an instance of discourse deviation. It is not linguistic deviation alone (as we encountered it in the advertisement 'Elizabeth Taylor's Passion'), nor is it conceptual deviation of the kind which may occur in scientific and other 'factual' writing (see pages 161–7).

In illustration of this, let us turn our attention to the noun phrase 'rolling level underneath him steady air' which creates in microcosm an effect of the poem as a whole. I shall analyse this as consisting of three adjectival premodifiers—'rolling', 'level underneath him', 'steady'—and one head-word—'air'. The second adjectival premodifier consists of a head word—'level'—which is itself postmodified by a prepositional phrase, 'underneath him'. Because this analysis is deviant in terms of existing grammars it is difficult to represent using my notation, but my reading is most nearly captured by:

(rolling (level (underneath (him))) steady air)

This is also semantically deviant, for how can a single entity, 'air', be at once rolling and level and steady? (Such semantic contradiction, we may recall (see pages 25–6), led Rumelhart to rule that the discourse in which a balloon had both burst and not burst was not 'well-formed'.) One answer to this problem is to say that the three premodifiers represent a process rather than a state: the air changes within the duration of the phrase. The deviation of this is startling, for usually such a change of state would be conveyed with several phrases, not within one. This construction disrupts both our schematic expectations about the language AND about narrative voice, for we expect the perception of the narrator to be more certain, rather than changing, as it were, in front of our eyes. (The effect is similar, in this respect, to the simultaneous assertion and denial of Raskolnikov's cowardice in *Crime and Punishment* (see pages 99–111).) This change in mid-phrase, however, prepares us for the change of attitude which takes place within the poem as a whole. It is a formal device enabling an apprehension of changing perception within, rather than prior to, the linguistic formulation. *This effect could not be rendered in a formal non-linguistic representation system such as Conceptual Dependency.* It exists within the interaction between the deviant linguistic form and a schematic preconception, namely that the situation described by a noun phrase has been analysed and perceived before its description. What happens here creates an illusion of access to the perceptual processes of the narrator, before their verbalization.

The process rendered by the semantic contradiction between the modifiers in this phrase may be rationalized if the reader perceives the air from the bird's point of view. As the kestrel rolls sideways, levels out, and comes to a hovering standstill (as kestrels do), the quality of the air changes for the bird. The narrator thus becomes, in this phrase, the bird, preluding the more explicit statement of this merger in one reading of 'My heart in hiding stirred for a bird' (interpreting 'for' to mean 'like' and not 'on behalf of'). A similar 'bird's eye view' is evident in 'shéer plód makes plough down sillion shine' which provokes (at least for this reader) an image of a field seen as though from above. Voices here merge and the narrator takes on whatever qualities of the bird may seem relevant to the reader: its mastery of the air and its 'pride'; or its obedience to the 'Lord' explicit in the dedication, and implicit in the description of it as 'dauphin' or 'minion', and in the schema of the knight. This ambiguity is emphasized by the double meaning of the preposition 'of' in the phrase 'the mastery of the thing'. This may mean either 'mastery belonging to the thing' or 'mastery over the thing' by someone else, presumably the narrator. The surprisingly dismissive and derogatory tone of 'thing', echoed by the negative connotations of 'brute' in the following line, suggest the latter reading, and mark a radical change in attitude to the bird.[20] $S FALCON here changes radically, the connection is no longer to the human, admirable $S KNIGHT, but to inanimate objects and inferior animals.

The grammatically simple noun phrases of the first line of the second stanza are in contrast with the complexity of the opening lines:

$_{NP}$(Brute beauty) and $_{NP}$(valour) and $_{NP}$(act), oh, $_{NP}$(air), $_{NP}$(pride), $_{NP}$(plume)

They evoke (depending on reader schemata) associations with all the major schemata. 'Here' becomes ambiguously either 'within the bird' or 'within the narrator's heart'; 'buckle' brings together (like 'CAUGHT' and 'drawn') a host of relevant meanings. 'Buckle' may mean 'to collapse under strain', 'come together', 'become obedient', or, as a nonce verb derived through class conversion and back-formation[21] from the noun 'buckler' (a kind of shield), 'to defend oneself as with a buckler'. (The extreme foregrounding of the word through the elision and the repeated stresses of 'air, pride, plume, here/Buck–' make it parallel to the word 'Falcon' in the first stanza.) All of the meanings of 'buckle' may contribute to an interpretation of the remaining lines as referring to the beauty which comes from striking opposed surfaces ('the fire that breaks'), hard work ('shéer plód makes plough down sillion shine'), or from the end of a fire ('blue-bleak embers . . . Fall, gall themselves, and gash gold-vermilion'). This last image contains another—a metaphor within a metaphor—in which the glowing of the dying fire is described as a wound, in language evocative of the wounding of Christ on the cross. The verbless 'No wonder of it' which introduces these last lines, may be interpreted either as a comment ('it is not surprising') or as a command to the self ('do not wonder at the bird'). A change of attitude is suggested by the regretful interjections 'oh', 'O', and 'ah my dear'. In Bakhtinian terms, what seems to be happening here is that the voice of the opening stanza is present in the closing two stanzas, though defeated and regretful. Conversely, the more disciplined, active voice of the second stanza is present in the first, in the active senses of 'CAUGHT' and of 'the mastery of the thing'. The change of voice reflects changes in the schemata through which the beauty of the bird is interpreted, and the plans which this beauty inspires. The original theme of being mastered by beauty has changed to one of mastering beauty. New plans have appeared in fulfilment of the theme of obedience to Christ: to reject ecstasy, to work hard, to control beauty. In this sense the poem deviates from the usual single voice of the lyric poem. Interestingly, the interjections in the second stanza are hard to incorporate into a grammatical (i.e. sentence-based) analysis, as is the dedication '*To Christ our Lord*', placed outside the poem as a whole. They are, however, more easily described as features of discourse.

The poem as discourse is text interpreted through a reader's schemata. It enters, however, into dynamic interaction with these schemata, both being interpreted through them, and simultaneously disrupting, recombining, and refreshing them. The narrator becomes the bird but also rejects the bird; the bird is like Christ but is also opposed to Christ; it is like a knight, who is like Christ. The bird is both controller of the narrator and of its own element, but also controlled, by the morning and finally by the poet. The bird is like a human—a knight, a skater—

but also a 'thing' of 'brute beauty'. The whole experience is fluid and changing, both physically in the flight of the bird, and emotionally in the mind of the observer and reader. Linguistic devices, such as those described above, convey the process of perception, itself a deviation from norms of narration. The overall effect of the interaction of these schemata is a disruption of plans and themes. In my reading, the relevant plan on the perceiving of beauty changes from wonder to control, from desire for mastery to acceptance of submission. The process of this change is effected through low-level devices, grammatical deviations, multiple meanings, ambiguities.

What I have attempted to describe is a small part of the process of the formation of an interpretation. I certainly do not propose the above as a fixed reading. Different initial schemata will, of course, yield different results.

'The Windhover': an ornithological schema

An interesting but neglected aspect of this poem, which well illustrates the dependency of interpretation on the schemata available to a given reader, is its ornithological accuracy. (Though it may seem pedantic to mention such details here, the accuracy of the reference to the world 'as it is', the 'realism' of the poem (in the sense defined on pages 67–8) is in interesting contrast to the use of language to disrupt and refresh such abstract schemata.)

'Windhover' is a dialect name for 'kestrel', a small and common falcon. (Another dialect name is 'standgale', a word motivated by the species' ability to fly accurately in strong winds.) The most distinguishing behavioural characteristic of this bird is its 'habit of protracted hovering'. This is 'the best pointer' to identification, a perceptual trigger in schema terms for the activation of a 'kestrel schema' for an ornithologist). While hovering, the bird hangs virtually stationary with extraordinary control, keeping its position through minute movements of its tail and primary feathers. Between hovers it flies to a higher point, then rolls away before braking to a standstill. In the words of one field guide (a text whose function is to communicate an appropriate schema of the species to those who do not have it), the kestrel 'flies with rapid wing beats, occasional short glides and frequent periods of hovering, head to wind; slants steeply down to catch mice, beetles, etc'. The male bird (and Hopkins's bird is a 'he') has 'spotted chestnut upper parts, warm buff lower-parts with scattered black spots' and a 'blue-grey head and tail'.[22]

The above description gives default and trigger elements of a 'kestrel schema'. The availability of this is, however, far less widespread than the other schemata I have suggested, as it will only be present in those observers with ornithological knowledge. I presume that Hopkins himself had this schema available. He may wrongly have assumed it to be available to readers. He was an accurate observer of wildlife, including birds, as the many references in his journals and papers make clear (House and Storey 1959). (I reject here the formalist and New Critical dogma of making no reference to biography.) The accuracy of the description is, moreover, unlikely to be coincidence. Hopkins correctly describes the bird as a falcon (in marked contrast to another literary representation of this species, Barry Hines's *Kes*, which wrongly describes it as a 'hawk'). The phrase I have already analysed, 'rolling level underneath him steady air', follows the stages of a kestrel's flight pattern, as does 'striding/High' and 'then off, off forth on swing'. 'Rung upon the rein of a wimpling wing' captures the sudden stopping, the immobility and control of the hover, and 'wimpling wing' the slight movements of the feathers. The habit of flying into the wind is present in 'Rebuffed the big wind'. Lastly, the colouring of the male bird is evoked by 'dapple', by 'blue-bleak', and by 'gash gold-vermilion'. These last two compounds—which also refer to the image of the dying embers, and, by association, to the wounds of Christ—are rather better descriptions of the species colouring than the ornithological descriptions cited above.

The extreme discourse deviation effected through phonological, orthographic, syntactic, and lexical innovations with changes in schemata is thus set firmly within a schematic framework which represents an aspect of the world 'as it is': predictable and true to form. The radical disruption of the usual (thematic) response to natural beauty is contrasted and replaced with a new plan—control, hard work, and obedience. This major change 'takes off' from this everyday sight. The process of change itself is conveyed through the syntactic choices: disturbingly for those used to a more stable narrative. The default elements of the kestrel schema evoke—through association and ambiguity—other schemata, interact with them, and refresh them. In the terms of the schema theory described in Chapter 3, this poem represents the replacement of one life-theme with another, but it is the disruption of linguistic norms and a very specific script-like world schema which both describe and institute this change.

Conclusion

In these analyses, I have attempted to show how these three complex texts can disrupt, change, combine, and refresh the schemata of a reader. That they do in fact do this, and that the changes they set in motion are both dynamic and self-perpetuating, is witnessed by the controversy and interest they have all provoked. Though they may represent aspects of the world, and of non-linguistic perception of that world (for example, 'The Windhover' accurately describes a kestrel), the changes they cause to high-level schemata are effected through linguistic and text-structural choices which are beyond expression in any other form. In this, my analyses bear out the formalist and Jakobsonian insistence on the primacy and uniqueness of form. Yet the forms of such discourses as these are most valuable to human beings, not in themselves, but for the effect they may have on schemata: though those schemata may be text or language schemata as well as schemata of the world. The minutest details of linguistic and textual form can reach through the intervening layers of the interpretative hierarchy to change our most fundamental approaches to language and to life. Thus the linguistic and pragmatic ambiguities of 'The Tyger' fuse contradictory views of the cosmos into one, leaving doubt where was certainty; in *The Turn of the Screw*, the juxtaposition of text types and the exploitation of a standard narrative sequence disrupt our expectations of other people, of the nature of truth, and of the act of story-telling itself; the patterns and multiple meanings of 'The Windhover' can represent and cause a change of 'life theme' from passivity to activity: a change effected through such devices as the dual senses of the verb 'CAUGHT', or the modifying phrase 'of the thing'. In this poem, the very process of change is captured in the altering perspective of a 'deviant' noun phrase, 'the rolling level underneath him steady air' which, while accurately describing the bird, also defies both schematic expectations about noun phrases, and schematic expectations about the stability of perception and attitude.

The degree of change caused by such discourse will vary with the schemata which a reader brings to it. Discourse deviation exists in the interaction of form and schemata, rather than in either one in isolation. A combination of schema theory and formalist analysis answers the charges of reader-response criticism against the validity of formal description. Yet the wide popularity and impact of texts such as these suggests that higher-level schemata are perhaps not so individual as is sometimes supposed.

As I have tried to show, linguistic and text-structural deviations from expectation are not in themselves any guarantee of schema refreshment. There are discourses which employ them to no greater effect than the addition of minor props to rigid social stereotypes. There are others, especially in the contemporary world, which use poetic devices to reinforce rather than break down the prejudices and preconceptions which limit our intelligence.[23] For these reasons, a formalist analysis of discourse needs to hypothesize about effects on schemata, just as much as an AI approach needs, when dealing with discourse deviation, to take account of form.

Though intelligence may need schemata to interpret and bring coherence to the world and the texts it perceives, it must also be capable of change. And change may be effected through form.

Notes

1 Doxey's interpretation is not cited by Fish, though it is by Epstein (1975:66, footnote). It is, however, similar in kind to the literary critical and scholarly interpretations cited by Fish.
2 Reminiscent, for example, of Brooks's ([1947] 1968) analysis of Donne's 'The Canonization' in her book *The Well Wrought Urn* in which she suggests that the poem is itself like the 'well wrought urn' which Donne describes as a better monument than 'half-acre tombs'. This New Critical principle is in fact inherited by Epstein (1975)—discussed at length in this chapter—in the title of his paper 'The Self-reflexive artefact'.
3 The words 'dread' and 'terror', for example, have shifted their meanings since the writing of this poem. They no longer collocate so readily with 'God'.
4 The Lamb—especially when written with a capital letter—is a Judaeo-Christian symbol of the Messiah (*Isaiah* 53:7). (The same symbol is used in the Edward Bond poem discussed on pages 167–73.) It is also the title of the sister poem in the *Songs of Innocence*. In our view, the connotations are not so specifically Christian or Jewish as to exclude other readings.
5 No patronizing depreciation of the ballad as an art form is intended by this remark.
6 *Ulysses* itself provides several examples of parallax. Bloom, on entering the library, is suddenly seen as though by Stephen and Buck Mulligan, and described as follows: 'A patient sillhouette waiting, listening'; 'a bowing, dark figure' ([1922] 1960:257).
7 Page references are to the Penguin edition (1969).
8 The governess frequently refers to her own life as a 'history' (pages 29, 72) and to her own reading (page 58), imagining herself as a character in a novel. At one point, she imagines:

> Wasn't it just a storybook over which I had fallen a-doze and a-dream? No; it was a big, ugly, antique, but convenient house. Was there a 'secret' at Bly—a mystery of Udolpho or an insane, an unmentionable relative kept in unsuspected confinement. (page 28)

Mrs Grose, on the other hand, is, significantly, illiterate.
9 A convention satirized in *Northanger Abbey*, but employed again in *Jane Eyre*. Comparisons between *The Turn of the Screw* and *Jane Eyre* have been frequently drawn. Sheppard (1974:42–61) devotes a whole chapter to the issue.
10 I use the term 'text schema' here for the sake of consistency with my tripartite division of schemata in Chapter 1. Previously the term

has been reserved for schemata representing text structure. Terms such as 'journal' and 'ghost story' should, strictly speaking, be described as 'discourse types' or 'genres' as they must take account of such factors as sender, communicative purpose, context, graphology, and physical substance (Cook 1989:95–102).

11 The oddity of the words 'brute' and 'thing' are discussed below.

12 Reasons for treating 'blue-bleak' and 'gold-vermilion' as properties of the bird as well as of embers and the 'gash' are discussed below.

13 The choice of a word of French origin (French *sillon* means furrow) associates it with '*chevalier*'.

14 From the poem 'Pied Beauty'.

15 For Hopkins's own comments on rhythm and scansion see Gardener and Mackenzie (eds.) (1967:255–6) and House and Storey (eds.) (1959:100–9, 267–83).

16 Figure 8.4 represents the orthographic lines as they are set out on the page. In Table 8.3 the very short orthographic lines are treated as part of the preceding line, following the numbers presented alongside the poem itself.

17 For comment on the effect of adverb fronting in another Hopkins poem, 'Inversnaid', see Short and van Peer (1989:54).

18 When the fronted clause is several words not one, as in 'disused mine'. Though in this case 'disused' can be treated as an adjective. So too can 'drawn' in the phrase 'drawn sword'.

19 Hopkins himself used the term 'parallelism' in its modern sense (House and Storey (eds.) 1959:108–14), see Chapter 2, note 7.

20 For a different interpretation of the word 'thing' and its extensive use in Hopkins's poetry, see Davies 1979:21.

21 Word-class conversion in literature is often remarked upon by stylisticians (see for example Widdowson 1975:15).

22 The quotations in this paragraph are from descriptions of the kestrel in four field guides: Fitter and Richardson 1952:71; Frohawk 1958: 252; Heinzel, Fitter, and Parslow 1979:94; Peterson, Mountfort, and Hollom 1983:79.

23 There is a paradox here of course, which may be easily deconstructed. The theory of schema change through formal deviation is itself schematic, and should itself be disrupted and refreshed.

9 What the theory means for literature teaching

In this book I have argued that it is through linguistic and textual details of an apparently purely formal or structural nature that literary discourse can refresh and change our preconceptions and prejudices. In the course of the argument, I have invoked some neglected theories of literature from the past, while also trying to move beyond the formal, structural, and stylistic choices which they so well describe, to see how these choices may act to destabilize preconceptions of a more global nature. This invocation of discarded voices is no accident, for the importance of form (indeed the liberating and disruptive function of unpredicted form for which I argue) is at odds with current emphases in both language and literature pedagogy, and in applied linguistics.

It is also, perhaps, no accident that those literary theoretical voices which emphasize form, are also often the voices of the radical and the rebel, from periods and places which have confronted established conventions with innovative, iconoclastic ideas.[1]

Approaches to literature teaching are inevitably influenced by current approaches to both language and education. Arguably, they are over-influenced, and it is the tendency to see literature as just another use of language, and literature study as just another subject on the curriculum, which has led to the neglect of features which mark literature as a discourse and an area of study demanding different techniques of description and different pedagogical approaches. The influence has been one-way: *from* theories of language use and education, *to* theories of literature and literature teaching.

Under the influence of ideas from language pedagogy, the retreat in literary study from an emphasis on linguistic and textual form has been hastened by the general shift of attention (following Hymes 1972) from what is *possible* in communication to what is *appropriate* or what is *performed*. Where literature has been introduced into the foreign language classroom as a means of furthering language development, it has also been influenced by theories of language acquisition stressing the importance of attention to meaning rather than form (despite the fact that these theories are based on disputable evidence and reasoning).

Our knowledge of what is appropriate and performed in communication is derived from social experience. It is inevitably concerned with conformity, normality, and convention, on the assumption that what has happened before is likely to happen again. A good deal of post-Hymesian work in applied linguistics has thus been concerned to show how expectations influence or even supply understanding, and the emphasis has been particularly upon how higher-level units condition or by-pass lower-level ones, thus reducing cognitive load and effecting ease and rapidity of communication. Work in this vein has been carried out at every level of description. In discourse analysis, attention has focused on schemata and upon genres (which can be described as discourse schemata). In semantics, there is the notion that prototypical concepts, assimilated from experience, and socially conditioned and variable, are used in assigning meaning to lexical items. At the syntactic level, lexical phrase theory (given impetus by the opportunities for the study of collocation provided by computer text analysis) has emphasized how many combinations of words are neither produced nor understood grammatically, but as ready-made chunks stored in memory. All these theories (of schema, genre, prototype, and lexical chunks) emphasize a top-down approach to both discourse understanding and production. They have generated a mood of excitement and enthusiasm, in which attention has shifted decisively away from bottom-up approaches to language acquisition and use.

This is understandably so. There is no doubt that these new approaches do significantly extend our understanding of, and our ability to describe, the process of communication. They are convincing explanations of routine language processing; they describe essential components of communicative competence (and are thus rightly stressed in foreign language teaching). In addition, they are an understandable reaction against the pre-Hymesian preoccupation, both in language description and pedagogy, with form in isolation from use, with what is grammatically possible rather than socially appropriate or performed. Yet a problem arises when these approaches are not only presented as *descriptions* of communication, but also as *prescriptions* for pedagogy, and it is implied that in all circumstances, and for all types of discourse, top-down approaches are to be preferred to bottom-up. When that happens, what was once a welcome revolution becomes, in its turn, an orthodoxy which can distract us from the plurality and variety of human language use. And when this orthodoxy spills over into literature teaching, its effect may be particularly limiting and detrimental.

For if, as I have argued, the relationship between top and bottom in literary discourse is different in kind, then in literature teaching there is a need to supplement these approaches with renewed recognition of the contribution of unpredictable form. Whereas top-down approaches may cope well with certain discourse types, we may need to move beyond this view in consideration of others. They certainly leave a number of important questions unanswered. How do new schemata, genres, and lexical phrases come into existence if not through communicative behaviour which is neither appropriate nor previously performed (though it may quickly become both)? And if the general function of top-down strategies is to aid speed and ease of processing, what is their relevance to literary discourses, which often seem wilfully difficult to process. In literary study it is not enough to see how conventional expectations predict what will happen, but also how deviation from expectation rebounds upon, and alters, those very predictive structures which literary form rejects. Schemata, genre conventions, prototypes, and lexical chunks are all socially conditioned and conditioning constraints, limiting possibility not only of language but of thought. To understand them is an essential *first* step in the use of language; but a *second* step is to move beyond them, to change and alter them. Inasmuch as the conventional forms reflect and create social conventions, deviation from these conventions reflects and creates a move beyond the constraints of a particular society towards new ways of seeing and thinking.

Given this link between global predictive structures and social conformity, and the capacity of original uses of form to disrupt them, it is strange to note the association which is often made in language-teaching theory between attention to form and authoritarian educational practice. Conversely, and equally surprisingly, there is an association between attention to global top-down processing and more liberal or progressive educational practice. Clark (1987), for example, distinguishes 'classical humanist' from 'progressivist' curriculum philosophies.[2] When describing the former, he makes a clear association between attention to the lower levels of language—pronunciation, grammar, and vocabulary—and authoritarianism and conservatism. When describing the latter, on the other hand, the converse is the case. In progressivism, attention is focused on the top levels—on meaning and function, on genre and social effect. Freedom and progress are thus associated with an approach which emphasizes the whole rather than the parts, the overall effect of an entire discourse rather than the abstracted rules and components which create that effect.

These associations are somewhat odd and, in my opinion, also the wrong way round. Knowledge of the larger social structures created through discourse is necessary for conventional and conformist language behaviour (the outcome sought by conservative and authoritarian education); but it is through manipulation of detail that the individual is able to move beyond them and gain freedom from the constraints they impose. Attention to the larger structures is a first step, and certainly an essential one to a student seeking to understand an unfamiliar culture, but a second step is to disrupt or refresh these structures, and this will demand use and understanding of inappropriate, innovative, never-before-performed manipulations of the code. Communication is often achieved through conformity to old patterns retrieved from memory, but there is also another side to human language use: a creative, original, liberating use which depends upon the form of language and its potential to generate an infinity of new and unforeseen higher-level ideas. In this view, grammar and textual form, far from being the tools of repression, are the guarantors of freedom.

The association between attention to form and authoritarian education perhaps confuses a causal or necessary relationship with one which is merely coincidental. Clark, for example, makes much of the historical association in Britain between his 'classical humanist' model and an élitist, socially divisive education system.[3] But this is not to say that the two necessarily accompany each other. The manifest injustices of the British (and other similarly élitist) educational systems could equally be combated by extending the classical humanist approach to all, rather than abolishing it for all.

Clark (and others who draw similar curriculum dichotomies for language teaching, e.g. White 1988; Breen 1987) are also influenced by an assumption that the teacher-centred classroom is necessarily an authoritarian one. Provided authority is not imposed only by sanctions and force, this is often far from the truth; the teacher-centred classroom can create a liberating environment for students, while the student-centred classroom can be the vehicle for an insidious and disguised authoritarianism, and also, if it imposes Western educational ideas upon other educational traditions, for cultural chauvinism (O'Neill 1991). Although, in any approach, some classes are inevitably boring for some students, the association of a teacher-centred approach with intellectual tedium contradicts many people's experience. It is often in the outwardly passive role of listening to the extended discourse of another person that moments of intellectual liberation and progress are achieved. Indeed, the act of silent and solitary reading, so often associated with personal and intellectual development, is an extreme example of allowing another person 'to do all the talking'. For the silent and *outwardly* passive reader, like the student listening in class, may *inwardly* be experiencing a mental revolution. This is very often the case in the reading of literature.

In literature teaching there is an additional justification for a degree of teacher-centredness. For as a good deal of literary effect is achieved through deviation from an established literary tradition, a knowledge of that tradition (or canon) will be needed by students before they can experience that effect. Time will need to be given to the transmission of knowledge of the canon. An angry reaction against this view has rightly been provoked by the specific canons which have been presented by educational establishments. This is particularly true where the canon is a national one.[4] The association of a literary canon with the tradition of a nation state often partakes of all the arrogance and militarism which is part and parcel of the nationalism it perpetuates. It often rides roughshod over the literary traditions of immigrant and minority communities within the nation, while also diminishing the traditions of other nations. In the colonial or post-colonial situation, it is often imposed upon nations with existing or emerging traditions of their own. Such a narrow approach to the construction of a canon is quite at odds with the civilizing effect of literature, which can stress the commonality rather than the particularity of the human condition, or, where it does associate with a particular culture, is unlikely to do so along boundaries conterminous with those of the politically defined nation. The narrow-minded notion of 'a national canon' has perhaps been instrumental in the declining popularity of the notion that literature teaching should present any canon at all. Yet opposition to a particular canon should not lead us to be oblivious to the way in which the literary discourse operates within, and achieves effect through, its conformity to, or deviation from, a particular tradition. But we do need to have more receptive, flexible, and less xenophobic notions of tradition.

In all of this, it might be argued, I am confusing issues in the teaching of foreign languages with issues in the teaching of literature. But the confusion, I reply, is not mine. It is often assumed that principles formulated for education in general, or for the teaching of foreign languages in particular, can be extended unchanged to the literature class, on the assumption that this, too, is a subject on the curriculum, and is an instance of language use. But the endeavour of this book has been to show that literary discourse is not just one more genre or social institution among others. It has a particular function in human life, especially for the inner mental world of the individual. It follows that it will demand particular approaches in the classroom.

Social uses of language demand rapid response and interaction. Therefore, in the teaching of a foreign language, there are good reasons to encourage constant student interaction and reaction. Similarly, in the interests of fast and efficient communication, there is an argument for concentration on higher-level predictive structures. Yet these principles may not necessarily be transferable to the literature class, at least where literature is studied as literature rather than as a way of improving language. The literary experience is one of mental disruption, refreshment, and play, more typically effected when the individual withdraws from the world of social and practical necessity than when he or she plunges into it. Arguably, this experience may not be suited to an educational environment at all; it is as much about rejecting social values as assimilating them. But given that the study of literature does form part of the curriculum, it demands very careful and responsible treatment.

To be always asking students for their reactions, and asking them to share these reactions with others, may stifle the whole mental process which literature can stimulate. This is especially so because, as I have argued throughout this book, the literary experience is not associated with any particular text, but with the interaction of text and individual. Certain works on the syllabus (however 'great') may simply not affect a particular reader, and this, too, should be respected. A teacher is a person who believes that the experiences he or she has found valuable may be so to others, and who, consequently, admirably, is driven by the desire to share them. In these circumstances, and in deference to the extraordinary effects of literary form upon the mind, perhaps all that a teacher can do is to present those works which he or she values, together with such information and explanation of the tradition and the language within which they exist, and from whose norms they may deviate. Then stand back, trust the power of literary form, through new works and for each new generation, to disrupt and refresh 'the glass armour of the familiar'.

Notes

1 I am thinking particularly of Russian formalism's opposition to both the pre- and post-revolutionary Russian establishment, and structuralism's association with the changes of the 1960s, particularly in France.
2 Clark also proposes a third curriculum philosophy, 'reconstructionism', in which education, as part of a political programme, is used as a means of changing society.
3 Because the course is content-driven, the class must move at the same pace. (Testing is norm-referenced, and curriculum content is dictated by examination.) This leads to streaming, which in turn leads to élitism and social division.
4 A good example of this is Leavis's notion of *The Great Tradition* which establishes an exclusively British tradition of the novel, rejecting and despising all foreign influence.

Appendix A: Grammatical notation: symbols and abbreviations

The grammatical notation used is as follows:

[ ] enclose clauses
( ) enclose phrases
< > enclose co-ordinated constructions

Function labels are written outside, in front of, and above the brackets enclosing the unit to which they refer. The following abbreviations are used:

S   = subject
Od = direct object
Oi = indirect object
P   = predicator
C   = complement
A   = adjunct
o   = object of a preposition

Form labels are written outside, in front of, and below the brackets enclosing the unit to which they refer. The following abbreviations are used:

Clauses
MCl = main clause
NCl = noun clause
ACl = adverb clause
RCl = relative clause

In non-finite clauses the following additional symbols are added:

t   = infinitive
ing = 'ing' form
en   = past participle.

Phrases
NP   = noun phrase
VP   = verb phrase
AjP = adjective phrase

PP   = prepositional phrase
AvP   = adverb phrase
cj   = conjunction

Symbols and abbreviations:

AI   = Artificial Intelligence
CD   = Conceptual Dependency
FSP   = Functional Sentence Perspective
SPGU   = *Scripts, Plans, Goals and Understanding* (Schank and
         Abelson 1977)

Schema types:

$ = script
$S   = script-like schema
Π   = plan
Γ   = goal
Θ   = theme

Appendix B: Conceptual dependency (CD) and semantics

Superficially, a system of conceptual representation such as CD would seem to have a great deal in common with approaches to semantics which also seek to present a formal representation of the 'content' of natural language, and thus inherit their weaknesses as well. It has certain similarities, for example, with 'truth-based semantics' (see Leech 1981: 76ff.; Lyons 1977:597), with componential analysis (see Leech 1981: 89–123; Lyons 1977:414; Cruse 1986:16–22), and with case grammar (Fillmore 1968).

Clearly, with its use of 'inferences', 'case relations', and 'primitives', it has made borrowings, if only terminological ones, although its pioneers claim to have reached their conclusions independently (Schank and Abelson 1977:11). Yet whether it may fairly be regarded as a further — and indeed, if one sees it in such terms, comparatively unsophisticated — variation of earlier systems of semantic representation, is open to dispute.[1] It is no more 'about the language' than it is 'about the world'. It seeks rather to reproduce the processing strategies of an intelligence in dealing with the world or with language about the world. Closely allied to this is its concern with encyclopaedic knowledge, and thus, in so far as they can be separated, with analytic rather than synthetic truth, which is sometimes regarded as beyond the boundaries of semantics altogether (Leech 1981:69).

Truth-based semantics is concerned with the static aspects of knowledge and with facts and inferences which are assumed to be true in all situations. As such, it is the epitome of a declarative system. Such systems contrast with procedural systems whose central concern is how and when to use knowledge and in which situations. Procedural systems match knowledge with a given situation through such heuristic devices as 'assuming a fact to be the case until proved otherwise' or 'trying a given inference' even in the absence of logical proof, and go some way towards avoiding the kind of combinatorial explosion which results from a procedure which tries every logical possibility. CD representations are derived from text by a combination of declarative representation and 'procedural attachments': that is to say, they contain instructions capturing strategies which are likely to work in a given context (Barr and Feigenbaum 1981:156; de Beaugrande and Dressler 1981:91;

Anderson 1983). Yet, although procedural representations have clear advantages over declarative ones when used to predict the contents of routine texts and situations, they will also have disadvantages in encounters with a situation or a text which is similar but subtly different from expectation. As this combination is a frequent characteristic of literary texts, which foster elements of surprise, and demand lateral or creative thinking, this shortcoming of procedural systems will need to be borne in mind in the application of Schankian schema theory (which is a development of CD) to literary analysis.

Notes

1 Woods, for example, (1975:36) and Pitrat ([1985] 1988:3) are unequivocal in describing CD as a descendant of earlier semantic systems, but there are other commentators who do not regard it as semantic—in the sense of being 'about the world'—but describe it as a model of processing (McTear 1987:33).

Bibliography

Dates in square brackets are those of an first or earlier edition than the one used, or, in the case of translations, of the original foreign language edition.

Abelson, R. 1987. 'Artificial Intelligence and literary appreciation' in L. Halasz (ed.): *Literary Discourse: Aspects of Cognitive and Social Psychological Approaches*. Berlin: Walter de Gruyter: 38–48.

Abrams, M. H. (ed.) [1962] 1986. *The Norton Anthology of English Literature* 2 (5th edn.). New York: Norton.

Achildiev, I. 1989. '*Idol: ocherk sotsiologii kulta lichnosti*' in *Yunost*, December 1989: 50–9.

Aitkenhead, A. M. and J. M. Slack (eds.) 1985. *Issues in Cognitive Modeling*. Hillsdale, NJ: Lawrence Erlbaum.

Allport, G. W. and L. Postman. 1947. *The Psychology of Rumour*. New York: Henry Holt.

Alshwani, H. 1987. *Memory and Context for Language Interpretation*. Cambridge: Cambridge University Press.

Amis, M. [1981] 1982. *Other People*. Harmondsworth: Penguin.

Anderson, J. R. 1983. *The Architecture of Cognition*. Cambridge, Mass.: Harvard University Press.

Appelt, D. E. 1985. *Planning English Sentences*. Cambridge: Cambridge University Press.

Atkinson, R. L., R. C. Atkinson, E. E. Smith, and E. R. Hilgard. 1987. *Introduction to Psychology*. New York: Harcourt Brace Jovanovich.

Atwood, M. 1971. 'You Fit Into Me' in *Power Politics*. Toronto: Anansi.

Austin, J. K. 1962. *How To Do Things with Words*. Oxford: The Clarendon Press.

Bakhtin, M. M. [1928] 1978. (See P. N. Medvedev, whose name he published under (Chapter 2, Note 2).)

Bakhtin, M. M. [1929] 1973. (See V. N. Volosinov, whose name he published under (Chapter 2, Note 2).)

Bakhtin, M. M. [1929] 1978. 'Discourse typology in prose' (trans. R. Balthazar and I. Titunik) in L. Matejka and K. Pomorska: 176–96.

Bakhtin, M. M. [1929, revised 1963] 1984. *Problems of Dostoevsky's Poetics* (trans. C. Emerson). Minneapolis: University of Minnesota Press.

Bakhtin, M. M. [1934] 1981. *The Dialogic Imagination* (ed. M. Holquist, trans. M. Holquist and C. Emerson). Austin: University of Texas Press.

Bakhtin, M. M. [1936] 1986. *Speech Genres and Other Late Essays* (ed. C. Emerson and M. Holquist, trans. V. McGee). Austin: University of Texas Press.

Bakhtin, M. M. [1940, 1965] 1968. *Rabelais and His World* (trans. H. Iswolsky). Cambridge, Mass.: MIT Press.

Barr, A. and E. A. Feigenbaum. 1981. *The Handbook of Artificial Intelligence* (3 Vols.). Los Altos, Calif.: William Kaufman.

Barthes, R. [1957] 1973. *Mythologies* (trans. A. Lavers). London: Paladin.

Barthes, R. [1966] 1977. 'Introduction to the structural study of narratives' (trans. S. Heath) in *Image, Music, Text*. London: Fontana 1977: 79–125.

Barthes, R. 1967. *Système de la Mode*. Paris: Seuil.

Barthes, R. [1968] 1977. 'The death of the author' (trans. S. Heath) in *Image, Music, Text*. London: Fontana: 142–9.

Barthes, R. [1970] 1974. *S/Z* (trans. R. Miller). New York: Hill and Wang.

Barthes, R. [1973] 1981. 'Textual analysis: Poe's Valdemar' (trans. G. Bennington), in R. Young (ed.): *Untying the Text: A Post-structuralist Reader*. London: Routledge and Kegan Paul: 133–61 (reprinted in D. Lodge 1988: 172–96).

Barthes, R. [1977] 1990. *A Lover's Discourse*. Harmondsworth: Penguin.

Bartlett, F. C. 1932. *Remembering*. Cambridge: Cambridge University Press.

Bates, E., W. Kintsch, C. R. Fletcher, and V. Guliani. 1980. 'The role of pronominalization and ellipsis in texts: some memory experiments.' *Journal of Experimental Psychology, Human Learning and Memory* 6: 676–691.

Batstone, R. F. 1994. *Grammar*. Oxford: Oxford University Press.

Bavelas, J. 1991. *Equivocal Discourse*. London: Sage.

de Beaugrande, R. 1987. 'Schemas for literary communication' in L. Halasz (ed.): *Literary Discourse: Aspects of Cognitive and Social Psychological Approaches*. Berlin: Walter de Gruyter: 49–100.

de Beaugrande, R. and W. Dressler. 1981. *Introduction to Text Linguistics*. London: Longman.

Bennet, T. 1979. *Formalism and Marxism*. London: Methuen.

Berry, M. 1981. 'Systemic linguistics and discourse analysis: a multi-layered approach to exchange structure' in M. Coulthard and M. Montgomery (eds.): 120–46.

Biber, D. 1988. *Variation across Speech and Writing*. Cambridge: Cambridge University Press.

Black, E. 1993. 'Metaphor, simile and cognition in Golding's *The Inheritors*', in *Language and Literature* 2/1: 37–49.

Blake, W. [1927] 1975. 'The Tyger', 'Ah! Sunflower', and 'The Garden of Love' in *Blake: Complete Poetry and Prose* (edited by G. Keynes). London: Nonesuch.

Bloom, H. 1973. *The Anxiety of Influence: A Theory of Poetry*. New York: Oxford University Press.

Bloomfield, L. [1933] 1935. *Language*. London: George Allen and Unwin.

Blume, R. 1985. 'Graffiti' in T. A. van Dijk 1985b: 137–47.

Blunden, E. (ed.) [1920] 1931. *The Poems of Wilfred Owen*. London: Chatto and Windus.

Boden, M. 1987. *Artificial Intelligence and Natural Man* (2nd edn.). London: Basic Books.

Boden, M. 1989. *The Philosophy of Artificial Intelligence*. Oxford: Oxford University Press.

Boden, M. 1990. *The Creative Mind*. London: Weidenfeld and Nicholson.

Bolinger, D. L. 1974. 'Meaning and memory.' *Forum Linguisticum* 1/1: 1–14.

Bolinger, D. L. 1975. *Aspects of Language* (2nd edn.). New York: Harcourt Brace Jovanovich.

Bond, E. 1978. 'First World War Poets' in *Theatre Poems and Songs*. London: Methuen.

Born, R. (ed.) 1987. *Artificial Intelligence: The Case Against*. Beckenham: Croom Helm.

Bower, G. H., J. B. Black, and T. R. Turner. 1979. 'Scripts in memory for text' in *Cognitive Psychology* 11: 177–220.

Bower, G. H. and R. K. Cirillo. 1985. 'Cognitive psychology and text processing' in T. A. van Dijk (ed.), Vol. 1: 71–107.

Bransford, J. D. and J. J. Franks. 1971. 'The abstraction of linguistic ideas' in *Cognitive Psychology* 2: 231–50.

Bransford, J. D. and M. K. Johnson. 1973. 'Considerations of some problems of comprehension' in W. G. Chase (ed.): *Visual Information Processing*. New York: Academic Press.

Breen, M. 1987. 'Contemporary paradigms in syllabus design' parts 1 and 2. *Language Teaching* 20/2 and 3:

Brik, O. [1923] 1977. 'The so-called formal method' in *Russian Poetics in Translation* 4: 90–1.

Brontë, E. [1847] 1963. *Wuthering Heights* (ed. W. Sale). New York: Norton.

Brooks, C. [1947] 1968. *The Well Wrought Urn*. London: Methuen.

Brown, G. and G. Yule. 1983. *Discourse Analysis*. Cambridge: Cambridge University Press.

Brown, P. and S. Levinson. 1987. *Politeness: Some Universals in Language Usage*. Cambridge: Cambridge University Press.

Brown, R. 1958. *Words and Things*. Glencoe, Ill. Free Press.

Browning, R. 1981. 'Meeting at Night' in J. Pettigrew (ed.): *Robert Browning: The Poems*. Harmondsworth: Penguin.

Buchan, D. 1972. *The Ballad and the Folk*. London: Routledge and Kegan Paul.

Bühler, K. 1934. *Sprachtheorie*. Jena: Fischer Verlag.

Buñuel, L. [1982] 1983. *My Last Breath* (trans. A. Israel). London: Fontana.

Burns, R. 1896. 'A Red, Red Rose', in *The Poems and Songs of Robert Burns* (edited by A. Long). London: Methuen.

Burton, D. 1980. *Dialogue and Discourse*. London: Routledge and Kegan Paul.

Carey, J. 1992. *The Intellectuals and the Masses*. London: Faber.

Carrell, P. 1988. 'Some causes of text-boundedness and schema interference in ESL reading', in P. Carrell, J. Devine, and D. Eskey: 93–101.

Carrell, P., J. Devine, and D. Eskey (eds.) 1988. *Interactive Approaches to Second Language Reading*. Cambridge: Cambridge University Press.

Carrell, P. and J. Eisterhold. 1983. 'Schema theory and ESL reading pedagogy.' *TESOL Quarterly* 17/4: 553–73, (reprinted in P. Carrell, J. Devine, and D. Eskey 1988: 72–92).

Carter, R. A. (ed.) 1982a. *Language and Literature*. London: George Allen and Unwin.

Carter, R. A. 1982b. 'Introduction' in R. A. Carter (ed.) 1982a: 1–17.

Carter, R. A. 1989. 'Directions in the teaching and study of English stylistics' in M. H. Short 1989b: 10–22.

Carter, R. A. and P. Simpson (eds.) 1989. *Language, Discourse and Literature*. London: Unwin Hyman.

Cazden, C. B. 1989. 'Contributions of the Bakhtin circle to communicative competence.' *Applied Linguistics* 10/2: 116–27.

Chandler, R. [1953] 1959. *The Long Goodbye*. Harmondsworth: Penguin.

Charniak, E. 1975. *Organisation and Inference in a Framelike System of Common Sense Knowledge*. Castagnola: Institute for Semantic and Cognitive Studies.

Chiaro, D. 1992. *The Language of Jokes: Analysing Verbal Play*. London: Routledge.

Ching, M. K., M. Haley, and R. Lunsford (eds.) 1980. *Linguistic Perspectives on Literature*. London: Routledge and Kegan Paul.

Chomsky, N. 1965. *Aspects of the Theory of Syntax*. Cambridge, Mass.: MIT Press.

Chomsky, N. 1988. *Language and Problems of Knowledge*. Cambridge, Mass.: MIT Press.

Cixous, H. and C. Clément. 1975. *La Jeune Née*. Paris: UGE.

Clark, J. 1987. *Curriculum Renewal in School Foreign Language Learning*. Oxford: Oxford University Press.

Clark, K. and M. Holquist. 1984. *Mikhail Bakhtin*. Cambridge, Mass.: Harvard University Press.

Cluysenaar, A. 1976. *Introduction to Literary Stylistics*. London: Batsford.

Conrad, J. [1902] 1963. *Heart of Darkness*. Harmondsworth: Penguin.

Cook, G. 1984. *Literary Translation: The Relevance of Theory to Practice*. Unpublished MA dissertation, London University Institute of Education.

Cook, G. 1986. 'Texts, extracts and stylistic texture' in C. J. Brumfit and R. A. Carter (eds.): *Literature and Language Teaching*. Oxford: Oxford University Press: 150–66.

Cook, G. 1988. 'Stylistics with a dash of advertising.' *Language and Style* 21/2: 151–61.

Cook, G. 1989. *Discourse*. Oxford: Oxford University Press.

Cook, G. 1990a. 'Transcribing infinity: problems of context presentation.' *Journal of Pragmatics* 14/1: 1–24.

Cook, G. 1990b. 'Adverts, songs, jokes and graffiti: approaching literary through sub-literary writing' in *Effective Teaching and Learning: The British Council 1989 Milan Conference*. London: Macmillan/MEP: 128–33.

Cook, G. 1992. *The Discourse of Advertising*. London: Routledge.

Cook, G. 1994a. 'Contradictory voices: a dialogue between Russian and western European linguistics' in R. Sell and P. Verdonk (eds.): *Literature and the New Interdisciplinarity*. Amsterdam: Rodopi.

Cook, G. 1994b. 'Language play in advertisements: some implications for applied linguistics' in D. Graddol and J. Swann (eds.): *Evaluating Language*. Clevedon, Avon: BAAL/Multilingual Matters.

Cook, G. 1994c. 'Repetition and knowing by heart: an aspect of intimate discourse and its implications.' *English Language Teaching Journal* 48/2: 133–41.

Cook, G. and E. O. Poptsova-Cook. 1989. 'Comparing translations.' *Journal of Russian Studies* 55: 223–35.

Cooper, D. 1986. *Metaphor*. Oxford: Blackwell.

Coulmas, F. (ed.) 1986 'Reported speech: some general issues' in F. Coulmas (ed.): *Direct and Indirect Speech*. Berlin, New York, and Amsterdam: Mouton de Gruyter.

Coulthard, M. and M. Montgomery (eds.). 1981. *Studies in Discourse Analysis*. London: Routledge and Kegan Paul.

Coulthard, M. 1981. 'Developing the description' in Coulthard and Montgomery: 13–31.

Cowie, A. P. 1981. 'The treatment of collocations and idioms in a learner's dictionary.' *Applied Linguistics* 2/3: 223–35.

Cowie, A. P. 1990. 'Multiword units and communicative language teaching' in P. Arnaud and H. Béjoint (eds.): *Vocabulary and Applied Linguistics*. London: Macmillan.

Cruse, D. A. 1986. *Lexical Semantics*. Cambridge: Cambridge University Press.

Crystal, D. 1985. *A Dictionary of Linguistics and Phonetics*. Oxford: Blackwell.

Culler, J. 1973. 'The linguistic basis of structuralism' in D. Robey (ed.): *Structuralism: An Introduction*. Oxford: The Clarendon Press: 20–37.

Culler, J. 1975a. 'Defining narrative units' in R. Fowler: 123–43.

Culler, J. 1975b. *Structuralist Poetics*. London: Routledge and Kegan Paul.

Culler, J. 1983. *On Deconstruction*. London: Routledge and Kegan Paul.

Culler, J. 1988. *Framing the Sign*. Oxford: Blackwell.

Dale, R. 1988. 'Generating referring expressions in a domain of objects and processes.' Unpublished PhD thesis, Edinburgh University.

Danlos, L. 1987. *The Linguistic Basis of Text Generation*. Cambridge: Cambridge University Press.

Dascal, M. 1981. 'Contextualism' in H. Parret, M. Sbisa, and J. Verschueren (eds.): *Possibilities and Limitations of Pragmatics*. Amsterdam: Benjamins: 153–79.

Davies, W. (ed.) 1979. *Gerard Manley Hopkins: The Major Poems*. London: Dent.

Davis, R. C. (ed.) 1986. *Contemporary Literary Criticism: Modernism through Post-Structuralism*. London: Longman.

Defoe, D. [1719] 1962. *Robinson Crusoe*. London: Purnell.

Derrida, J. [1967] 1976. *Of Grammatology* (trans. G. C. Spivak). Baltimore, Md.: Johns Hopkins University Press.

Derrida, J. [1967] 1978. 'Structure, sign and play in the discourse of the human sciences' (trans. A. Bass) in *Writing and Difference* (reprinted in D. Lodge (ed.) 1988: 107–24).

Derrida, J. [1972] 1982. *Margins of Philosophy* (trans. A. Bass). Brighton: Harvester.

van Dijk, T. A. 1972. *Some Aspects of Text Grammars*. The Hague: Mouton.

van Dijk, T. A. 1977. *Text and Context*. London: Longman.

van Dijk, T. A. (ed.) 1982. *New Developments in Cognitive Models of Discourse Processing* (special issue of *Text* 2–1/3). Amsterdam: Mouton.

van Dijk, T. A. (ed.) 1985a. *A Handbook of Discourse Analysis* (4 Vols.). New York: Academic Press.

van Dijk, T. A. (ed.) 1985b. *Discourse and Literature*. Amsterdam: Benjamins.

van Dijk, T. A. and W. Kintsch. 1983. *Strategies of Discourse Comprehension*. New York: Academic Press.

Dimter, M. 1985. 'On text classification' in T. A. van Dijk 1985b: 214–29.

Dostoevsky, F. M. [1862] 1989. *Notes from the Dead House* (trans. G. Cook and E. Poptsova-Cook). Moscow: Raduga.

Dostoevsky, F. M. [1871] 1953. *The Devils* (trans. D. Magarshak). Harmondsworth: Penguin.

Doxey, W. S. 1970. 'William Blake and William Herschel: the poet, the astronomer and The Tyger.' *Blake Studies* 2/2: 5–13.

Dresher, B. E. and N. H. Hornstein. 1976. 'On some supposed contributions of artificial intelligence to the scientific study of language.' *Cognition* 4: 321–98.

Dreyfus, H. 1987. 'Misrepresenting human intelligence.' R. Born (ed.) 1987: 41–55.

Dreyfus, H. and S. Dreyfus. 1986. *Mind over Machine*. London: Macmillan.

Dunne, T. 1976. *Gerard Manley Hopkins: A Comprehensive Bibliography*. Oxford: The Clarendon Press.

Duranti, A. and C. Goodwin (eds.) 1992. *Rethinking Context: Language as an Interactive Phenomenon*. Cambridge: Cambridge University Press.

Eagleton, T. 1983. *Literary Theory*. Oxford: Blackwell.

Eco, U. 1979. *The Role of the Reader*. Bloomington, Ind. and London: Indiana University Press.
Eco, U. 1989. *Reflections on 'The Name of the Rose'*. London: Secker and Warburg.
Edelman, G. 1989. *The Remembered Present: A Biological Theory of Consciousness*. New York: Basic Books.
Edelman, G. 1992. *Bright Air, Brilliant Fire: On the Matter of the Mind*. Harmondsworth: Penguin.
Edwards, D. and D. Middleton. 1987. 'Conversation and remembering: Bartlett revisited.' *Applied Cognitive Psychology* 1: 77–92.
Edwards, D. and J. Potter. 1992. *Discursive Psychology*. London: Sage.
Eikhenbaum, B. M. [1926] 1978. 'The theory of the formal method' in L. Matejka and K. Pomorska: 3–37.
Ellis, A. and G. Beattie. 1986. *The Psychology of Language and Communication*. London: Weidenfeld and Nicolson.
Ellman, R. [1959] 1982. *James Joyce*. New York: Oxford University Press (page reference is to 1982 edition only).
Empson, W. 1956. 'Missing Dates' in *The Penguin Book of English Verse* (ed. J. Hayward). Harmondsworth: Penguin.
Epstein, E. L. 1975. 'The self-reflexive artefact: the function of mimesis in an approach to a theory of value for literature' in R. Fowler 1975: 40–79.
Erlich, V. [1955] 1980. *Russian Formalism: History, Doctrine*. The Hague: Mouton.
Eskey, D. 1988. 'Holding in the bottom: an interactive approach to the language problems of second language readers' in P. Carrell, J. Devine, and D. Eskey (eds.): 93–101.
Eysenk, M. W. and M. T. Keane. 1990. *Cognitive Psychology*. Hove: Lawrence Erlbaum.

Fabb, N., D. Attridge, A. Durant, and C. MacCabe (eds.) 1987. *The Linguistics of Writing*. Manchester: Manchester University Press.
Feldman, C. F. 1991. 'Oral Metalanguage' in D. R. Olson and N. Torrance (eds.) 1991: 47–66.
Fillmore, C. J. 1989. 'Two dictionaries.' *International Journal of Lexicography* 2/1: 57–83.
Firth, J. R. 1957. *Papers in Linguistics 1934–1951*. Oxford: Oxford University Press.
Fish, S. 1972. *Self-Consuming Artefacts*. Berkeley and Los Angeles, Ca.: California University Press.
Fish, S. 1980. *Is There a Text in This Class?* Cambridge, Mass.: Harvard University Press.
Fish, S. 1981. 'Why no-one's afraid of Wolfgang Iser.' *Diacritics* 11: 2–13.
Fitter, R. S. R. and R. A. Richardson. 1952. *Collins Pocket Guide to British Birds*. London: Collins.
Fleischman, S. 1990. *Tense and Narrativity: From Medieval Performance to Modern Fiction*. London: Routledge and Kegan Paul.
Fodor, J. A. 1976. *The Language of Thought*. New York: Harvester.
Forgacs, D. 1982. 'Marxist literary theory' in A. Jefferson and D. Robey: 134–69.
Foucault, M. [1969] 1979. 'What is an author?' (trans. J. V. Harari) in J. V. Harari (ed.): *Textual Strategies: Perspectives in Post-Structuralism* (reprinted in D. Lodge (ed.) 1988: 197–210).
Fowler, R. 1966. *Essays on Style and Language*. London: Routledge and Kegan Paul.

Fowler, R. (ed.) 1975. *Style and Structure in Literature: Essays in the New Stylistics.* Oxford: Blackwell.

Frazer, J. G. [1922] 1949. *The Golden Bough* (abridged edition). London: Macmillan.

Frohawk, F. W. 1958. *British Birds.* London: Ward, Lock.

Gadamer, H.-G. [1960] 1975. *Truth and Method* (trans. G. Barden and J. Cumming). London: Sheed and Ward.

Garnham, A. 1987. *Mental Models as Representations of Discourse and Text.* Chichester: Ellis Horwood.

Garnham, A. 1988. *Artificial Intelligence: An Introduction.* London and New York: Routledge and Kegan Paul.

Genette, G. [1982] 1988. 'Structuralism and literary criticism' in G. Genette: *Figures of Literary Discourse* (trans. A. Sheridan) New York: Columbia University Press (reprinted in D. Lodge 1988: 63–78).

van Gennep, A. [1908] 1960. *The Rites of Passage.* London: Routledge and Kegan Paul.

de George, R. and **F. de George** (eds.) 1972. *The Structuralists from Marx to Lévi-Strauss.* New York: Doubleday, Anchor.

Gibson, J. J. 1950. *The Perception of the Visual World.* Boston: Houghton Mifflin.

Grabwicz, G. 1973. 'Translator's introduction to Roman Ingarden's "The Literary Work of Art"' in Ingarden [1931] 1973.

Greene, J. 1987. *Memory, Thinking and Language.* London: Methuen.

Gregory, M. 1967. 'Aspects of varieties differentiation.' *Journal of Linguistics* 3/2: 177–274.

Greimas, A. J. 1966. *Sémantique Structurale.* Paris: Larousse.

Grice, H. P. [1967] 1975. 'Logic and conversation' in P. Cole and J. L. Morgan (eds.): *Syntax and Semantics. Vol. 3: Speech Acts.* New York: Academic Press: 41–59.

Grosz, B. J. 1986. 'Attention, intention, and the structure of discourse.' *Computational Linguistics* 12/3: 175–204.

Haberlandt, K. and **G. Bingham.** 1982. 'The role of scripts in the comprehension and retention of texts' in T. A. van Dijk: 29–46.

Halliday, M. A. K. [1964] 1967. 'The linguistic study of literary texts' in S. Chatman and S. R. Levin (eds.): *Essays on the Language of Literature.* Boston: Houghton Mifflin: 302–7.

Halliday, M. A. K. 1973. *Explorations in the Function of Language.* London: Edward Arnold.

Halliday, M. A. K. 1975. *Learning How to Mean.* London: Edward Arnold.

Halliday, M. A. K. 1976. *System and Function in Language* (ed. G. Kress). Oxford: Oxford University Press.

Halliday, M. A. K. 1985. *An Introduction to Functional Grammar.* London: Edward Arnold.

Halliday, M. A. K. and **R. Hasan.** 1976. *Cohesion in English.* London: Longman.

Halliday, M. A. K., A. McIntosh, and **P. Strevens.** 1964. *The Linguistic Sciences and Language Teaching.* London: Longman.

Halverson, J. 1991. 'Olson on Literacy.' *Language in Society* 20: 619–40.

Hasan, R. 1989. *Linguistics, Language, and Verbal Art.* Oxford: Oxford University Press.

Harris, R. 1987. *The Language Machine.* London: Duckworth.

Harris, Z. 1952. 'Discourse analysis.' *Language* 28: 1–30.

Hatch, E. 1992. *Discourse and Language Education.* Cambridge: Cambridge University Press.

Hawking, S. 1988. *A Brief History of Time*. London: Bantam.

Head, H. 1920. *Studies in Neurology*. London: Henry Frowde.

Heinzel, H., R. S. R. Fitter, and J. L. F. Parslow. 1979. *The Birds of Britain and Europe* (4th edn.). London: Collins.

Hillary, R. 1943. *The Last Enemy*. London: Macmillan.

Hirsch, E. D. 1964. *Innocence and Experience*. New Haven: Yale.

Hobsbaum, P. 1964. 'A rhetorical question answered: Blake's Tyger and its critics.' *Neophilologus* 48/2: 154.

Hobsbawn, E. J. 1975. *The Age of Capital: 1848–1875*. London: Weidenfeld and Nicolson.

Holub, R. C. 1984. *Reception Theory*. New York and London: Methuen.

Hopkins, G. M. [1918] 1967. 'The Windhover' and 'Pied Beauty' in W. H. Gardener and N. H. Mackenzie (eds.): *The Collected Poems of Gerard Manley Hopkins*. London: Oxford University Press.

House, H. and G. Storey (eds.) 1959. *The Journals and Papers of Gerard Manley Hopkins*. Oxford: Oxford University Press.

Hunter, I. 1985. 'Lengthy verbatim recall' in A. W. Ellis (ed.): *Progress in the Psychology of Language*. London: Lawrence Erlbaum.

Hymes, D. [1964] 1977. 'Towards ethnographies of communication' in J. J. Gumperz and D. Hymes (eds.) 1964. *The Ethnography of Communication*. Washington DC: American Anthropological Association: 1–34. Revised version in D. Hymes (1977): *Foundations in Sociolinguistics*. London: Tavistock Press: 3–66.

Hymes, D. 1972a. 'On communicative competence' in J. B. Pride and J. Holmes (eds.): *Sociolinguistics: Selected Readings*. Harmondsworth: Penguin.

Hymes, D. 1972b. 'Models of the interaction of language and social life' in J. J. Gumperz and D. Hymes (eds.): *Directions in Sociolinguistics*. New York: Holt, Rinehart and Winston: 5–71.

Hymes, D. 1989. 'Postscript.' *Applied Linguistics* 10/2: 244–50.

Ingarden, R. [1931] 1973. *The Literary Work of Art: An Investigation on the Borderlines of Ontology, Logic and the Theory of Literature* (trans. G. Grabwicz). Evanston, Ill.: Northwestern University Press.

Iser, W. 1974. *The Implied Reader: Patterns of Communication in Prose Fiction from Bunyan to Beckett*. New York and London: Columbia University Press.

Iser, W. 1978. *The Act of Reading: A Theory of Aesthetic Response*. Baltimore and London: Johns Hopkins University Press.

Jakobson, R. [1921] 1978. 'On realism in art' (trans. K. Magassy) in L. Matejka and K. Pomorska: 38–46.

Jakobson, R. [1935] 1978. 'The dominant' (trans. H. Eagle) in L. Matejka and K. Pomorska (eds.): 83–7.

Jakobson, R. 1960. 'Closing statement: linguistics and poetics' in T. A. Sebeok (ed.): *Style in Language*. Cambridge, Mass.: MIT Press: 350–77.

Jakobson, R. and C. Lévi-Strauss [1962] 1972. 'Charles Baudelaire's Les Chats' (trans. R. de George and F. de George) in R. de George and F. de George: 124–67.

James, H. [1898] 1969. *The Turn of the Screw*. Harmondsworth: Penguin.

Jefferson, A. and D. Robey. [1982] 1986. *Modern Literary Theory: A Comparative Introduction* (page references are to the 1982 edition). London: Batsford.

Jespersen, O. 1949. *A Modern English Grammar* (Vol. VII). London: George Allen and Unwin.

Johnson-Laird, P. N. 1983. *Mental Models: Towards a Cognitive Science of Language, Inference and Consciousness.* Cambridge: Cambridge University Press.

Johnson-Laird, P. N. 1988. *The Computer and the Mind: An Introduction to Cognitive Science.* London: Fontana.

Johnson-Laird, P. N. and R. Stevenson. 1970. 'Memory for syntax.' *Nature* 227: 414.

Joyce, J. [1922] 1960. *Ulysses.* London: Bodley Head.

Keenan, J. M., B. McWhinney, and D. Mayhew. 1977. 'Pragmatics in memory: A study of natural conversation.' *Journal of Verbal Learning and Verbal Behaviour* 16: 549–60.

Kennedy, S. 1971. *Murphy's Bed.* Bucknell University Press.

Kholodovich, A. A. (ed.) 1977. *Editor's Introduction to Ferdinand de Saussure: Trudy po Yazikoznaniyu.* Moscow: Progress.

Kintsch, W. 1974. *The Representation of Meaning in Memory.* Potomac: Lawrence Erlbaum.

Kirk, G. S. 1970. *Myth: Its Meanings and Functions.* Cambridge: Cambridge University Press.

Kobsa, A. 1987. 'What is explained by AI models?' in R. Born: 174–90.

Kramsch, C. 1993. *Context and Culture in Language Teaching.* Oxford: Oxford University Press.

Kruisinga, E. 1932. *A Handbook of Present Day English. Part II: English Accidence and Syntax (Volume 2).* Noordhoff: Groningen.

Kuhn, T. 1962. *The Structure of Scientific Revolutions.* Chicago: University of Chicago Press.

Krzeszowski, R. P. 1975. 'Is it possible and necessary to write text grammars?' in S. P. Corder and E. Roulet (eds.) 1975. *Theoretical Linguistic Models in Applied Linguistics.* Brussels, Aimav, and Paris: Didier.

Lachter, J. and T. G. Bever. 1988. 'The relationship between linguistic structures and associated theories of language learning—A constructive critique of some connectionist learning models.' *Cognition* 28: 195–247.

Lakoff, G. 1987. *Women, Fire and Dangerous Things: What Categories Reveal About the Mind.* Chicago: Chicago University Press.

Lakoff, R. 1973. 'The logic of politeness: on minding your p's and q's' in *Proceedings of the Ninth Regional Meeting of the Chicago Linguistic Society*: 292–305.

Lapochkin, G. K. 1992. 'Ob'yasnit ya vam mogu.' Moscow: Yagoda.

Lawrence, D. H. [1913] 1961. *Sons and Lovers.* Harmondsworth: Penguin.

Lecercle, J.-J. 1990. *The Violence of Language.* London: Routledge and Kegan Paul.

Leech, G. N. 1966. *English in Advertising.* London: Longman.

Leech, G. N. 1969. *A Linguistic Guide to English Poetry.* London: Longman.

Leech, G. N. 1981. *Semantics* (2nd edn.). Harmondsworth: Penguin.

Leech, G. N. 1983. *Principles of Pragmatics.* London: Longman.

Leech, G. N. and M. H. Short. 1981. *Style in Fiction.* London: Longman.

Lehnert, W. G. 1979. 'The role of scripts in understanding', in D. Metzing (ed.): *Frame Conceptions and Text Understanding.* Berlin: de Gruyter: 79–95.

Lemon, L. T. and M. J. Reis. 1965. *Russian Formalist Criticism: Four Essays.* Lincoln: University of Nebraska Press.

Lentricchia, F. 1980. *After the New Criticism.* London: Athlone.

Lévi-Strauss, C. [1949] 1962. *The Elementary Structures of Kinship* (trans. J. H. Bell, J. R. van Sturmer, and R. Needham). London: Eyre and Spottiswoode.

Lévi-Strauss, C. [1955] 1972. 'The structural study of myth.' *Journal of American Folklore* 78/270: 428–44 (page references are to reprint in de George and de George: 168–94).

Lévi-Strauss, C. [1960] 1972. 'Four Winnebago myths' in S. Diamond (ed.): *Culture in History: Essays in Honour of Paul Radin.* New York: Columbia University Press: 351–62 (page references are to reprint in de George and de George: 195–208).

Lévi-Strauss, C. [1962] 1972. 'History and dialectic' in de George and de George: 209–37.

Levinson, S. 1983. *Pragmatics.* Cambridge: Cambridge University Press.

Linde, C. and W. Labov. 1975. 'Spatial networks as a site for the study of language and thought.' *Language* 51: 924–39.

Litman, D. J. and J. F. Allen. 1987. 'A plan recognition model for sub-dialogues in conversations.' *Cognitive Science* 11/2: 163–201.

Lodge, D. 1987. 'After Bakhtin', in Fabb et al.: 89–103.

Lodge, D. (ed.) 1988. *Modern Criticism and Theory: A Reader.* London: Longman.

Loftus, G. R. and E. F. Loftus. 1976. *Human Memory: The Processing of Information.* Hillsdale, NJ: Lawrence Erlbaum.

Longacre, R. E. 1983. *The Grammar of Discourse.* New York and London: Plenum.

Lord, A. B. 1960. *The Singer of Tales.* Harvard: Harvard University Press.

Lyons, J. 1968. *Introduction to Theoretical Linguistics.* Cambridge: Cambridge University Press.

Lyons, J. 1973. 'Structuralism and Linguistics' in D. Robey (ed.): *Structuralism: An Introduction.* Oxford: The Clarendon Press: 5–20.

Lyons, J. 1977. *Semantics* (2 Vols.). Cambridge: Cambridge University Press.

Lytenin, S. L. and R. C. Schank. 1982. 'Representation and translation' in T. A. van Dijk: 83–111.

Mann, W. C. 1984. *Discourse Structures for Text Generation.* Information Sciences Institute Research Report RR–84–127: University of Southern California.

Mann, W. C. 1987. *Text Generation: The Problem of Text Structure.* Information Sciences Institute Reprint Series RS–87–181: University of Southern California.

Martin, J. R. 1985. *Factual Writing: Exploring and Challenging Social Reality.* Oxford: Oxford University Press.

Martindale, C. 1991. *Cognitive Psychology.* Pacific Grove, Calif.: Brooks/Cole.

Matejka, L. and K. Pomorska (eds.) 1978. *Readings in Russian Poetics.* Ann Arbor, Mich.: Michigan University Press.

Matejka, L. and R. Titunik. 1986. 'Translators' preface 1986' in V. N. Volosinov [1929] 1973. Cambridge, Mass.: Harvard University Press (in the 1986 edition only: vii–xiii).

Mauriac, F. 1927. *Thérèse Desqueyroux.* Paris: Bernard Grasset.

McCarthy, M. 1991. *Discourse Analysis for Language Teachers.* Cambridge: Cambridge University Press.

McCarthy, M. 1993. 'Spoken discourse markers in written text' in J. M. Sinclair, M. Hoey, and G. Fox: 170–83.

McKeown, K. R. 1985. *Text Generation.* Cambridge: Cambridge University Press.

McTear, M. 1987. *The Articulate Computer.* Oxford: Blackwell.

Medvedev, P. N. (name used by M. M. Bakhtin) [1928] 1978. *The Formal Method in Literary Scholarship* (trans. A. J. Wherle). Baltimore, Md.: Johns Hopkins University Press.

Melchuk, I. A. 1988. 'Semantic description of lexical units in an explanatory combinatorial dictionary: basic principles and heuristic criteria.' *International Journal of Lexicography* 1/3 1988: 165–88.

Miller, G. A. 1966. *Psychology: The Science of Mental Life*. Harmondsworth: Penguin.

Miller, J. R. and W. Kintsch. 1980. 'Readability and recall of short prose passages: a theoretical analysis.' *Journal of Experimental Psychology: Human Learning and Memory* 6: 335–54.

Milroy, J. 1977. *The Language of Gerard Manley Hopkins*. London: Deutsch.

Minsky, M. L. 1975. 'A framework for representing knowledge' in P. Winston (ed.): *The Psychology of Computer Vision*. New York: McGraw-Hill: 211–27.

Nattinger, J. R. and J. S. DeCarrico. 1992. *Lexical Phrases and Language Teaching*. Oxford: Oxford University Press.

Neumaier, O. 1987. 'A Wittgensteinian view of Artificial Intelligence' in R. Born 1987: 132–74.

Newman, M. 1986. 'Poetry processing.' *Byte*, February 1986: 221–8.

Odier, D. 1970. *The Job: An Interview with William Burroughs*. London: Cape.

Olson, D. R. and N. Torrance (eds.) 1991. *Literacy and Orality*. Cambridge: Cambridge University Press.

O'Neill, R. 1991. 'The plausible myth of learner-centredness: or the importance of doing ordinary things well.' *ELT Journal* 45/4: 293–305.

Ong, W. 1982. *Orality and Literacy*. London: Methuen.

O'Toole, L. M. and A. Shukman. 1977. 'A contextual glossary of formalist terminology.' *Russian Poetics in Translation* 4: 13–38.

Patten, T. 1988. *Systemic Text Generation as Problem Solving*. Cambridge: Cambridge University Press.

Pawley, A. and F. Syder. 1983. 'Two puzzles for linguistic theory: nativelike selection and nativelike fluency' in J. Richards and J. Schmidt (eds.): *Language and Communication*. London: Longman.

van Peer, W. 1986. *Stylistics and Psychology: Investigations of Foregrounding*. London: Croom Helm.

van Peer, W. 1993. 'Typographic foregrounding', in *Language and Literature* 2/1: 49–61.

Penrose, R. 1989. *The Emperor's New Mind*. Oxford: Oxford University Press.

Peterson, R., G. Mountfort, and P. A. D. Hollom. 1983. *A Field Guide to the Birds of Britain and Europe* (4th edn.). London: Collins.

Petofi, J. S. 1976. 'A frame for frames: a few remarks on the methodology of semantically guided text processing' in *Proceedings of the Second Annual Meeting of the Berkeley Linguistics Society*. Berkeley, Ca.: University of Calfornia Institute of Human Learning: 319–29.

Pinker, S. and A. Prince. 1988. 'On language and connectionism: analysis of a PDP model of language and acquisition.' *Cognition* 28: 73–193.

Pitrat, J. [1985] 1988. *An Artificial Intelligence Approach to Understanding Natural Language* (trans. E. F. Harding). London: North Oxford.

Popper, K. R. 1972. *Objective Knowledge: An Evolutionary Approach*. Oxford: The Clarendon Press.

Propp, V. [1928] 1968. *The Morphology of the Folk Tale* (trans. L. Scott). Austin, Tex.: University of Texas Press.

Putnam, H. 1988. *Representation and Reality*. Cambridge, Mass.: MIT Press.

Quillian, R. 1968. *Semantic Memory*. Cambridge, Mass.: Bolt, Berenak and Newman.

Quirk, R., S. Greenbaum, G. N. Leech, and **J. Svartvik.** 1972. *A Grammar of Contemporary English*. London: Longman.

Quirk, R., S. Greenbaum, G. N. Leech, and **J. Svartvik.** 1985. *A Comprehensive Grammar of the English Language*. London: Longman.

Raine, C. 'The Behaviour of Dogs', in B. Morrison and B. Motion (eds.) *The Penguin Book of Contemporary Poetry*. Harmondsworth: Penguin.

Raine, K. 1954. 'Who made the tyger?' *Encounter*, June 1954.

Reichman, R. 1985. *Getting Computers to Talk Like You and Me: Discourse Context, Focus and Semantics*. Cambridge, Mass.: MIT Press.

Reiser, B. J., J. B. Black, and **R. P. Abelson.** 1985. 'Knowledge structures in the organization and retrieval of autobiographical memories.' *Cognitive Psychology* 17: 89–137.

Rice, P. and **P. Waugh** (eds.). 1989. *Modern Literary Theory: A Reader*. London: Edward Arnold.

Rich, E. 1983. *Artificial Intelligence*. New York: McGraw-Hill.

Richards, I. A. 1926. *Science and Poetry*. London: Kegan Paul, Trench and Trubner.

Richards, I. A. 1929. *Practical Criticism* London: Routledge and Kegan Paul.

Rist, R. R. 1989. 'Schema creation in programming.' *Cognitive Science* 13/3: 389–414.

Robey, D. 1973. *Structuralism: An Introduction*. Oxford: The Clarendon Press.

Robinson, F. N. (ed.) [1957] 1966. *The Works of Geoffrey Chaucer*. London: Oxford University Press.

Rosch, E. 1973. 'Natural categories.' *Cognitive Psychology* 4: 328–506**Rosch, E.** 1977. 'Classification of real world objects: origins and representations in cognition' in P. N. Johnson-Laird and P. C. Wason (eds.): *Thinking: Readings in Cognitive Science*. Cambridge: Cambridge University Press: 212–23.

Rosch, E. and **C. B. Mervis.** 1975. 'Family resemblances: studies in the internal structure of categories.' *Cognitive Psychology* 7: 573–605.

Rumelhart, D. E. 1975. 'Notes on a schema for stories' in D. G. Bobrow and A. M. Collins (eds.): *Representation and Understanding: Studies in Cognitive Science*. New York: Academic Press: 211–37.

Rumelhart, D. E. 1977. 'Understanding and summarising brief stories' in D. Laberge and J. Samuels (eds.): *Basic Processes in Reading: Perception and Comprehension*. Hillsdale, NJ: Lawrence Erlbaum.

Rumelhart, D. E., J. L. McClelland, and **the PDP Research Group** (eds.). 1986a. *Parallel Distributed Processing: Explorations in the Microstructure of Cognition. Vol. 1: Foundations*. Cambridge, Mass.: Bradford Books/MIT Press.

Rumelhart, D. E., J. L. McClelland, and **the PDP Research Group** (eds.). 1986b. *Parallel Distributed Processing: Explorations in the Microstructures of Cognition. Vol. 2: Psychological and Biological Models*. Cambridge, Mass.: Bradford Books/MIT Press.

Rumelhart, D. E. and **A. Ortony.** 1977. 'The representation of knowledge in memory' in R. C. Anderson, R. J. Spiro, and W. E. Montague (eds.): *Schooling and the Acquisition of Knowledge*. Hillsdale, NJ: Lawrence Erlbaum.

Rumelhart, D. E., P. Smolensky, J. L. McClelland, and G. E. Hinton. 1986. 'Schemata and sequential thought processes in PDP models' in Rumelhart et al. 1986b.

Ryan, M. L. 1991. *Possible Worlds, Artificial Intelligence and Narrative Theory.* Bloomington and Indianapolis, Ind.: Indiana University Press.

Rylance, R. (ed.) 1987. *Debating Texts: A Reader in Twentieth Century Theory and Method.* Milton, Keynes: Open University Press.

Sacks, J. S. 1967. 'Recognition memory for syntactic and semantic aspects of connected discourse.' *Perception and Psychophysics* 2: 437–42.

Sanford, A. J. and S. C. Garrod. 1981. *Understanding Written Language.* Chichester: Wiley.

de Saussure, F. [1916] 1960 (new edition 1974). *Course in General Linguistics* (translated by W. Baskin). London: Fontana/Collins.

Schachtel, E. G. 1949. 'On memory and childhood amnesia' in F. Mullahy (ed.): *A Study of Interpersonal Relations.* New York: Grove: 3–49.

Schank, R. C. 1972. 'Conceptual dependency: A theory of natural language understanding.' *Cognitive Psychology* 3: 552–631.

Schank, R. C. 1975. *Conceptual Information Processing.* Amsterdam: North Holland.

Schank, R. C. 1980. 'Language and memory.' *Cognitive Science* 4: 243–84.

Schank, R. C. 1982a. *Dynamic Memory.* Cambridge: Cambridge University Press.

Schank, R. C. 1982b. *Reading and Understanding: Teaching from the Perspective of Artificial Intelligence.* Hillsdale, NJ: Lawrence Erlbaum.

Schank, R. C. 1984. *The Cognitive Computer.* Reading, Mass.: Addison-Wesley.

Schank, R. C. 1986. *Explanation Patterns.* Hillsdale, NJ: Lawrence Erlbaum.

Schank, R. C. and R. Abelson. 1977. *Scripts, Plans, Goals and Understanding.* Hillsdale, NJ: Lawrence Erlbaum.

Schank, R. C. and M. Burstein. 1985. 'Artificial Intelligence memory for language understanding' in T. A. van Dijk 1985 (Vol. 1): 145–67.

Schank, R. C., G. C. Collins, E. Davis, P. N. Johnson, S. Lytinen, and B. J. Reiser. 1982. 'What's the point?' *Cognitive Science* 6: 255–75.

Schegloff, E. 1972. 'Notes on a conversational practice: formulating place' in D. Sudnow (ed.): *Studies in Social Interaction.* New York: Free Press: 75–119.

Schlechta, K. (ed.) 1966. *Nietzsche: Werke* (3 Vols.) Munich: Hauser.

Scott, P. [1971] 1973. *The Towers of Silence.* London: Panther.

Scura, D. M. 1979. *Henry James: A Reference Guide.* Boston, Mass.: G. K. Hall.

Searle, J. R. 1969. *Speech Acts: An Essay in the Philosophy of Language.* Cambridge: Cambridge University Press.

Searle, J. R. 1975a. 'Indirect speech acts' in P. Cole and J. L. Morgan (eds.): *Syntax and Semantics. Volume 3: Speech Acts.* New York: Academic Press: 59–82.

Searle, J. R. 1975b. 'A taxonomy of illocutionary acts' in K. Gunderson (ed.): *Language, Mind and Knowledge.* Minnesota Studies in the Philosophy of Science 7. Minneapolis, Mn.: University of Minnesota Press: 344–70.

Searle, J. R. 1975c. 'The logical status of fictional discourse.' *New Literary History* 6: 319–32.

Searle, J. R. [1980] 1987. 'Minds, Brains and Programs.' *The Behavioural and Brain Sciences* 1: 417–24 (also in R. Born (ed.) 1987: 18–41).

Shanker, S. G. 1987. 'The decline and fall of the mechanist metaphor' in R. Born (ed.): 72–132.

Sheppard, E. A. 1974. *Henry James and 'The Turn of the Screw'*. Oxford: Oxford University Press.
Shippey, T. A. 1993. 'Principles of conversation in Beowulfian speech' in J. M. Sinclair, M. Hoey, and G. Fox (eds.): 109–27.
Shklovsky, V. B. [1917] 1965. 'Art as Technique' in L. T. Lemon and M. J. Reis: 3–24.
Shklovsky, V. B. [1921] 1965. 'Sterne's *Tristram Shandy*: stylistic commentary' in L. T. Lemon and M. J. Reis: 25–61.
Shklovsky, V. B. [1940] 1974. *Mayakovsky and His Circle*. London: Pluto.
Shklovsky, V. B. 1966. *Povesti o Prose*. Moscow: Khudozhestvenaya Literatura.
Short, M. H. 1989a. 'Discourse analysis and drama' in R. A. Carter and P. Simpson (eds.): 139–71.
Short, M. H. (ed.) 1989b. *Reading, Analysing and Teaching Literature*. London: Longman.
Short, M. H. 1989c. 'Introduction' in M. H. Short 1989b: 1–9.
Short, M. H. and J. C. Alderson. 1989. 'Reading literature' in M. H. Short 1989b: 72–120.
Short, M. H. and W. van Peer. 1989. 'Accident! Stylisticians evaluate: aims and methods of stylistic analysis' in M. H. Short 1989b: 22–72.
Shorter Oxford English Dictionary (3rd edn.) 1944. (ed. C. T. Onions.) Oxford: Oxford University Press.
Simon, H. A. 1979. 'Information-processing theory of human problem solving' in W. Estes (ed.): *Handbook of Learning and Cognitive Processes. Vol. 5.* Hillsdale, NJ: Lawrence Erlbaum (reprinted in A. M. Aitkenhead and J. M. Slack (eds.) 1985).
Sinclair, J. M. 1991. *Corpus, Concordance, Collocation*. Oxford: Oxford University Press.
Sinclair, J. M. and M. Coulthard. 1975. *Towards an Analysis of Discourse: The English Used by Teachers and Pupils*. London: Oxford University Press.
Sinclair, J. M., M. Hoey, and G. Fox (eds.). 1993. *Techniques of Description: Spoken and Written Discourse*. London: Routledge and Kegan Paul.
Skehan, P. 1989. *Individual Differences in Second Language Learning*. London: Edward Arnold.
Slobin, D. 1979. *Psycholinguistics*. Glenview, Ill.: Scott Foresman.
Sperber, D. and D. Wilson. 1986. *Relevance*. Oxford: Blackwell.
Steiner, G. 1972. 'After the Book' in *On Difficulty and Other Essays*. Oxford: Oxford University Press: 186–205.
Stern, H. H. 1983. *Fundamental Concepts of Language Teaching*. Oxford: Oxford University Press.
Stevenson, W. 1969. 'The Tyger as Artefact' in *Blake Studies* 2/1.
Stone, G. O. and G. C. van Orden. 1989. 'Are words represented by nodes?' *Memory and Cognition* 17: 511–24.
Swales, J. 1990. *Genre Analysis*. Cambridge: Cambridge University Press.

Tannen, D. 1986. 'Introducing constructed dialogue in Greek and American conversational and literary narrative' in F. Coulmas (ed.): 311–60.
Tannen, D. 1989. *Talking Voices: Repetition, Dialogue, and Imagery in Conversational Discourse*. Cambridge: Cambridge University Press.
Terras, V. 1985. *A Handbook of Russian Literature*. New Haven, Conn: Yale University Press.
Thomas, D. 1954. *Under Milk Wood*. London: Dent.
Todorov, T. [1966] 1988. 'The typology of detective fiction' reprinted in D. Lodge 1988: 157–66.

Todorov, T. 1966b. *Theorie de la Literature: Textes des Formalistes Russes*. Paris: Seuil.

Todorov, T. [1969] 1987. 'Structural analysis of narrative' in *Novel: A Forum on Fiction*: 70–6. (Reprinted in R. C. Davis (ed.) 1986: 323–30).

Tomashevsky, B. V. [1923] 1978. 'Literature and biography' in L. Matejka and K. Pomorska: 47–55.

Tomashevsky, B. V. [1925] 1965. 'Thematics' in L. T. Lemon and M. J. Reis: 61–99.

Turing, A. M. 1950. 'Computing machinery and intelligence' in *Mind* 59: 433–60.

Tynyanov, Y. N. [1929] 1978. 'On literary evolution' in L. Matejka and K. Pomorska: 66–78.

Vachek, J. (ed.) 1964. *A Prague School Reader in Linguistics*. Bloomington: Indiana University Press.

Vestergaard, T. and K. Schroder. 1985. *The Language of Advertising*. Oxford: Blackwell.

Volosinov, V. N. (name used by M. M. Bakhtin) [1929] 1973. *Marxism and the Philosophy of Language* (trans. L. Matejka and R. Titunik). Cambridge, Mass.: Harvard University Press (translators' preface in 1986 reprint only). (See Chapter 2, Note 2.)

Wales, K. 1989. *A Dictionary of Stylistics*. London: Longman.

Wallace, C. 1992. *Reading*. Oxford: Oxford University Press.

Wanner, E. and M. Maratsos. 1978. 'An A. T. N. approach to comprehension' in M. Halle, J. Bresnan, and G. Miller (eds.): *Linguistic Theory and Psychological Reality*. Cambridge, Mass.: MIT Press: 119–62.

Werlich, E. 1976. *A Text Grammar of English*. Heidelberg: Quelle and Meyer.

Werth, P. W. 1976. 'Roman Jakobson's verbal analysis of poetry.' *Journal of Linguistics* 12: 21–73.

White, H. 1973. *Metahistory: The Historical Imagination in Nineteenth Century Europe*. Baltimore, Md. and London: Johns Hopkins University Press.

White, R. V. 1988. *The ELT Curriculum*. Oxford: Blackwell.

Widdowson, H. G. 1975. *Stylistics and the Teaching of Literature*. London: Longman.

Widdowson, H. G. 1978. *Teaching Language as Communication*. Oxford: Oxford University Press.

Widdowson, H. G. 1983. *Learning Purpose and Language Use*. Oxford: Oxford University Press.

Widdowson, H. G. 1984. *Explorations in Applied Linguistics 2*. Oxford: Oxford University Press.

Widdowson, H. G. 1987. 'On the interpretation of poetry' in Fabb et al.: 241–52.

Widdowson, H. G. 1990. 'Discourse of inquiry and conditions of relevance' in *Proceedings of the Georgetown Round Table: Linguistics, Language Teaching, and Language Acquisition: The Interdependence of Theory, Practice and Research*. Washington DC: Georgetown University Press.

Widdowson, H. G. 1992. *Practical Stylistics*. Oxford: Oxford University Press.

Willen, G. (ed.) 1960. *A Casebook on Henry James's 'The Turn of the Screw'*. New York: Thomas Crowell.

Williams, R. 1983. *Keywords*. London: Fontana.

Wimsatt, W. K. and M. C. Beardsley. 1954. 'The affective fallacy' in *The Verbal Icon*.

Winograd, T. 1977. 'A framework for understanding discourse' in P. Just and P. A. Carpenter (eds.): *Cognitive Processes in Comprehension*. Hillsdale, NJ: Lawrence Erlbaum.

Winograd, T. 1983. *Language as a Cognitive Process. Vol. 1: Syntax*. Reading, Mass.: Addison-Wesley.

Wittgenstein, L. [1953] 1968. *Philosophical Investigations*. Oxford: Blackwell.

Wolfson, N. 1988. 'The bulge: a theory of speech behaviour and social distance' in J. Fine (ed.): *Second Language Discourse: a Textbook of Current Research*. Norwood, NJ: Ablex.

Woods, W. A. 1975. 'What's in a link?' foundations of semantic networks' in D. G. Bobrow and A. Collins (eds.): *Representation and Understanding: Studies in Cognitive Science*. New York: Academic Press: 35–82.

Zamyatin, Y. I. [1924] 1970. *We* (trans. R. Guerney). Harmondsworth: Penguin.

Index

Introductory note: The following abbreviations are used: AI = Artificial Intelligence. CD = conceptual dependency. *SPGU* = *Scripts, Plans, Goals, and Understanding*. Material from chapter endnotes is included where there is new information not included in the main text. Page locations in bold indicate tables or figures.